# Material Ambitions

# Material Ambitions

Self-Help and Victorian Literature

REBECCA RICHARDSON

Johns Hopkins University Press

*Baltimore*

© 2021 Johns Hopkins University Press
All rights reserved. Published 2021
Printed in the United States of America on acid-free paper

2  4  6  8  9  7  5  3  1

Johns Hopkins University Press
2715 North Charles Street
Baltimore, Maryland 21218-4363
www.press.jhu.edu

Library of Congress Cataloging-in-Publication Data

Names: Richardson, Rebecca, 1983– author.
Title: Material ambitions : self-help and Victorian literature / Rebecca Richardson.
Description: Baltimore : Johns Hopkins University Press, 2021. |
Includes bibliographical references and index.
Identifiers: LCCN 2021011251 | ISBN 9781421441962 (hardcover ; acid-free paper) |
ISBN 9781421441979 (paperback ; acid-free paper) | ISBN 9781421441986 (ebook)
Subjects: LCSH: English fiction—19th century—History and criticism. |
Ambition in literature. | Self-actualization (Psychology) in literature. |
Conduct of life in literature. | LCGFT: Literary criticism.
Classification: LCC PR468.S43 R53 2021 | DDC 820.9/353—dc23
LC record available at https://lccn.loc.gov/2021011251

A catalog record for this book is available from the British Library.

*Special discounts are available for bulk purchases of this book. For more information,*
*please contact Special Sales at specialsales@jh.edu.*

# CONTENTS

# ACKNOWLEDGMENTS

It seems appropriate to begin in the same way that so many self-help narratives do—with a moment of inspiration. Mine came while reading Samuel Smiles's *Self-Help*, with its overflowing examples of men who persevere despite setbacks, failures, and poverty—whether that means sleeping only four hours a night, or working two jobs, or, in one memorable case, copying Newton's *Principia* by hand. We know how these stories end, but there's still some allure to reading the familiar trajectory from rags to riches—or if not riches, at least, in Victorian terms, respectability. They reassure us that hard work pays off, that merit is rewarded, and that those who are successful earned it. Of course, despite the popularity of such stories in the nineteenth century and our own, we don't live in a meritocracy. Spending too much time with Victorian self-help texts—which preach that you should work hard, and, when you reach an obstacle, you should just work even harder—could be disastrous. Especially so in the context of Silicon Valley during the years when an entire generation was attempting to establish themselves in an economy that never recovered from the 2008 financial crisis (and then, of course, the pandemic hit).

But I was fortunate to have circles of friends, colleagues, and mentors who provided a counternarrative to that story of the bootstrapping individual. In its place, they modeled an expansive and generous intellectual community. And so the story of this book is not the story of a lone individual writing in a garret (although the size of my apartment might sometimes make it feel that way). I have many people, organizations, and institutions to thank for their support and collaboration. The project began as a dissertation advised by Denise Gigante, Franco Moretti, and Alex Woloch, who always offered wise counsel and pointed me to more promising paths. I have also deeply benefited from the conversations and friendships that started in those years, and especially with Irena Yamboliev, Meredith Castile, Sarah Allison, Stephen Osadetz, Kenny Ligda, Natalie Phillips, Amir Tevel, Ben Wiebracht, Lindsey D. Felt, Abigail Droge, and Justin Tackett. Friends, colleagues, and students in the Program in Writing and Rhetoric and the Hume Center for Writing and Speaking at Stanford have further taught me how deeply the work of writing, researching, and communicating depends on community. My students have been in the work of these revisions with me even when they didn't know it. Their willingness to always revise is an inspiration. To my writing group turned family, the Round Table—Jillian Hess, Hannah Doherty Hudson, Bronwen Tate, and Bridget Whearty—who read and discussed so many drafts from the dissertation prospectus to the book chapters to these acknowledgments, I want to express my deepest friendship and thanks.

I have also benefited from far-flung intellectual communities, presenting work in progress at meetings of the Wordsworth Summer Conference, the North American Society for the Study of Romanticism, British Women Writers, Interdisciplinary Nineteenth-Century Studies, the Association for the Study of Literature and Environment, the North American Victorian Studies Association, the Nineteenth Century Studies Association, the Pacific Coast Conference on British Studies, and Dickens Universe. I was especially lucky to participate in a National Endowment for the Humanities seminar led by the wonderful Sharon Aronofsky Weltman, where I was fortunate to have Kirsten Andersen, Taryn Hakala, and Carrie Sickmann for roommates. Looking back, I am struck by how many serendipitous conversations have shaped this project in important ways, from a seminar at Dickens Universe—thanks especially to Tabitha Sparks, Jason Rudy, and Jessica Valdez—to one of the many lively discussions at the Wordsworth Summer Conference with Richard Lansdown, to whom I am indebted for his feedback and for his notes on unpublished material by Miles Franklin—especially as circumstances prevented me from taking a much-anticipated trip to Australia to see them for myself.

This project took its final shape with Johns Hopkins University Press. I am grateful to the anonymous readers, who inspired me to further develop so many of the ideas in this final version, and to Catherine Goldstead, who always illuminated the path to get there. I also owe many thanks to Carrie Watterson for her brilliant copyediting and to the entire team that made this book a real, material thing in the world. After such thoughtful and careful feedback and collaboration, any errors are my own.

A key moment in the development of this project was writing what is now chapter 5. This work appeared in earlier and shorter form in the *Fortnightly*

*Review* as "A Competitive World: Ambition and Self-Help in Trollope's *An Auto-biography* and *The Three Clerks*," the winner of the 2012 Trollope Prize. My thanks to the committee for their thoughtful feedback and to Denis Boyles and the *Fortnightly Review* for permission to reprint this material in its current form.

Financial and institutional support has made possible the space and time to complete this project. I want to thank the Stanford Department of English, the Stanford Humanities Center and Mellon Foundation, the Tom Killefer Dissertation Fellowship Fund, and the National Endowment for the Humanities. I am also grateful for the Research Awards in the Program in Writing and Rhetoric at Stanford, which allowed such things as a trip to access materials held at the British Library, the Armitt Museum and Library, the Cadbury Research Library at the University of Birmingham, and the London School of Economics Women's Library. That I have been able to write about these texts— particularly those Victorian self-help texts that have been preserved and digitized despite how rarely they are checked out—is thanks to the work of librarians, archivists, and staff near and far. I am also especially grateful to everyone at Stanford Libraries and HathiTrust Digital Library who made it possible to complete this project—and to double-check so many footnotes and citations—during a pandemic.

I also want to acknowledge how much this project has depended on my time at Stanford and how I've benefited from the too-often-unacknowledged people and work behind this institution—the Muwekma Ohlone Tribe who have been the stewards of this land and continue to offer their knowledge, the Chinese workers who built the railroads that made the Stanford fortune. This history and present that I'm still learning about illustrates another danger of the self-help myth: focusing on the successful individual almost always elides fuller stories.

Finally, because they have laid the deepest foundation for my work and its inspiration, I want to thank my closest circle. Brad McGowan not only cheered me on across revisions but also provided a lived example of the inventor at work—in case I ever lost sight of why Samuel Smiles and the like were so fascinated by people driven by a passion to create something new. My step-father, Timothy Chambers, reminded me to trust—and also reminded me that I always had a room of my own in Oregon to write from when I needed it. My mother, Richelle Duckwall, believed in me and taught me that the best sort of upward mobility is climbing a mountain—may we climb many more soon. My sister, Merrie Richardson, has been that most necessary person—the one who pretends to let you teach them even as they teach you. And finally, because the loss of his example is too recent and deep for brief anecdotes, my father, Steven Richardson, showed me what it is to love books and art and ideas. He passed in 2021. I wish I could share this book with him; I think he'd get a kick out of it. This book is for all my family, but especially for him.

# Material Ambitions

# Introduction

## Self-Help and the Story of the Ambitious Individual

Today, readers of Victorian literature tend to know about self-help texts like George Lillie Craik's *The Pursuit of Knowledge under Difficulties* and Samuel Smiles's *Self-Help* only from allusions and footnotes. To take just one prominent example, Charles Dickens used "The Pursuit of Knowledge" as a running chapter title in *Great Expectations* and played on it elsewhere[1]—from Sam's father asking, "But wot's that, you're a-doin' of? Pursuit of knowledge under difficulties, Sammy?" in *The Pickwick Papers* to Boffin readying himself for "the pursuit of knowledge" in *Our Mutual Friend*.[2] Victorian readers would have encountered these allusions differently: for them, Craik's and Smiles's titles were household words on par with Dickens's own. In fact, with *Self-Help*, Smiles rivaled the sales of even such popular novelists as Dickens and George Eliot. *Self-Help* sold twenty thousand copies in its first year—one-third more than the "literary sensation" also released in 1859, Eliot's *Adam Bede*,[3] and roughly five times the sales of *Great Expectations* in its first year.[4] It also easily outsold those other well-known titles from 1859, John Stuart Mill's *On Liberty* and Charles Darwin's *On the Origin of the Species*.[5] Craik and Smiles were initial developers of self-help, a genre that, then and now, spans a variety of topics and audiences. Early examples centered on a shared set of ingredients and norms that are still recognizable in today's versions—a mix of inspirational biographies, maxims, and advice designed to encourage readers to work hard, develop their character, and persevere.

Such texts are premised on the idea that, as Smiles puts it, "any man can do what any other man has done."[6] Smiles offered many examples in *Self-Help* of what men had accomplished in a range of fields, from the arts to business, to suggest that readers could emulate such outcomes by similarly developing their characters and work habits. Smiles especially held up examples who had persevered despite failures, illnesses, and poverty, sometimes sleeping only four hours a night, or working multiple jobs, or, in one particularly strange case, subsisting entirely on walnuts for weeks. Given how frequently studies of Victorian literature, particularly the novel, have focused on concepts like character and individualism, it is striking how little attention the self-help genre has received. If we recenter these texts, we can better see how tropes about the hardworking and ambitious subject were employed across genres— and how these tropes participated in a larger cultural debate about the value and limits of ambition. While ambition had long been associated with sin and criminality, it was also, increasingly and paradoxically, seen as driving individual and national progress.[7] The self-help text played a key role in reimagining ambition by centering example after example of hard work leading to success that is both well deserved and, ultimately, beneficial for all. But ambition still suggested dangerous potential, particularly when it was imagined working not in a short anecdote in a self-help text but in a crowded nation and empire.

To make the case for reapproaching Victorian literature through the lens of self-help texts, it's useful to return to the example of Dickens, both because he so self-consciously engaged with the genre and its associated stories about upward mobility, and because he so clearly had complicated ideas about ambition. Across his work, Dickens suggests the difficulties of imagining the wider and longer story of an individual's ambition, specifically how one can both actively pursue and deserve eventual success. While Dickens's novels frequently center characters who escape their early poverty and obscurity, as many critics have argued, Dickens's protagonists turn out to be more passive than ambitious.[8] Instead, Dickens's characters—even his favored and upwardly mobile protagonists, like Pip and David Copperfield—turn out to be more lucky than actively ambitious, benefitting from all the forms in which that recurring character, what George Orwell called "the Good Rich Man," appears in Dickens's fiction.[9] Most typically, characters like Oliver Twist end up rising not through their own ambitious work but through fortunate twists of family inheritance, patronage, or marriage. If they break this mold by actively pursuing a better station, like Bella Wilfer in *Our Mutual Friend*, they are educated out of their ambition before being rewarded with the upward mobility they have learned not to desire.

Dickens still employs ambition in his narratives. But it is more apparent and more active at the margins—in the many antagonists and villains who desire the good things that will ultimately go to the more deserving characters. Characters like Uriah Heep, Josiah Bounderby, and Bradley Headstone embody the energy and ambition that is lacking in Dickens's saintly protagonists. These characters' desires seem to overwhelm them, resulting in an overbearing and superfluous physicality: the clammy hands, sweaty brows, and bloody noses; the sexual desires that repulse both the women they harass or assault and Dickens himself;[10] the aggressive attacks they launch on the favored protagonists. From the margins, then, ambition becomes a material and integral part of Dickens's plots, which so frequently pair an aggressive character against a passively deserving one: Orlick against Pip, Heep against David, Headstone against Eugene. Critics have often read such pairings as a way of disavowing, repressing, or redirecting ambition.[11] It is also a way of using that disavowed ambition to drive a narrative, as the actions of a Heep or a Headstone can finally push the more passive and genteel rival into action. Even more than this, what motivates such characters are the plotted, structural conditions that give them (and the reader) the sense that there aren't quite enough prizes to go around. Dickens's crowded novels are suggestive of so many zero-sum games, with characters pitted—often quite physically—against one another to compete for spouses, careers, and inheritances. Such plotlines implicitly critique the self-help narrative, instead suggesting that ambition (especially of the wrong sort, or, perhaps more accurately, in the wrong subject) can turn individuals against one another in a crowded system.

Dickens's novels are also suffused with these questions about ambition and competition because of the way they refract his own biography. Critics have often had recourse to biographical readings to explain what seems to be everywhere in Dickens's writing, and yet nowhere easily pinned down. As Rosemarie Bodenheimer observes, criticism "has become ever more attentive to the revealing and concealing intelligence that lurks somewhere—but where, exactly?—in Dickens's writing."[12] For Bodenheimer, and for many critics of Dickens, the "where" turns out to be the space between his life and his fiction. And the starting point for understanding Dickens's ambition is the autobiographical fragment that John Forster included in the biography he published after Dickens's death. The fragment concentrates on Dickens's early stint at the blacking warehouse—the setting for his later, ambitious rise—and this has become the single narrative readers of Dickens will have in mind when reading his novels. As Alexander Welsh puts it, "Any reasonably attentive student of literature believes that the single most important event in the life of Dickens was not the writing of any novel, or his attaining of independence, or his marriage and the births of his children, but the four months he spent in Warren's Blacking warehouse at the age of twelve."[13]

The autobiographical fragment includes those ingredients so common to the Dickensian novel: the promising child in unpromising circumstances, the absent or sabotaging parents, the sense that there isn't enough money or attention or opportunities. And much like Dickens's protagonists—those good, aspiring characters that have to be patronized or pushed into success—Dickens portrays his younger self as the passive center of the narrative, dutifully becoming the "self-dependent" worker that his situation and his parents demand.[14] Dickens acknowledges his early desires, as when he sees his sister, Fanny, win a spot at the Royal Academy of Music and prays "to be lifted out of the humiliation and neglect in which I was." But, he swiftly adds, "there was no envy in this."[15] Dickens carefully contrasts two ways of imagining ambition: he distances himself from the sort who "envy" and perhaps even seek to take from another's advancement, while instead claiming that he desires a sort of vertical "lifting," as if by some higher power. Such rhetorical maneuvering is suggestive of how Dickens represented his own ambition with awareness of the larger cultural debates about this drive's potential value and potential dangers—pointing to why Dickens was at such pains to manage the ambitions of his characters.

In this book, I argue that the self-help narrative offered a way around the problem of ambition by asserting that the persevering individual could indeed lift himself out of poverty or obscurity—and not by taking away from anyone else but by lifting the larger society as well. This narrative effectively avoided imagining ambition as a source of envy, competition, or selfishness. Dickens tapped into the power of such self-help tropes to describe his own rise when he addressed working men at mechanics' institutes, where he was frequently invited to lecture and give out prizes. In a speech delivered on December 3, 1858, at the prize-giving of the Institutional Association of Lancashire and Cheshire, in Manchester, Dickens seems to find real inspiration in the accounts of the prize winners: the men who worked by day in a coalpit and walked eight miles a night (three nights a week) to take classes, or the molder who worked in an iron foundry for twelve hours a day but woke up at 4 a.m. to learn drawing.[16] As Dickens put it in an 1843 speech at the First Annual Soiree of the Athenaeum in Manchester, self-improvement builds a certain "property of soul": "The man who lives from day to day by the daily exercise in his sphere of hand or head, and seeks to improve himself in such a place as the Athenaeum, acquires for himself that property of soul which has in all times upheld struggling men in every degree, but self-made men especially and always."[17] Such passages center the hardworking individual who deserves their improvement (while conveniently leaving out how, exactly, this work leads to socioeconomic advancement, if at all).

At such events, Dickens also patterned his own success on such tropes: "The one serviceable, safe, certain, remunerative, attainable quality in every study and in every pursuit is the quality of attention. My own invention or imagination, such as it is, I can most truthfully assure you, would never have served me as it has, but for the habit of commonplace, humble, patient, daily, toiling, drudging attention."[18] True to the self-help ethos, Dickens attributes his success not to genius—not to "invention or imagination"—but to his "attention," a "commonplace" quality that is imagined as available to all through patient and persevering hard work. Dickens gives a similar line to David Copperfield, who explains that he owes his writing career to "steady, plain, hardworking qualities."[19] From the fragment to his speeches to his most autobiographical novel, Dickens helped lay the groundwork for the story of his own ambition and persevering work.

The extent to which Dickens's life was understood in terms of the Victorian self-help narrative is demonstrated by the number of biographers and early critics who fashioned the story of his career as, in fact, a lesson demonstrating the power of hard work. For example, the volume *Risen by Perseverance; or, Lives of Self-Made Men* includes Dickens among its handful of biographies, explaining that his "early untoward surroundings only strengthened him to put forth the most determined and preserving energy to overcome them."[20] Dickens was also held up as a model specifically for aspiring writers. In his 1898 *Charles Dickens: A Critical Study*, George Gissing writes that the biography of Dickens is inspiring for the "young man"—because these authors are so often coded as men—"beginning his struggle in the world of letters." Gissing claims that the biography "stirred" his own ambition—"not to imitate Dickens as a novelist, but to follow afar off his example as a worker," to imitate "the strenuous spirit in which Dickens wrought."[21] Similarly, G. K. Chesterton fashions Dickens as an inspiring story of self-help, imagining how his "resolution to rise" led him to work "all day at law, and then all night at shorthand" to become a reporter: "Learning the thing under every disadvantage, without a teacher, without the possibility of concentration or complete mental force, without ordinary human sleep, he made himself one of the most rapid reporters then alive."[22] In such anecdotes, Dickens's ambitious spirit overcomes all material obstacles, defying socioeconomic conditions and physical needs. These tropes, closely aligned with the discourse circulating in self-help texts, focus our attention entirely on the successful individual and their hard work— work that tends to be overtly physicalized, implicitly or explicitly coded as masculine, and premised on being able bodied, with the subject disciplining both mind and body to ever-greater feats of productivity.

When ambition backfires in these narratives that so entirely center the successful subject, it tends to do so not on others but on the individual who wields it. Even according to Forster's idolizing biography, as much as Dickens's early hardships inspired this ambitious drive "to rise," it was "not without alloy." While Dickens forged his ambitious character in those blacking warehouse fires, his ambition entailed a latent danger: "The fixed and eager determination, the restless and resistless energy, which opened to him opportunities of escape from many mean environments . . . brought with it some disadvantage among many noble advantages." Dickens, by this account, seemed to risk a certain excess of confidence and even aggression: "A too great confidence in himself, a sense that everything was possible to the will that would make it so, laid occasionally upon him self-imposed burdens greater than might be borne by any one with safety. In that direction there was in him, at such times, something even hard and aggressive; in his determinations a something that had almost the tone of fierceness; something in his nature that made his resolves insuperable."[23]

These ideas about Dickens's aggressive will and determination all became part of the narrative of his death as well as his life. To his friends, Dickens seemed to be speaking himself into poor health during his public tours. These tours eventually came to a halt after Frank Beard diagnosed Dickens with "overwork." As Dickens admits in a letter to Forster, "the tremendously severe nature of this work [in his public readings] is a little shaking me. At Chester last Sunday I found myself extremely giddy, and extremely uncertain of my sense of touch, both in the left leg and the left hand and arms."[24] Much as Dickens's novels imagine that ambition is always pushing against not only the limits of the larger society and its laws, but even against the ambitious individual's body, so too did Dickens and his acquaintances worry that his ambition and energy would overflow his physical abilities. While in his ambitious villains this excess energy drove plots pitting him against a too-passive protagonist, in the fashioning of Dickens's biography, such energy and activity seem to turn not against others but against Dickens himself.

I start with this example not only because Dickens is such a foundational figure for a study of Victorian literature and ambition but also because this analysis foregrounds the methodology underpinning this book. Dickens self-consciously employed these tropes about self-help and the hardworking individual to different ends across his novels, his speeches, and the story of his own life. As noted above, critics have long recognized the need to think across

Dickens's biography and his novels. Such an approach is all the more necessary when tracking the self-help narrative in the Victorian era, and not only in the case of Dickens. First, this narrative immediately implicates an author's own ambition in a competitive literary marketplace. All the authors I focus on in this study were very much aware of their own ambitions as writers, and each made or regained their fortune (or at least a living) by writing. Second, as these authors fashioned the story of their successes, they patterned themselves on (or subverted) the sorts of narratives circulating in the popular genres of self-help and inspirational biographies. In fact, most of the authors I discuss wrote an autobiography or memoir, including Smiles, Harriet Martineau, Anthony Trollope, and Miles Franklin, often with the explicit intention of offering up their life as an example for others to learn from. Finally, all this self-fashioning indeed worked on the wider public, with readers and critics repeating inspirational stories (as we've seen with self-help texts, biographies, and literary criticism focusing on Dickens). The genres of biography and autobiography are thus important for understanding the story of the ambitious and successful individual that was shaped in the Victorian era. Even if the ambitious individual was typically portrayed as dangerous or villainous in their fiction—where the drive tends to turn outward on others—these authors imagined themselves as positive examples of such persevering work when they told the story of their own rise. Still, this drive posed risks. As the biography of Dickens in *Risen by Perseverance* notes, "The immediate cause of [Dickens's] death was from effusion of blood on the brain, brought on by overwork."[25]

When we read self-help texts, biographical writing, and fiction together, the paradox of ambition in the Victorian era emerges in fuller context. Ambition had long been understood as double sided: manifesting itself in admirable perseverance toward individual goals and national progress or in ruthless self-seeking after money, power, and accomplishments. Even a supposedly admirable ambition can blur into its opposite, when a passion becomes an obsession that leads to overwork or, scaling up, when national or imperial progress is quite literally built on the destruction of others. Narratives about ambition took up both these strands, as well as the lurking suspicion that ambition always does violence to someone, somewhere. This suspicion comes through most clearly when authors imagine the material limits to their own or their characters' ambition—the limits posed by one's own body, by socioeconomic barriers, or by the environment.

In making this argument, I want to speak to two larger and related critical conversations in Victorian studies. First, this book reapproaches long-standing questions about the liberal or, later, neoliberal individual via the lens of self-help texts and discourse. Critics from Ian Watt to Franco Moretti to Nancy Armstrong have tended to center the novel in discussions about the individual and individualism. According to these readings, the novelistic protagonist must discipline or compromise their desires to adapt to a wider cultural and economic system. The limit of individualism in the novel is the wider society, and the trespasser is the figure of the criminal. Even as recent studies have developed our understanding of how the modern liberal subject is defined by categories like character (Amanda Anderson) and through developing ideas about the state, sovereignty, and empire (Bruce Robbins, Lauren M. E. Goodlad), such studies have largely centered the novel.[26] If we attend to a range of genres, from biography and self-help to the novel, a more nuanced picture emerges. Self-help texts like Craik's *The Pursuit of Knowledge under Difficulties* (1830–31), the anonymously published *Success in Life* (1858), William Anderson's *Self-Made Men* (1861), and, most famously, Smiles's *Self-Help* (1859) all quite explicitly sought to build their readers' characters. They praised perseverance and hard work, holding up the biographies of successful men—and, on occasion, women—for readerly admiration and emulation. As this book will argue, the self-help genre provided a narrative structure for ambition and a moralized cover story, a way of centering and also valorizing the individual and their success. Works like Smiles's *Self-Help* explicitly linked individual ambitions to the nation and empire, suggesting a one-to-one relationship between the success of the individual and the group—even if, in actuality, this was a far more fraught relationship.

Second, recentering this self-help narrative—and how it frames the relationship between the individual and the wider system—offers a new perspective on long-standing questions about the rise of individualism in relation to the aggregate, whether the aggregate is understood to be the nation, the corporation, or the population. Recent work in this area has drawn attention to the underlying tensions between representing the individual and the group in nineteenth-century literature. For example, Daniel Stout analyzes "how the corporate and the collective appeared as an analytical problem for individualism,"[27] while Emily Steinlight focuses on "mass life" and the way fiction "strategically exacerbates the conditions of crowding and superfluity, and turns these conditions into sources of narrative energy."[28] To add to this critical conversation, I would suggest the importance of looking to a genre that, while overlooked in criticism now, loomed large for the Victorians themselves. The self-help narrative offered a rosy cover story for how a crowd of individuals might succeed together. At the same time, this narrative also points to the limits of individualism in overtly material and physical terms—the limits of the larger socio-economic system and environment, as well as one's own physical and psychological well-being. As seductive as the story of the individual triumphing against all odds has proven, the version popularized by self-help discourse highlights just how much this story depends on ideas about ability and able bodiedness, on the exploitation of natural resources and, all too often, on eliding the failure or losses of someone else.

As I'll argue, in these narratives the distance between ambition and its realization originates in the body's capabilities as well as the affordances of the socioeconomic and material environment. Our understanding of individualism and how it's fashioned in narrative requires greater attention to ambition and to the cultural history of this drive. Self-help texts are well positioned to flesh out such a history, as they seek to inspire and manage the excessive ambition that pushes against the limits of human ability and finite material resources. In thinking about physical and material limits, I want to foreground the importance of work in gender and disability studies, ecocriticism, and settler colonial studies to this book. These theoretical lenses importantly draw attention to systems of power relations and agency—or, translated into the terms of my own argument, to the way an individual's abilities are imagined in relation to the limits of the body, the collective, and the built and natural environment.

While Armstrong has importantly situated the rise of individualism alongside theories of gender, this history parallels and often intersects with the period's—and the novel's—interest in juxtaposing and defining ability through and against representations of disability. Since David T. Mitchell and Sharon L. Snyder's argument in *Narrative Prosthesis* that the novel in fact depends on representations of disability,[29] critics have analyzed how the Victorian novel was particularly concerned with portrayals of disability and illness—from Martha Stoddard Holmes's *Fictions of Affliction: Physical Disability in Victorian Culture* to Karen Bourrier's *The Measure of Manliness: Disability and Masculinity in the Mid-Victorian Novel*.[30] The examples I explore in this book illustrate the importance, specifically, of self-help texts to this ongoing critical conversation—with their mythologies about the all-powerful individual, about hard (and overtly physicalized and gendered) work, and about the ultimate value of "difficulties" (which often take the shape of physical illnesses or disabilities).

What has also often been lacking in literary studies of ambition and individualism is the role of the setting and environment—the material surroundings that the ambitious individual acts upon. This absence is striking when we consider the importance of geography in the age of the British empire, and the interest, both in reality and in the novel, in portraying colonial spaces as so many playing fields for ambition, waiting to receive the overflow of the British population. These questions about limitations take on further urgency when imagined via the logic of settler colonialism, which relied on appropriating land from Indigenous people around the world. As Patrick Wolfe theorizes, settler colonialism has always been essentially "a winner-take-all project whose dominant feature is not exploitation but replacement."[31] With these theories in mind, I argue that representations of the ambitious individual acting on a limited environment suggest the zero-sum mentality of imperialism, as well as a more general competition for scarce resources.

While bodies always exist in physical environments, the discourses of competitive and even Malthusian or Darwinian natural forces in the Victorian period—in an age that saw the violent spread of imperial and colonial expansion, and the growth of an increasingly global capitalist economy—amplified the stakes of representing ambitious individualism. Across the chapters, across analyses of self-help texts, autobiographies, and novels, I point to how these limits are rendered into form, whether in compressed biographies that imagine how the subject is overwhelmed by their own ambition or in fictional narratives that use zero-sum games and competitions to structurally enact the sense that there isn't quite enough room for everyone's ambitions. Texts like Smiles's *Self-Help* focus, by stated design, on success stories—and, in the process, they tend to trace a straight line from an individual's actions to their eventual triumph. This hides the fuller picture of ambition and its costs. Smiles of course entirely leaves out stories about failure or losing out to a successful rival. He also leaves out the wider cast of characters who propped up the success stories by quietly helping from the sidelines.[32] And in fact even the individual seems to fade into the background as their ambition takes over—with the drive to work frequently verging on self-destructive obsession or monomania. Smiles was particularly fascinated by people whose pursuits took "complete possession" or "firm possession" over them (131 and 66). These are recurring phrases in *Self-Help*, where the ambition to chart the stars or discover the chemical composition of porcelain or paint the next masterpiece takes possession of the subject—even if it means risking one's health or even life in the process.

Fictional narratives, and especially multiplot Victorian novels, with their notoriously baggy plots and large casts of characters, were well suited to widening the lens beyond the individual. But even in the "baggy monster" of the Victorian novel that seems to offer plenty of space, ambitious individuals get in one another's way. As one character worries in Trollope's *The Three Clerks*, the world "will soon be like a fishpond, very full of fish, but with very little food for them."[33] Authors dramatized concerns about ambition by representing its physical and material limits. Such limits are figured first in the individual body and become all the more pressing (literally and metaphorically) as the individual enters into competition with others. Many of the era's most popular plots function like competitions, from marriage plots to courtroom trials. The nineteenth-century novel seems drawn to the limited system—in terms of both character systems (Austen's "3 or 4 Families in a Country Village") and settings (Eliot's town of Middlemarch). And readers and authors have in fact approached these narratives with an eye to which character most deserves the novel's prizes. For example, Frances Ferguson notes the many readings (or misreadings) of *Emma* that "stress the clarity of the victory through which Emma is awarded Knightley, the husband who counts as the finest trophy in the marriage competition."[34]

Across fictional and nonfictional narratives, the obstacles individuals face to fulfilling and deserving their goals points to material realities in the Victorian era—the limits of a person's energy or ability, competitions with others, and a socioecological system of finite resources. As a result, to portray the ambitious subject in the Victorian era is to imagine not only their abilities but also the workings of local and global economies, which gesture to the violence underlying the nation and the empire. Far from the self-help genre's celebration of noble or laudable ambitions that might overcome all obstacles for the greater good—even if, in the process, the individual sacrifices their time or health—ambition in the novel emerges as always already compromised in an increasingly global socioecological system. The aim of this book is to show how reading across popular Victorian narratives about the successful individual highlights the era's ambivalence about the value of ambition.

## Ambition, Self-Help, and the Nation

I want to turn now to those key terms that I've suggested need more attention: first, to contextualize ambition and self-help, and second, to speak more specifically to what centering these terms means for our understanding of Victorian literature as well as the history of individualism. As much as studies of nineteenth-century British literature have focused on ideas about the self and its improvement—from Armstrong's work on desire and individualism to Andrew

Miller's work on perfectionism to Robbins's work on upward mobility—they have tended to overlook self-help (as a term and a genre) as well as the concept of ambition. These are particularly important gaps to fill because the concept of ambition has such a long and fraught history in the West, while the term and genre of self-help were specifically developing in the nineteenth century and attempting to manage readers' ambitions.

Readers were thought to need such management because ambition was a Janus-faced drive. This duality is built into the Anglo-American history of ambition, as William Casey King has recently explored. For much of this history, ambition was seen as irredeemably sinful. The Geneva Bible, across text and annotations, attributes Adam's fall not to pride but to ambition, thus aligning this original sin with Lucifer's. On the stage, across *Macbeth*, *Julius Caesar*, and *Doctor Faustus*, the ambition to have more power or more knowledge or more life is portrayed as a tragic flaw. It is not until Francis Bacon's *Novum Organum*, King suggests, that we get the "possibility of 'noble ambition'"—the possibility that this drive could be used to good ends without tipping into a dangerous passion.[35] Meanwhile, the closely associated term "avarice" was similarly undergoing a conceptual shift, as Albert O. Hirschman has famously argued: reframed as "interest" in the eighteenth century, avarice was presented as a quality that might actually keep more violent passions in line.[36] These appetitive drives, though, never entirely shed their original sin. In fact, writing about how ambition has been understood in philosophy and ethics today, Glen Pettigrove closely adheres in spirit as well as terminology to these earlier conceptualizations: ambition "has the potential to be a crucial virtue as well as a devastating vice"; it might provide "direction and meaning," "supplying a normative framework that encourages creativity, industry, discipline and perseverance," or it might become all consuming and "supplant the moral point of view."[37]

While this duality is a long-standing one, it was particularly fraught in the Victorian age, as ideas about upward mobility were being worked out amid all the changes that came with the rise of a middle class and the expansion of industrial capitalism in a global empire. Many writers, across philosophical and literary as well as popular writing, openly confronted the duality of ambition. As the *Mirror Monthly Magazine* put it, "Ambition is one of those feelings of the human breast which may become a virtue or a vice."[38] No wonder the word "ambition" was always being modified, whether to signal a "high ambition" or a "selfish ambition." For a rough big picture, British works published from 1800 to 1900 and searchable through Google Books show that popular adjectives include, on the one hand, "highest," "noble," "laudable," "honourable," "honest," and "proud"; and, on the other hand, "selfish," "insatiable," "worldly," "inordinate," "private," "vain," "wild," "mad," "unprincipled," "vulgar," and "earthly."[39] At a more fine-grained level, we see this duality over and over in the way Victorian writers meditated on the value of ambition. For example, Thomas Carlyle sought to separate "the two kinds of ambition; one wholly blamable, the other laudable and inevitable," and proposed that "to decide about ambition, whether it is bad or not, you have two things to take into view. Not the coveting of the place alone, but the fitness of the man for the place withal."[40]

The attempt to distinguish between these types of ambition also led to the use of two terms, "ambition" and "aspiration." Although these are synonyms, their etymology and connotations offer a stark contrast. Whereas the root of "ambition" in Latin and French—"going round," in the sense of a compass or circumference—is suggestive of "getting around" others in a competitive system, "aspiration" carries suggestions of other meanings of "aspire," such as "to rise," "soar to," or "mount up."[41] Or, as William Rounseville Alger succinctly puts it, "Aspiration is a pure upward desire for excellence, without side-references; ambition is an inflamed desire to surpass others."[42] Alger depicts a clear and tidy break between the two modes of striving—the sort of distinction Dickens seems to make when he insists there is "no envy" in his desire to be lifted out of obscurity. Other thinkers point to what a faint line this distinction could be. Reflecting on the expression "All claret would be port if it could," Thackeray writes that "a desire to excel, a desire to be hearty, fruity, generous, strength-imparting—is a virtuous and noble ambition; and it is most difficult for a man in his own case, or his neighbour's, to say at what point this ambition transgresses the boundary of virtue, and becomes vanity, pretence, and self-seeking."[43]

The invention of "self-help," as a term and a genre, can be read as a strategy for separating out and cultivating "high" or "laudable" ambitions, without relying on a word that, as we've seen, was so ambiguous. Unlike "ambition," "self-help" was associated with entirely positive qualities, including self-reliance, self-education, and persevering dedication. Early uses of the term branched from two sources. First, there is the philosophical branch: Carlyle was among the first to use the word in the early 1830s in letters and in *Sartor Resartus*. Tellingly, whereas Carlyle worried about how to distinguish between laudable and not-so-laudable ambitions, when it came to "self-help," he saw only positive connotations, using the term to praise figures like J. P. Richter, Sir Walter Scott, and Samuel Johnson.[44] Self-help is, for Carlyle, the "highest of all possessions," the quality that Teufelsdröckh cultivates as he teaches himself languages and literatures.⁴⁵ Such self-help becomes coded as resistant to the dominant culture. As Vladimir Trendafilov argues, Carlyle seems to use the term to describe the "self-reliant, self-subsistent individual aiming to stay unchanged against the advance of urban civilization and polite society"—in short, a sort of "noble savage on the margins of the social contract, a set of human qualities extolled because uncontaminated by cultivation."⁴⁶ These ideas easily traveled or rhymed with those across the Atlantic. Smiles's use of the term "self-help" may also have been influenced or reinforced by American reformers, including the Unitarian minister William Ellery Channing and Ralph Waldo Emerson, with their arguments for self-culture and self-education as ends in themselves.⁴⁷ Across these influences, there is an emphasis on holding up the independent man—gendered and physicalized as a sort of masculine self-reliance—from Henry David Thoreau on the margins of society in *Walden,* to Emerson's vision, in pieces like "Man the Reformer" and "Self-Reliance," of the "self-helping man" who seems to command instant respect: "For him all doors are flung wide; him all tongues greet, all honors crown, all eyes follow with desire."⁴⁸ This first branch of usage around "self-help" thus imagines someone independent of the usual social norms, able to cultivate his own intellectual—and often quite physicalized—self-reliance.

The second origin point for the term "self-help" stems from radical politics. According to this branch, the self-helper is figured not as some rare hero but as all those working people who persevere and help themselves. While critics have debated which line of thought and which particular thinkers most immediately influenced Smiles's use of the term, Trendafilov has importantly filled in this history from both sides: he notes that Smiles may have encountered the neologism "self-help" not only through Carlyle but also through a source close to him—the *Leeds Times.* About two years before Smiles himself became the editor of this newspaper, the young Robert Nicoll wrote a piece titled "The Duties of the People" with the pithy line, "Heaven helps those who help themselves, and self-help is the only effectual help."⁴⁹ Further backing up Trendafilov's theory, this line is "practically quoted" in the first paragraph of Smiles's *Self-Help.*⁵⁰

Regardless of the exact mix of influence from these two early strands of usage, Smiles exhaustively defines the term in his 1859 *Self-Help: With Illustrations of Character and Conduct*: the book contains "lessons of industry, perseverance, and self-culture." ("Perseverance" proved important enough for a promotion, joining the title in Smiles's revised edition.) In a departure from the Carlylean strand, Smiles importantly emphasizes hard work in any sphere: far from re-serving the quality for the famous heroes of history, Smiles illustrates what he means by "self-help" with hundreds of examples of success across business, reli-gion, the arts, and industry. In the process, Smiles became, as Asa Briggs writes, "one of the most important propagandists" in mid-Victorian England, preach-ing a wildly popular and adaptable "gospel of work."[51] These ideas easily fed into the mythology of the self-made man, which, especially in the Victorian context, paralleled and worked to reimagine ideas about the gentleman.[52] In fact, Smiles dedicates a whole chapter to "character—the true gentleman," insisting that "the poor man may be a true gentleman,—in spirit and in daily life. He may be hon-est, truthful, upright, polite, temperate, courageous, self-respecting, and self-helping,—that is, be a true gentleman" (327–28).

Smiles's version of the genre had an outsized influence, in and beyond his immediate context. As noted above, *Self-Help* sold well above many of the ti-tles we're more familiar with today: twenty thousand copies in its first year, fifty-five thousand copies by 1864, and more than a quarter of a million by 1905.[53] And Smiles went on to publish similar works, such as *Character* (1871), *Thrift* (1875), *Duty* (1880), and *Life and Labour* (1887). The self-help message was amplified in a variety of ways, by authors who were inspired by Smiles, or who were happy to lift from him, or who were eager to translate or adapt the work for other audiences. The writer Orison Marden remembered be-ing "thrilled and inspired" by the "stories of poor boys climbing to the top," which led him to seek the title of "the Samuel Smiles of America."[54] His own take on the genre, *Pushing to the Front* (1894), went through 250 editions. Tipping his hat to Smiles, Marden even included him as an example of some-one to emulate for his work ethic.[55] Others outright borrowed and plagiarized: as Irvin G. Wyllie observes, American authors regularly copied from England's "success cult," with Smiles proving an "inexhaustible mine."[56]

Smiles's work was also widely translated. In 1887, the *Athenaeum* claimed that "Turkey is the only country of Europe in which the book has not been translated."[57] (And even Turkey eventually got its own version.) In his *Auto-biography* (1905) Smiles proudly recalls the many translations of his work around the world—including editions in Buenos Aires, Portugal, and Russia. There were also translations into Arabic and into "several of the languages of India, more specially into Tamil, Marati, Gujarati, Hindustani, and Canarese." Smiles especially delighted in the story behind the popular Japanese transla-tion, which could itself have been included as an example of persevering work: Nakamura Masanao brought a copy of *Self-Help* back to Japan after his 1868 visit to England, translating it during his journey home and publishing it upon his arrival.[58] Passages from *Self-Help* even made their way onto the walls of an Egyptian palace, rubbing elbows with inscriptions from the Koran.[59] By the end of the Victorian era, the *Saturday Review* claimed that "Smiles' books have had a wider circulation through translations into foreign languages than any other English author, barring Shakespeare."[60] Far beyond his own lifetime, Smiles's influence has been felt across many traditions. Sir John Lubbock added *Self-Help* to his popular list of one hundred books best worth reading, where it appeared alongside Burke and Voltaire.[61] By 1891, a description of a South African library includes *Self-Help* among the "works without which 'no gentleman's library is complete.'"[62] In her recent work on self-help and modern literature, Beth Blum chooses Smiles as a key case study for how the genre sparked cross-cultural exchanges in Japan, China, and Nigeria.[63] Smiles's message proved to be lasting as well as adaptable, emphasizing such widely valued qualities as hard work, honesty, and perseverance.

Given this immediate success and lasting influence, it is not surprising that Smiles's work is the best-known Victorian example of the genre today. Though the volume hasn't received much attention in relation to Victorian literature or the history of ambition, it is still regularly invoked in discussions of the self-help genre and its history. The text is available in a modern Oxford edition with an excellent introduction by Peter Sinnema, and the title often crops up in footnotes to critical editions of nineteenth-century texts and occasionally in criticism (particularly by historians). But to get at how pervasive the self-help narrative was in the Victorian era—and how this narrative imagined a path for the "right" sort of ambition—it's important to resituate *Self-Help* within a broader constellation of texts and to think of self-help as a genre rather than a single title, while also considering the deeper traditions that informed its rise.

To acknowledge the persistence of this genre today, and to recall the importance of Smiles's work in particular, I refer to the nineteenth-century version of the genre under the umbrella of "self-help." Other critics have referred to Victorian texts like *Self-Help* as "success literature" or "self-improvement biography" or "advice books." The Victorians themselves sometimes also used the catchall category of "self-culture," which was closely associated with self-education. Across these terms, the emphasis on actively shaping the self echoes ideas about "self-fashioning" in the Renaissance, a tradition that has continuities with advice and conduct manuals in the eighteenth century (such as Lord Chesterfield's *Letters to His Son* and Hester Chapone's *Letters on the Improvement of the Mind, Addressed to a Young Lady*). Other adjacent terms include "self-improvement," which is closely associated with the eighteenth century, and "self-development," which has affinities with the Romantic era.[64] Unlike these related terms, "self-help" emerged as a popular term and concept in the Victorian era, implying a different understanding of the "self" and who should have one. For example, many of these earlier terms are suggestive of a more organic process of self-formation, and they tend to imagine a better-heeled subject. While self-improvement had been part, as John Brewer notes, of the eighteenth-century project of "general enlightenment," it was aimed at merchants, tradesmen, and skilled artisans "refining and cultivating" their knowledge and taste. In contrast, "self-help" embraced a wider audience, appealing to working- as well as middle-class readers.

Self-help texts thus responded to a specifically nineteenth-century interest in education and advancement for the masses. To be sure, self-help texts drew on a tradition of more general life advice or "wisdom literature"—with Victorian versions like Martin Tupper's *Proverbial Philosophy* (1838) running into forty editions just in Britain—but self-help writers tended to frame this wisdom in terms of "useful knowledge" and practical advice for socioeconomic advancement. Interest in this improvement came from multiple directions. The middle class sought to "diffuse" knowledge to the lower classes, often simply to make them better behaved and more productive workers. At the same time, radicals across classes looked to adult education, cooperative movements, and labor unions to actively improve conditions, sometimes directly challenging the interests of the higher middle and managerial class. With its roots in lectures that Smiles gave to local youth and workers' mutual improvement organizations, *Self-Help* participated in this movement for wider education, particularly for the working and lower-middle classes. Other similar texts explicitly addressed mechanics' institutions, such as Timothy Claxton's *Hints to Mechanics on Self-Education and Mutual Instruction* (1839), which includes a mix of biographies and advice, a history of mechanics' institutes, and practical suggestions for lecture topics and discussion questions. An emphasis on education is also clear in William Robinson's *Self-Education, or The Value of Mental Culture, with the Practicability of Its Attainment under Disadvantages* (1845), with Robinson's revised edition citing the "awakened attention to the importance of mental culture" and particularly addressing itself to "the humbler classes."[65] George Jacob Holyoake's *Self-Help by the People. History of Co-operation in Rochdale* (1857) offered an example and guide for how the people could enact principles valuing shared interests, cooperation, and justice over selfishness.

Children and young adults were also especially targeted with the self-help message. The Christian Knowledge Society offered the title *Higher and Higher: A Book for Children* (1876), which included stories "by Mr. Smiles' permission, adapted from 'Self-Help.'" Other titles include the anonymously published *The Elements of Success: Illustrated in the Life of Amos Lawrence and Others; A Book for Young Men* (1862) and James Hogg's *Men Who Have Risen: A Book for Boys* (1861) and *Brave Men's Footsteps: A Book of Example and Anecdote in Practical Life, for Young People* (1872). Other writers offered versions specifically for women, sometimes complementing or adapting titles that implicitly or explicitly addressed themselves to men. Craik issued a follow-up, *The Pursuit of Knowledge, Illustrated by Female Examples* (1847). W. H. Davenport Adams offered both *The Secret of Success; or, How to Get On in the World* (1879) as well as titles aimed at women, including *Woman's Work and Worth in Girlhood, Maidenhood, and Wifehood* (1880) and the abridged version, *Exemplary Women: A Record of Feminine Virtues and Achievements* (1882). Jessie Boucherett's *Hints on Self-Help: A Book for Young Women* (1863) invokes and quotes at length from Smiles's work. We might also consider texts addressed to particular tasks or professions, like *Mrs Beeton's Book of Household Management* (1861), as self-help texts—particularly given the genre's overlapping roots with conduct manuals and outgrowth into all sorts of "how to" guides. But these sorts of more specific guides often lack that ingredient that proved so fundamental to texts like Craik's and Smiles's—exemplary biography.

The practice of collecting biographies to celebrate great men and women has a long history, stretching back to Plutarch's *Lives* and Christine de Pizan's *The Book of the City of Ladies*. Closely adjacent is the tradition of saints' lives (in fact, Smiles's work has been likened to a secular hagiography).[66] The nineteenth century saw a renewed interest in collected biographies, from Mary Hays's *Female Biography; or, Memoirs of Illustrious and Celebrated Women, of All Ages and Countries* to Carlyle's *On Heroes, Hero-Worship, & the Heroic in History*. This interest came with an intense focus on using such biographies to mold one's own character, as both Alison Booth and Juliette Atkinson have demonstrated. Booth traces the interest to Henry Fielding and Samuel Johnson and "the demand for prosopographies as both self-help and collective historiography."[67] As Atkinson observes of the Victorian era, the use of "exemplary biography was pervasive, and the belief in the emulative power of biography was rarely questioned."[68] Of course, didactic fictional and allegorical tales, before and after the novel, also offer up examples—even if fictional— from Christian in *Pilgrim's Progress* to Laura Montreville in Mary Brunton's

*Self-Control*. But, as Booth notes, "while the novel was regarded with suspicion, there was a consensus that biography had a beneficent effect," via what we might now call identification.[69] Smiles himself seems to have experienced such identification when reading Craik's *The Pursuit of Knowledge under Difficulties*, which collected exemplary biographies and was written for the Society for the Diffusion of Useful Knowledge.[70] As Craik explains of his method, "every man is interested in learning what are the real hindrances which have opposed themselves to the progress of some of the most distinguished persons, and how those obstacles have been surmounted."[71] Smiles similarly lauds biography because it offers "helps, guides, and incentives to others": "Some of the best are almost equivalent to gospels—teaching high living, high thinking, and energetic action for their own and the world's good." Such biographies illustrate "what it is in the power of each to accomplish for himself" (21). Texts like *Self-Help* explicitly employ biography to form the reader's habits—a key term for Smiles, who recites the commonplace that man "is a bundle of habits" (319).

As many of the above examples of self-help texts already make clear, the genre was particularly fixated on the rags-to-riches narrative, with titles like R. A. Davenport's *Lives of Individuals Who Raised Themselves from Poverty to Eminence or Fortune* (1841), Anderson's *Self-Made Men* (1865), Hogg's *Small Beginnings, or The Way to Get On* (1859), or, on the American side, Charles C. B. Seymour's *Self-Made Men* (1858). Self-help books were at pains to frame these successes as more than simply financial. While Smiles readily acknowledges that "comfort in worldly circumstances" and the maintenance of one's family are important (242), he warns that money should not be made into "an idol," but rather, regarded as "a useful agent" (246). Still, one offshoot of self-help explicitly took up "money-making," with titles like *Millionaires and How They Became So* (1884), *Fortunes Made in Business* (1891), *Money-Making Men, or How to Grow Rich* (1886), *Great Fortunes and How They Were Made* (1871), and P. T. Barnum's *The Art of Money-Getting* (1882). Even among such titles, authors frequently stress the importance of hard work and character over mere financial success. For example, *Fortunes Made in Business* reminds the reader that each story "carries with it the lessons of small beginnings and noble aspirations—of resolute perseverance and commanding integrity—and reveals achievements of far greater importance than the acquisitions of individual riches."[72]

The concern about financial motives is indicative of the larger concern about ambition that the self-help genre had to navigate: how to keep self-interest from turning into selfishness and how to get ambition to work for (rather than against) others. For example, *Fortunes Made in Business* is care-ful to frame financial success as extending far beyond the individual, since "no great industrial concern can be built up without its benefits extending to the community as well as to its founders and heads."[73] This need to frame and manage the reader's ambition is clear across self-help discourse. *Success in Life* urges readers to develop "a well regulated ambition": "To supply at once a guide and a stimulus to the youthful reader, in this path of honourable ambition, is the purpose of the following work."[74] In supplying this "guide," *Success in Life* distinguishes between the "laudable" (51) and the "false" (178) varieties of am-bition. Similarly, Boucherett's *Hints on Self-Help: A Book for Young Women* argues that "a noble self-supporting ambition should be aroused, a truthful spirit encouraged, and obedience to lawful authority inculcated."[75] As William Anderson advises in *Self-Made Men*, "he who can control and regulate his ap-petites and passions is nobler far" than a Caesar or an Alexander, whose "overweening and insane ambition flung them prostrate in degradation and death."[76] These texts tend to clarify which type of ambition they have in mind, holding up the "well regulated," "honourable," and "laudable"[77] ambitions while warning against the "immoderate" (Craik 1.282).

What makes ambition "noble" (versus "overweening and insane") is the link between an individual's success and that of a collective, usually imagined as the family and the nation. To take two immensely popular examples: William Arthur's biography of Samuel Budgett analyzes his subject's "natural ambi-tion," which, helped by "the grace of God," manifests in his "sacred resolve to employ his gains, not in hoarding up wealth for himself, but in promoting the happiness, first of his family, then of his neighbours."[78] The first chapter in Smiles's *Self-Help* explicitly connects the individual and the nation in its very title: "Self-Help—National and Individual." As Smiles argues, "The spirit of self-help, as exhibited in the energetic action of individuals, has in all times been a marked feature in the English character, and furnishes the true measure of our power as a nation" (20). Although not extending into as many editions as Arthur's and Smiles's works, Boucherett similarly moves between the individual and the group, linking her readers specifically through their identity as women: "Every piece of good work done by a woman raises the character of the sex" (120). As a genre, self-help set out to shape the read-er's ambition, justifying this focus on individual success by reframing it as service to a wider group. This message seemed to be heard loud and clear. As Horace Mayhew advised in *Punch*, there are two main paths for improving one's lot: "You can do it a la STEPHENSON, or a la ROBESPIERRE. If you want to know what is the final reward of such men, read two great books:—*Self-Help* and the *French Revolution*."[79] Whereas reading about the French Revolution could teach one to weaponize one's ambition against the system that had deprived one of a good position to start with, reading Smiles's *Self-Help* instructs the reader to funnel his ambition into a project of individual as well as national uplift (with George Stephenson, as the "Father of Railways," being a much-loved subject for Smiles—so much so that he wrote a stand-alone biography).

This strategy for reframing the value of ambition via the self-help narrative is surely one reason Ian Watt cites *Self-Help* as a turning point in the history of the concept of individualism in England.[80] It's important to pause here at how the term "individualism"—like "ambition"—evolved with such opposed meanings. "Individualism" had previously conjured up negative associations: as Steven Lukes has argued, the French *individualism* "grew out of the general European reaction to the French Revolution" and subsequently came to signify "individual isolation and social dissolution."[81] As Watt recounts, when the term came to England in the 1830s, "it was dyslogistic—it carried an invidious or a hostile sense: it put the individual person in implied opposition to human solidarity." In distinction, far from seeing individualism as a threat to a harmonious society, Smiles uses the term with positive connotations. At one point he observes that "daily experience shows that it is energetic individualism which produces the most powerful effects upon the life and action of others, and really constitutes the best practical education" (20). Or, as Smiles later wrote in *Thrift*, if you stop "the advancement of individualism," you also stop that of "society at large."[82] Such messages must have easily blended with John Stuart Mill's *On Liberty*, imagining how individualism is not only good for the one but also good for the larger society.

The self-help genre's focus on regulating ambition and developing a sense of prosocial individualism via the use of exemplary biography thus constitutes a crucial shadow movement to the other genre typically read as creating individuals—the novel. The rise of the novel and the rise of individualism have long been read as entangled histories, reaching back to *Robinson Crusoe* as well as to the development of the bildungsroman, a genre that celebrates the individual even as it tracks the compromises he must make to live in society rather than on a deserted island. As Watt puts it, "The novel is the form of literature which most fully reflects this individualist and innovating reorientation."[83] More recently, Armstrong has seen individualism as both the subject of eighteenth- and nineteenth-century novels and, by modeling such individualism, what "novels were acquiring the power to endow their readers with" (3). The novel has also, going back to Benedict Anderson, long been associated with the nation: both link subjects through the sense of being "embedded in 'societies'" and "in the minds of the omniscient readers." As Anderson famously theorized, "The idea of a sociological organism moving calendrically through homogenous, empty time is a precise analogue of the idea of the nation."[84] Armstrong makes this argument more specifically for the British novel after the second decade of the nineteenth century, when it "could no longer tell the story of subject formation without telling the story of nation formation as well."[85] Both projects—building the modern liberal individual and the nation-state—have come in for much overdue scrutiny, yet self-help texts remain an important understudied link.

The history of individualism becomes clearer when the lens widens to consider not only the novel but also the rise of popular texts like *Self-Help* that deliberately and self-confessedly set out to build individuals as well as nations. As Beth Blum points out in her *Self-Help Compulsion: Searching for Advice in Modern Literature*, self-help's "literary import has not received the attention it demands."[86] Although Blum importantly contributes to this overlooked area, she concentrates on a later period and, more specifically, on the way self-help texts and literature positioned themselves as compared to the ways readers blurred the distinctions between popular and literary texts. These distinctions between genres and audiences were less clear cut in the Victorian era, with authors as well as readers happily disregarding them. Many authors, from Trollope to Smiles, quite explicitly imagined their role as inspiring readers to improve their characters—whether they held up a real or a fictional example for the reader to emulate. (If anything, it was self-help writers who worked to separate themselves from novelists, and novelists who sought the moral legitimacy of genres like biography and self-help.) Despite our different focuses and the resulting distinctions in our arguments, I agree with Blum's assessment that critics have been too quick to condemn (and thus, perhaps, to simplify or ignore) self-help as a genre—writing off "self-help as an instrument of neoliberal governance, a tool of systemic oppression, or an agent of colonial subjection."[87] Victorian self-help texts were of course more complicated than this, springing from and serving different political ends. This flexibility, as chapter 1 explores in greater detail, is built into the form of these texts. As a result, I'm especially interested in analyzing the formal and stylistic features associated with these popular texts—an approach that has not typically been employed because self-help is so often treated, unlike the "Literature" it is compared with, as a transparent sort of writing that wears its message on its sleeve.

As I hope to show, self-help texts both engaged with larger cultural debates about the value and limits of ambition, and they established narrative structures and tropes about the successful individual that could be adapted across genres.

In the process of making these arguments I also speak, specifically, to studies of the Victorian novel and, more broadly, to narrative studies. While many critics of the novel have gestured to the importance of other similar and understudied genres such as the conduct book—including Armstrong's *Desire and Domestic Fiction: A Political History of the Novel* and Kent Puckett's *Bad Form: Social Mistakes and the Nineteenth-Century Novel*—self-help texts are an important gap to fill, getting at key questions about ambition, individualism, and self-development. Whereas conduct books purported to help readers affect the manners of a certain socioeconomic class, the self-help book addressed how to improve one's station (for the right reasons, of course) as well as how to form character itself. My aim in this book is also to include more analysis of these "popular" genres—which have tended to be sidelined in favor of the novel. In taking this approach, I hope to show the actual continuity across these genres. After all, self-help texts relied heavily on biographical sketches that attempted, like the bildungsroman, to focus on the formation of the real individual in the real world. In short, self-help texts, biographies of the exemplary individual, and fictional narratives like the bildungsroman all relied on the market for realistic depictions of the individual's rise, and on the inherent narrativity contained in the ambitious subject.

This "narrativity" typically involves the ambitious individual encountering obstacles. Craik's very title, *The Pursuit of Knowledge*, insists on holding up success stories that unfold "*under Difficulties.*" And, as Sinnema observes, the "mini-biographies" of *Self-Help* all follow "a similar narrative trajectory"— early years and influences, adversity, perseverance, and success (xvii). Both the self-help narrative and the novel seem then to demand that the ambitious individual encounter adversity and obstacles. Presumably, entirely happy ambitions, like Tolstoy's happy families, are not the stuff of self-help texts or novels. Then again, happiness and ambition might be in tension: as Pettigrove defines it, "ambition" signals a longer-lasting and more onerous project than what we tend to signal by a word like "desire." An ambition involves a "commitment or determination to obtain its object"—an object that "cannot be achieved overnight" and is "difficult to achieve."[88] These difficulties strewn in the path of ambitious characters thus point to real, material limits. Reading across self-help texts, biographies, and fictional narratives, I argue, demonstrates how representations of ambitious individuals raised questions about the ethics of the drive to be and do more in a finite world. At the level of the individual, ambition points to the economy of one's body, abilities, and time. Zooming out, the meeting of many ambitious subjects on the same playing field immediately suggests competition.

## Ambitions in a Crowd: Rivalry, Competition, and Zero-Sum Games

I've suggested that the self-help genre provided a moralized cover story for ambition by focusing on the exemplary individual, who proves hardworking and deserving of success. This tightly focused narrative has the additional benefit of avoiding concerns about what might happen if many ambitious self-helpers were to become rivals or competitors. But these concerns still haunted self-help texts. In fact, we can see this anxiety at work in the choice of Craik's title, *The Pursuit of Knowledge under Difficulties*. If Craik's work serves as an origin story for the self-help genre—given that it was an influence Smiles directly claims in his *Autobiography* and given that Smiles had an outsized influence on the larger genre—then it is telling that Craik concentrated on examples of men and women who pursued *knowledge*. As Craik puts it, this is one pursuit where "it matters not how many be the competitors":

> In other pursuits, the most unremitting endeavors often fail to secure the object sought; that object, generally being some worldly advantage, is equally within the grasp of other competitors, some one of whom may snatch it away before it can be reached by him who best deserves it. But in the pursuit of knowledge, it matters not how many be the competitors. No one stands in the way of another, or can deprive him of any part of his chance, we should rather say of his certainty, of success; on the contrary, they are all fellow-workers, and may materially help each other forward. The wealth which each seeks to acquire, has, as it were, the property of multiplying itself to meet the wants of all. (1.286)

Craik imagines this "pursuit of knowledge" as the rare case that does not set up a competition: this sort of "wealth," like Jesus' loaves and fishes, multiplies to meet demands—in fact, the more pursuers the better, since they may "materially help each other forward." This desire to frame ambition in such a way that the individual's gains do not take away from others is deeply rooted in the self-help genre. Even when Smiles and others broadened the genre to celebrate all sorts of other pursuits, including inherently competitive fields like business, the desire to avoid thinking about competition is still apparent. On the rare occasions when Smiles addresses the question of how success is allotted among his self-helpers, there is a note of discomfort: "All may not rise equally, yet each, on the whole, very much according to his deserts. 'Though all cannot live on the piazza,' as the Tuscan proverb has it, 'every one may feel the sun'" (224). The transitions between plural and individual subjects are telling, in both Smiles's phrasing and the proverb's: the "all"'s quickly turn into "each" and "every one"—as if even grammatically Smiles cannot bear to imagine self-helping men competing in a common space or economy and keeps shifting to focus on individuals. This is of course the form of *Self-Help*: the succession of discrete biographies prevents the individuals from ever encountering one another on the same piazza.

Smiles continually struggled with the idea of competition. In *Thrift*, he points out that competition can be seen in a positive or a negative light (much like ambition). As he quips, "It is charged with lowering prices, or almost in the same breath with raising them" (199). Smiles goes on to defend competition, which he sees as conducive to individualism: "Put a stop to competition, and you merely check the progress of individuals and of classes . . . Stop competition, and you stop the struggle of individualism. You also stop the advancement of individualism, and, through that, of society at large" (200). Here, again, there is the desire to link the individual's advancement with the nation's—via and thus justifying competition. The problem with competition is that it tends to produce losers as well as winners, something that Smiles is at pains to reframe: "If one man prospers more than others, or if some classes of men prosper more than others, they leave other classes of men behind them. Not that they leave those others worse, but that they themselves advance" (200). Smiles teases out a careful distinction between leaving others *behind* versus leaving them *worse*. The structuring metaphor here points to how tricky this distinction is: if we understand it to be a journey and the way is open to everyone, then Smiles's reasoning makes sense; if we take it to be a race, then those who pass others might indeed be winning all the prizes.

Smiles repeatedly distances the concept of self-help from the selfish, competitive sort of ambition that seeks to take away from others. Instead, he imagines self-help, like Craik's knowledge, as something that raises the collective. Smiles's rhetoric sometimes takes on a spiritualizing quality, as when he argues that the "healthy spirit of self-help" would raise working people "as a class, and this, not by pulling down others, but by levelling them up to a higher and still advancing standard of religion, intelligence, and virtue" (*Self-Help*, 245). The more radical strand of self-help concretizes this ethos by recommending cooperative action: as Holyoake puts it, "How much higher is the morality of co-operation than that of competition" (50–51). Other writers more directly confronted these concerns about whether advancement is available to all or whether it is a limited resource. For example, *Millionaires and How They Became So* cautions readers that "there is not wealth enough in the world for every man to be rich"—even going so far as to do the math and conclude that, if "all the money in the world were equally divided, there would be about £100 for everybody."[89] Again, thinking about success in terms of socioeconomic advancement (vs. developing one's character, virtue, or ability at some task) seems to raise this concern about competition most acutely.

Such quandaries in the self-help ethos point us back to debates about the relation between self-interest or ambition and a wider, competitive economy that are important to contextualize here even if briefly. The era's political economy offered starkly different understandings about how self-interest and competition worked. On the one hand, as Hirschman argues, Adam Smith's *Wealth of Nations* broadly rehabilitated "avarice" into "interest." Smith lumped all desires into the catchall of "interest" and established "a powerful *economic* justification for the untrammeled pursuit of individual self-interest."[90] Many thinkers, including Montesquieu and Smith, believed that individuals and nations following their various interests would lead to mutual dependency and peace. As Hirschman sums up, such early theories of capitalism imagined not only an "uneasy *balance,* but a strong *web* of inter-dependent relationships. Thus it was expected that expansion of domestic trade would create more cohesive communities while foreign trade would help avoid wars between them."[91] The complexity of trade and finance made it difficult to parse out how, exactly, one's ambition or self-interest functioned in the larger system to create this greater good. Meanwhile, as capitalism advanced, such early and rosy theories were not exactly vindicated. On the contrary, comparisons between economic activity and war became increasingly ubiquitous. I'm thinking especially of Mill's description of a "struggle for riches" and Friedrich Engels's visceral "battle for life," where the individual seeks "to crowd out all who are in his way, and to put himself in their place."[92] This all culminates of course in Karl Marx's vision of how capitalism compels people within and across classes to compete.

Across the conceptual frameworks of political economy, natural selection, and war, the potential for violence is built into the idea of competition. As William Davies has theorized, competitors must "remain constrained by norms of equality, playing the same rules," while also "resist[ing] these norms at all costs, in search of inequality." Competition thus hovers between "completely

peaceful, normative fairness" and "violent, existential combat."[93] Eighteenth-
and nineteenth-century ideas about capitalism tap into exactly this tension
when they toggle between visions of competition—as a force that benignly
weaves everyone together through mutual needs or one that violently pits actors and classes against one another.

Many thinkers tried to reconcile these views by theorizing how competition works at different scales. Both political economy and natural selection
offered theories of how competition could benefit collectives, if not always
individuals. Competition might be bad for certain individuals (like sellers
who find themselves undercut in the market by others or members of a species
with a less advantageous adaptation), even if it was good for the aggregate (a
more efficient market and affordable goods for buyers or a gene pool with a
higher rate of the advantageous adaptation). Mill took a more psychological
interest in this solution. In his discussion of liberty, he reminds the reader
that one's success in a crowded field is predicated on another's failure:
"Whoever succeeds in an overcrowded profession, or in a competitive examination; whoever is preferred to another in any contest for an object
which both desire, reaps benefit from the loss of others, from their wasted
exertion and their disappointment." Mill wraps up as cheerily as he can, noting, "It is, by common admission, better for the general interest of mankind,
that persons should pursue their objects undeterred by this sort of consequences."[94] Such a philosophy could offer solace to anyone with a sort of
proto–"survivor's guilt": it's for the greater good that they succeeded, even if
their success directly "reaps benefit from the loss of others." In this way, the
failures as well as the successes become linked to the good of the collective.

Concerns about how economic competition worked became more urgent
as the economy rapidly grew, both in Britain and the wider empire, across the
nineteenth century. In his *Origins of Modern English Society*, Harold Perkin
frames his discussion of modern industrialism with a reminder of the sheer
acceleration of economic growth across the nineteenth century: "Exports rose
sevenfold (allowing for falling prices, tenfold) from about 40 million to over
280 million a year; imports still faster, from about 30 million to over 500 million a year . . . Total industrial production may have grown as much as
fourteen-fold during the century."[95] Even in the midst of this collective growth,
limits were hard to ignore. W. D. Rubinstein reveals in his study of fortunes
made in this era how deeply entrenched the interests of the aristocracy and the
rich still were. Only 21.6 percent of the era's non-landed millionaires could be
considered "self-made." And although "the rise in top fortunes at this time was

unparalleled in previous British experience," these British fortunes "were not, on an international scale, all that vast." As Rubinstein sums up, "Britain's wealthiest men never did attain that level of wealth [as the fortunes in the United States], measured not in tens of millions but in hundreds of millions of pounds."[96] At the same time, as much as the British empire had grown, the continual rebellions and wars (more than two hundred separate wars during Queen Victoria's reign) were a constant reminder of its cracks.[97] The British were thus keenly aware of limits as well as the risk of collapse, despite—or perhaps more accurately because of—the economy and empire's rapid growth.

Adding to these anxieties was the fact that Britain simply felt more crowded in the nineteenth century. Britain was generally understood as a closed system, with an excess population in search of opportunities in the larger empire, in the colonies, and in the United States (all of which were frequently and deceptively portrayed as open and empty spaces). As much as Malthus's warnings were based on faulty assumptions, he was responding to a marked demographic shift in the nineteenth century and to enduring concerns about the allocation of finite natural resources across a growing population. Europe and North America both experienced a "demographic transition" from high fertility and mortality to low fertility and mortality. In the midst of this transition the birth rate was still high even as mortality fell, resulting in a "population explosion."[98] Compounding these realities, the nineteenth century also saw more people moving to the towns and cities for economic opportunities—literalizing Mill's "struggle for riches," with ambitious individuals "trampling, crushing, elbowing, and treading on each other's heels."[99] In this context, even the "laudable" ambitions of self-helpers are less likely to drive collective progress than to lead to bloody conflict over scarce opportunities and resources in Britain and the wider world.

Although this context is important, my focus in this book is less on how economic thought imagined ambition (or self-interest) and competition in economic treatises and more on how popular texts, relying on biographical or fictional narratives, represented the ambitious individual—from Smiles's *Self-Help*, to Martineau's *Illustrations of Political Economy*, to Craik's *John Halifax, Gentleman*. Such texts, besides outselling political economy, also more explicitly set out to manage readers' ambitions while shaping their characters. With this in mind, I want to build on recent studies of political economy and the novel[100] by considering how other genres, particularly self-help texts and biographies, explicitly set out to manage and imagine ambition at the scale of the individual and against the backdrop of a competitive milieu.

In the process, my argument also dovetails with recent interest in crowds and the collective. As I briefly outlined above, critics have long been interested in how Victorian literature imagines the crowd, from destructive mobs—a recurring ingredient in Condition of England novels and a mainstay of Dickens's imagination—to, in Steinlight's terms, "surplus life," to, in Armstrong's reading, the hordes of vampires and cannibals that threaten individuality.[101] As Alex Woloch's *The One vs. the Many* contends, narrative always conceptualizes the relation between the individual and the collective through character systems that put subjects into competition for finite narrative space and readerly attention. Woloch writes that "the discrete representation of any specific individual is intertwined with the narrative's continual apportioning of attention to different characters who jostle for limited space within the same fictive universe."[102] As this book will argue, when Victorian authors dramatized ambitious self-help and its ensuing competitions, they emphasized how literal this jostling is, portraying ambition as an embodied drive acting on a material and finite environment.

Victorian narratives explored these questions by relying on forms that stage zero-sum games. In self-help texts, the individual works ever harder, straining against the limits of their own physical ability—and, in the process, concentrating our attention on the successful subject. In the longer form of the Victorian novel, writers obsessively returned to plots about inheritance and primogeniture, legal cases that decide for the prosecution or the defense, career narratives that stress the scarcity of opportunities, and marriage plots that imagine a limited number of eligible young people (which, in the case of scarce men, again responded to actual concerns about demographics, given the "superfluous women" of the Victorian era). These plots set up competitions that launch and demand narrative. Novels like Dickens's *David Copperfield* and Thackeray's *Vanity Fair* draw attention to this imperative, asking us to read for who will emerge as the hero or setting characters up in a system where one's gains require another's losses.

As these examples already suggest, zero-sum thinking has real dangers—in our own time, for example, the rise of populists who employ the rhetoric of scarcity and competition to demonize immigrants, women, and people of color. Perhaps in part as a response to such dangers, a number of critics have recently downplayed or hoped to move past the zero-sum thinking associated with upward mobility and narrative form. Robbins in *Upward Mobility and the Common Good* emphasizes the role the patron and the state play in stories ostensibly about ambitious individuals. In the process, he addresses and hopes we might finally lay to rest "the zero-sum necessity according to which a post-colonial migrant's upward mobility can only happen at the expense of some-one at home."[103] More recently, Caroline Levine has concurred that "Robbins is right to reject the zero-sum game . . . because no single hierarchy governs all others, nor do they all work together, successfully reinforcing Western imperi-alism, or the ruling class, or patriarchy." Instead, Levine argues, forms can dis-rupt as well as reinforce power relations, meaning "there is no need to assume that one person's rise necessarily comes at the expense of another."[104]

As much as I agree in spirit and share such hopes, I want to pause over why so many Victorian narratives do in fact imagine how one person's rise comes at the expense of another. The use of the zero-sum game—whether it is his-torically let alone universally accurate and whether such thinking is employed ethically or unethically in our own time—importantly points to a concern with the sustainability of individual ambitions. By considering Victorian lit-erature's use of these formal, felt, and often real limitations, I suggest that we might better see not only the era's concerns about ambition and its ensuing competitions but also how they feed into our own moment. It offers further correctives for acknowledging and conceptualizing the role of the zero-sum game. Many situations do function as competitions for limited prizes, in lit-erature as in life. And to think about how one's ambition might compete with or take away from others could usefully acknowledge an interconnected econ-omy and a finite environment. As Alf Hornborg argues, "Only when the world is viewed as a finite and in certain respects closed system are we able to discover what is locally perceived as a cornucopia may in fact be a component in a global zero-sum game."[105] From this widened view, we can better see "how the accumulation of money and technology in core areas of the world-system occurs at the expense of the natural resources, environment, and health of their peripheries."[106] Considered in this light, zero-sum thinking can offer a needed corrective to economic theories that imagine abstract growth without considering the costs and limits of communities and ecosystems—as well as to narratives about the successful individual that focus on "deserving" success versus the larger, structural allocation of such successes.

In my reading, the zero-sum game also importantly offers an analogy for how ambitious individualism works at the level of the body. Even if self-help texts tend not to imagine individuals struggling in competitions with others, they do imagine individuals struggling with themselves and their physical lim-its—to work two jobs, or study all night, or live in poverty for years. Such tropes were also common in the autobiographies of writers like Martineau and

Trollope, who emphasized the hard work of writing, meaning they had to gauge not only their ambition but also their ability—with the body emerging as the ultimate closed system. The novelists I engage with in this project were very aware of how their writing competed for readers' money and attention. They were also keenly aware of the embodied work they put into their writing and the toll this might take on their health.

While we tend to think of writing as an entirely intellectual activity, Victorian writers repeatedly emphasized the physical demands involved, as well as their ensuing dangers—as outlined above in the example of Dickens. Trollope's celebration of his work ethic in *An Autobiography* details his physical self-discipline: to write, as he claimed, the most of any living author (while working a day job!), he had to be "at my table every morning at 5.30 A.M.," "allow[ing] myself no mercy."[107] Thackeray complained of his exhaustion while producing *The Luck of Barry Lyndon*, writing that the manuscript was "lying like a nightmare on [his] mind."[108] Dinah Craik has been compared to her hard-working protagonist, John Halifax, because of the way she drafted and revised her most enduring novel—while giving up evenings and social engagements.[109] As a young author in London, Martineau sought to pace her writing in order to guard her health. She justified her decisions by citing Walter Scott's recent death of (presumably) overwork.[110] The potentially dangerous physical effects of their work haunted Victorian authors, who worried that taxing the mind could result in brain fevers, strokes, and an early death. Such fears culminate in a figure like George Gissing's Alfred Yule in *New Grub Street*, whose literary ambitions "devour" him, allowing him but "three or four hours of sleep" and resulting in "dyspepsia, and many another ill that literary flesh is heir to."[111] No wonder, when Samuel Smiles suffered a stroke one night while working on a manuscript, he attributed it to overwork.[112]

## Shaping Ambition, from Self-Help to the Novel

Across the following chapters, I argue that we can better understand Victorian literature and the mythology of individualism through the genre that explicitly sought to guide readers in becoming ambitious individuals at the height of industrialization and laissez-faire policies—the self-help text. This important popular discourse already hinted at how even a "laudable" ambition might take over one's life or end in illness. Ultimately, fictional narratives, in imagining how ambitious characters might crowd limited opportunities, confronted questions about not only the embodiment but also the wider context of ambition. Chapters of this book analyze how ambition was rendered, formally and stylistically, across self-help texts, biographies, and short as well as long fictional narratives. Among the many genres that imagine the ambitious individual in a wider competitive milieu, I suggest that these most directly grappled with the potential tensions that ensued. Self-help texts quite explicitly set out to manage readers' ambitions; both inspirational biographies and autobiographies imagined the development of an exemplary individual; and fictional narratives, particularly the multiplot Victorian novel, questioned not only *which* but also how *many* individuals can exercise their ambition.

The first chapter analyzes and suggests the interconnections among the style, form, and politics of Smiles's *Self-Help*. Although Smiles initially seems to preach the gospel of hard work unequivocally, his text also gestures to the potential dangers of ambition. In seeking the most determined and persevering of men to hold up as models, Smiles's examples begin to strain at the limits of physical ability. For example, Bernard Palissy spends sixteen years in the pursuit of the formula for Chinese porcelain (and eventually burns the family furniture to keep the kiln going), while Elihu Burrett learns eighteen ancient and modern languages and twenty-two European dialects—all while earning his living as a blacksmith. These figures walk a fine line between genius and mental illness—specifically monomania, a condition first defined in the nineteenth century. The tendency for these figures' ambition to overlap with monomania is largely due to the form of Smiles's biographies: intentionally kept short and teleological, they emphasize the single-mindedness of each character's drive to work. But by celebrating such pathological ambitions, the self-help genre subtly undermined its own advice, showing how the drive threatened to become dangerously all encompassing, subsuming the individual even while defining him.

The second chapter turns to a didactic genre that effectively bridged the self-help text and the Victorian novel. Martineau established her career and her financial independence through her popular *Illustrations of Political Economy*, a series of short novels that explained economic principles through fictional illustrations. These stories, not unlike Smiles's *Self-Help*, emphasize the agency of individual economic actors. But Martineau's lessons about self-reliance are complicated by her attention to how protagonists remain dependent upon material conditions beyond their control—suffering from disasters like droughts, famines, and storms. This tension between individual ambition and external conditions parallels the one between ambition and the body. Such tensions were familiar to Martineau. An ambitious woman writer, Martineau imagined her own career as both inspired and limited by her body's illnesses and disabilities. This chapter ultimately poses questions that the rest will seek to answer—about how more sustained narratives represent ambitions that are dependent on the body, on the socioeconomic system, and on the environment.

The first two chapters focus on how both Martineau and Smiles used short narratives—whether fiction or nonfiction—to illustrate principles and maxims that would help the individual develop and navigate the wider system (the nation, the economy). The third chapter turns to the longer Victorian novel, specifically the bildungsroman, which expands the individual ambition plot to explore the consequences of that drive in a larger competitive and hierarchical system. Dinah Craik's popular *John Halifax, Gentleman* has long been read as the novelistic analogue to Smiles's *Self-Help*.[113] But in adapting the self-help plot, the novel faces a difficulty Smiles avoided: how to value success when it might be predicated on another's loss. Across Victorian novels, it frequently falls to characters who have an illness or disability to reveal the latent violence behind ambition in a limited system. In *John Halifax, Gentleman*, Craik disables the ambitious hero's competition: Phineas Fletcher narrates the story of his best friend's rise in the Fletcher family business, a business Phineas himself is too ill to run. Although Craik suggests alternate routes for ambition's fulfillment—Phineas is able to take on the task of writing the biography of John Halifax because of his position—she also exposes the implicit violence behind even the most high minded of ambitions.

The fourth chapter turns to the multiplot Victorian novel—and to an example that explicitly pits characters against one another. Importantly, Thackeray's *Vanity Fair* centers two women who are suggestive of the limits placed on individual ambitions. Although Becky Sharp is one of the most famously ambitious characters in Victorian literature, her larger-than-life character is continually figured in terms of her physically diminutive presence. She is short and overtly feminized, and Thackeray's repeated epithet associates her with this quality— she is a "little upstart" and "little adventuress." Thackeray's belittling both feminizes and domesticates the threat of Becky Sharp's ambition (as exemplified in his vignette of Becky dressed up as Napoleon). In continually contrasting Becky and Amelia, Thackeray suggests where the imperative to "help oneself" creates a double bind for women—and perhaps individuals in general—who are either too ambitious and thus comical or diabolical (like Becky) or not ambitious enough (like Amelia). This novel is also indicative of Thackeray's interest in using scale—most notably, the "puppet show" of the frame—to judge the ambitions of his characters, a recurring strategy in Thackeray's work, from *The Book of Snobs* to *Barry Lyndon.* As this chapter argues, Thackeray's use of shifting perspectives and scales dramatizes the pursuit of a critical distance from which one might accurately gauge the value of ambition.

Whereas chapters 3 and 4 concentrate on novels that contrast two key characters, the fifth chapter turns to a novel that pits an entire group of ambitious characters, who are also friends and relatives, into competition. In *The Three Clerks,* Trollope asks the reader to sympathize with all three clerks, whose high aspirations often conflict with their desires to get around one another and to succeed, usually at one another's expense. Such a disconnect between aspirations and material limits troubles the plots we associate with the Victorian novel—the career plot, the marriage plot, and the trial or test—by revealing how our diffusive readerly sympathies are at odds with plots that rely on zero-sum games and binaries that reward one individual as the "winner." These competitions force the characters to recognize how they are scrambling over scarce resources, be they jobs, promotions, or marriage partners. Through this novel's representation of competitions among friends, Trollope reveals the psychological violence caused by such everyday competitions. I suggest that the tension between characters' lofty aspirations and the realities of the material competitions they engage in dramatizes the period's debates about the value of ambition. These tensions were essential to Trollope's work and to his classic vacillation plot. They are also key to the Victorian novel's strategies of characterization and narration, revealing how persistent such questions about ambition were in the era, and how they suggested their own formal or narrative logic.

When faced with such a crowded economic playing field, a popular solution—both in British politics and in the Victorian novel—was to release the pressure by sending the "overflow" to make their fortunes in the colonies. In the concluding chapter, I consider the aftermath of colonial ambition in Miles Franklin's *My Brilliant Career* and *My Career Goes Bung.* Franklin's novels overtly thematize the limitations placed on women's ambitions, taking up themes of the New Woman novel in the Australian context. Franklin also suggests, particularly in the latter, follow-up novel, how women might realize their ambitions by displacing them onto the nation—with this second version of Sybylla dedicating herself to forging a specifically Australian literature. Franklin sets both novels during the "hot, dry, pitiless" drought of the 1890s, a reality that rarely aligns with how the heroine, Sybylla, imagines the land as an analogue for her own ambitions: "My ambition was as boundless as the mighty bush in which I have always lived."[114] It is in these depictions of the hostile Australian environment that Franklin gestures to the stakes of settler colonialism, which relied on a literal competition over land in order to practice the sort of pastoral settlement that, in Franklin's novels and in reality, goes terribly awry.

Across the chapters, this book seeks to elucidate how Victorian self-help discourse sought to inspire and manage ambition or individualism, even as it raised questions—taken up in the very form of the era's fiction—about the value and sustainability of such ambitions in a bounded and material world. In considering such tensions, I also want to raise questions about our own moment—what stories we tell about ambition and the successful individual, about the playing field, and about competition. The potential for socioeconomic mobility in both the United States and the United Kingdom has declined in recent decades, while, especially since 2008, study after study has critiqued the neoliberal rhetoric of meritocracy.[115] The COVID-19 pandemic has again revealed deepening gaps: between those fortunes that have grown and those that have been demolished, between who can pay their way out of a crisis and who is forced to put their lives on the line, between our rhetoric about "essential workers" and our society's way of compensating those workers (or not, as it turns out). At the same time, the pandemic has newly insisted on our interconnections and dependencies not only across societies and economies but also across larger ecological systems. This moment seems to invite more reflection on conceptions about the individual and the socioecological system.

As much as ambition has been revalued as a nearly unalloyed good, this drive still raises questions about its relation to ability, competition, and sustainability. The increasing sense of scarcity, whether real or imagined—of good jobs, of housing near those jobs, of "room" in the United States for immigrants and refugees—puts ever more pressure on individuals and society. According to neoliberal logic, if an individual "hustles," they will be both well rounded and angular enough to earn a spot among the 5 percent of applicants admitted to an elite university, or they will find enough investors for their start-up while piecing together gigs in the 1099 economy, or, in our academic context, they will publish enough as an adjunct to land one of the handful of tenure-track jobs in their field that year. At the same time, workers are also tasked with finding time to take care of themselves, with imperatives like, to take an example from the program I work in, "Caretaking Your Own Well-Being,"[116] or, from a Stanford-wide initiative in 2018, "enjoy the power of the pause."[117] As Blum has further documented, the "self-helpification of academe" is on the rise alongside increasing precarity.[118] Such precarity has only been exacerbated by the pandemic, as workloads increased and childcare evaporated—forcing many people, especially women, to leave their jobs or cut back their hours.

While the above examples are drawn from my immediate context (Silicon Valley, academia, the pandemic), they are in keeping with longer and wider trends in the US economy (and beyond). As Rachel Greenwald Smith has recently put it, the neoliberal agenda touts "the necessity of personal initiative" while "pathologizing" "structures of dependence," "call[ing] upon subjects to see themselves as entrepreneurial actors in a competitive system."[119] And despite all the data and think pieces explaining that we are not, in fact, living in a meritocracy, mythologies about successful individuals seem to outshout them—all the more so when these narratives frame such success as the well-deserved reward for hard work. Perhaps such stories simply appeal to us more, given tendencies for people across cultures to believe in a just world and the power of hard work over luck or chance (especially when we're sitting in the winner's seat).[120] Banking on these tendencies, the self-help market is more profitable than ever, selling emotional fulfillment, financial independence, and the promise of self-efficacy. As much as groups like FIRE (Financial Independence, Retire Early), including cult figures like Mr. Money Mustache, get into the details of saving and investing, they rarely point to the real culprits that have made it necessary to "hack" our way into sufficient leisure time and retirement funds in the first place. Nor do they address how policy changes could solve these problems. The self-help genre, then and now, largely elides the systemic issues of liberal or neoliberal capitalism that make all this advice both profitable and, ultimately, woefully insufficient.

Much has of course changed between nineteenth-century liberalism and twenty-first-century neoliberalism. But in significant ways the Victorian context undergirds or rhymes with our own stories about both the playing field and our agency within it. Unlike classical liberalism's pursuit of a natural, laissez-faire market, neoliberalism is thoroughly and self-confessedly constructed, relying on state intervention rather than its absence to enforce continual competition.[121] At the same time, however, the rhetoric of "the market" as a naturalized, impersonal force is alive and well whenever corporations, politicians, and the billionaire class seek to justify policies that disadvantage workers. There are also parallels in conceptions of the self and how it is put to work. A typical distinction is that classical liberalism was built on a labor theory of value while neoliberalism "reduces the human being to an arbitrary bundle of 'investments.'"[122] Sianne Ngai notes how, with the neoliberal shift in the 1970s, "human competences once viewed as outside capital—affect, subjectivity, and sociability—are systematically put to work for the extraction of surplus value (however directly or indirectly)."[123] And yet, a "bundle of investments" sounds much like Smiles's "bundle of habits." The subject who results from all this, with their affect, subjectivity, and sociability being just so much more to put to work in today's economy, is the update on Smiles's way of imagining character as beyond price, even as it is rewarded in the marketplace for being above expecting such a thing (like one of Dickens's dutifully chastised upstarts).

Smiles's emphasis on the individual and their ability to control their mind, body, and outcome always too easily toggled between an empowering message with radical political roots and a justification for framing everything in terms of "personal responsibility" in a way that would appeal to Thatcher, Reagan, and subsequent generations of right-wing politicians (as chapter 1 will take up). These ideas have become uncannily timely once again in the context of neoliberal policies, manifested to such extremes in the context of the United States but common to many others—as inequalities in wealth continue to grow; as we hit glass ceilings or regress in the supposed progress toward a society that does not simply recreate hierarchies around class, race, gender, disability status, sexuality, and so on; and as entrenched powers deny the environmental consequences of constant economic growth powered by fossil fuels. To better understand the pervasiveness of mythologies about the successful individual and ambition, it is useful to return to the Victorian age—and to the narratives that represented and questioned how the individual embodied ambition in a finite world.

# CHAPTER 1

# Forming the Ambitious Individual in Samuel Smiles's *Self-Help*

Samuel Smiles's *Self-Help* is a key site for understanding Victorian narratives about ambition and individualism. This text and the wider genre explicitly set out to shape readers' characters and to channel their ambitions—to lift not only the individual but also the wider nation. In the process, as the introduction argued, self-help texts offered a moralized cover story for ambition: a way to center the individual and their success while avoiding concerns about selfishness—as well as concerns about how ambitious individuals might come into competition. Such a tight focus on the individual has made it difficult to determine *Self-Help*'s ultimate politics, as Smiles tends to imagine his nation of self-helpers interacting only in the abstract. (This also conveniently removes any risk of competition, as most of Smiles's examples are safely in the past.) We can see this dynamic in the form of *Self-Help*, which collects example after example that paints a clear cause-and-effect relationship between a person's hard work and their well-deserved success. Smiles repeatedly explained the thinking behind these rhetorical decisions. He thought that short, striking biographies were the most likely to inspire, so he compressed his examples. And he hoped to show "examples of what other men had done, as illustrations of what each might, in a greater or less degree, do for himself,"[1] so he tended to tout the commonplace and replicable traits that seemed to lead to success. Through these strategies, Smiles encouraged a simple lesson: if readers cultivate these common qualities, they too can be successful. All this of course necessarily reduces the complexity of both success stories and their protagonists: narrowly focusing on the scale of the individual, defining that individual by a handful of traits, ignoring any fuller context, and then claiming that such success is highly replicable. The ultimate message, as Lauren M. E. Goodlad has succinctly put it, is "a fantasy of limitless individual autonomy."[2] Even in the pages of *Self-Help*, as I'll argue, this narrative ends up backfiring on the individual, in ways that suggest the physical limits to ambition.

For a number of reasons, Smiles's examples of hard workers blur into examples of overworkers. In part because these stories so entirely focus on the individual—rather than on a larger cast of characters, whether of rivals or collaborators—the ambition drive in *Self-Help* takes an inward turn. And since the qualities these characters are meant to illustrate tend to boil down to supposedly replicable traits like energy and perseverance, Smiles exaggerates them while downplaying the role of anything harder to replicate—including innate ability and genius. The result is an emphasis on very physicalized and often gendered work. Even pursuits that we tend to think of as intellectual rather than physical become, in Smiles and in the self-help genre, examples of "mind work" or "brain work" that rely on a well-disciplined body. Smiles's self-helpers thus overwork themselves into amazing feats, limiting their sleep to four hours a night or working two jobs at full speed. The fantasy of "limitless autonomy" thus depends on the assumption that the mind will bend the body, society, and environment to its will. These representations of excessive work frequently blur into what were symptoms of mental illness—specifically, in nineteenth-century terminology, monomania, which was emerging as a category of illness. Even as the ambitious individual—in Smiles's writing, generally a man—pursues work that will individuate him and set him apart from the crowd, this work threatens to subsume him—with ramifications for thinking about how ambition and able-bodiedness were conceptually merging in this period.

## "Busts Rather Than Full-Length Portraits": Forms of Exemplarity in *Self-Help*

In the introduction, I suggested that ambition needed to be managed because it was just as liable to manifest in competitively seeking to get around others as in laudable and magnanimous aspirations. I want to pause here to explore how this concern about ambition manifested, even more specifically, in Smiles's writing, and the implications this has for an understanding of how self-helpers might actually interact (or not, as the case turned out). Although Smiles uses the term "ambition" infrequently, he dedicates entire chapters to qualities that were closely associated with ambition but didn't carry the drive's vestiges of selfishness and sin. Some of Smiles's most frequently praised qualities include "energy," "application," "industry," and "perseverance."[3] When Smiles does use the word "ambition," he is careful to show by context how he is separating the "high" from the "low." Ambition is "low" when it is a selfish desire for money, status, or power for their own sakes. For example, Smiles warns that there is "a dreadful ambition abroad for being 'genteel,'" with many par-ents harboring an "ambition to bring up boys as gentlemen" (250). In another passage, Smiles describes Wellington's "great character" as "untarnished by ambition, by avarice, or any low passion." Ambition is similarly guilty by as-sociation when Smiles lists the ways that power can be misused—"fanaticism, despotism, and ambition" (270). In distinction, Smiles praises ambition when it is directed toward a goal that benefits others as well as oneself. He puts spe-cial emphasis on redefining and redirecting selfish or financial ambitions: "And if a working man have high ambition and possess richness in spirit,—a kind of wealth which far transcends all mere worldly possessions—he may not only help himself, but be a profitable helper of others in his path through life" (254). The difference between "low" and "high" ambition in Smiles's *Self-Help* thus has to do with whether one is merely seeking to benefit oneself—perhaps even at the expense of others—or whether one's work will improve others' lives as well as one's own. And a key concept that assists in framing ambition as a "helper of others" is the nation.

The first chapter of *Self-Help* is titled "Self-Help—National and Individual," and Smiles repeatedly asserts this link: "The spirit of self-help is the root of all genuine growth in the individual; and, exhibited in the lives of many, it con-stitutes the true source of national vigour and strength" (17). A few pages later, again linking these key terms—"the spirit of self-help," the individual, and the nation—Smiles observes, "the spirit of self-help, as exhibited in the energetic action of individuals, has in all times been a marked feature in the English character, and furnishes the true measure of our power as a nation" (20). Or, in a more succinct version of this message, "National progress is the sum of individual industry, energy, and uprightness" (18). But, as noted above, as much as Smiles insists on conceptually linking the individual to the nation, we don't get many concrete examples of how exactly individuals come together to help one another. Instead, in a sort of analogue of the invisible hand, self-helpers work by a diffusive power—spurring others on by their good exam-ple, often indirectly or from a distance. For instance, Smiles praises Josiah Wedgwood for is how his creations, those "articles in daily use," "may be made the vehicles of education to all": "The most ambitious artist may thus confer a greater practical benefit on his countrymen than by executing an elaborate work which he may sell for thousands of pounds to be placed in some wealthy man's gallery where it is hidden away from public sight" (153). As the introduc-tion argued, the self-help genre was at pains to avoid imagining ambitious individuals as part of a crowd—which would immediately suggest how ambition might turn against others in a competitive system. In obscuring how self-helpers might come together in real life—rather than in the pages of *Self-Help* or via a nice piece of pottery—Smiles elides the larger political stakes of the project.

The politics of Smiles and his bestselling text have been the focus of most of the critical work on *Self-Help* and this genre. Critics and historians have carefully traced Smiles's earlier radical politics and his later movement away from such causes—but have come to different conclusions about how to read *Self-Help*'s ultimate message.[4] I want to briefly contextualize such criticism and how it's influenced the reception of this text up to our own moment. This context is important for any study of Smiles's *Self-Help* and the wider genre, but particularly so when it highlights the need for more close reading of a text (and genre) that has long been seen as entirely transparent. While *Self-Help* and the larger genre is often quoted from as if it wears its meaning on its sleeve, this is clearly not the case if critics and readers have disagreed so fundamentally over Smiles's ultimate message. These disagreements are the result of, and parallel, two key features of Smiles's text: the structure of a series of discrete, compressed biographies, and the emphasis on individuals who interact only through the abstraction of the nation. Of course, such disagreements also stem from Smiles's often messy, contradictory thinking across a long career. Even restricting ourselves to *Self-Help*, this text's focus on the individual becomes something of a Rorschach test. *Self-Help*'s emphasis on the all-powerful individual can seem radically empowering, or it can further justify doing nothing to help those who have been disadvantaged by economic and political systems.

Smiles repeatedly downplays the role of institutions that might bring self-helping individuals together and direct their ambition to the collective good. For example, he warns that patriotism and philanthropy should be less concerned with "altering laws and modifying institutions" and more focused on "helping and stimulating men to elevate and improve themselves by their own free and independent individual action" (18). It's easy to imagine Smiles's message as a precursor to ideas about the neoliberal subject as "entrepreneur of himself." And many have read or misread Smiles in this way. The politician Ian Gilmour named Smiles "the Victorian hero of Thatcherism,"[5] and Thatcher herself used the term "self-help"—as in "I believe that the national motto should be self-help, not help-yourself at someone else's expense."[6] No wonder, then, that a critic jabbed back with, "We have a Prime Minster who, if she recommends anyone to undertake any reading at all, can only recommend them, judging by what we have heard of her, to read Samuel Smiles's 'Self

Help.'"[7] And in fact Smiles's text has frequently been framed by conservative voices. Ralph Harris, Baron of High Cross, wrote a foreword for a 1996 edition, where he proclaims that Smiles anticipated "the cumulative failure" of the welfare state. Harris laments that "multiplying social benefits have spread the chronic malaise of dependency that has come perversely to stunt the lives of growing numbers of able-bodied young people and the deprived off-spring of so many never-married parents."[8] The term "able-bodied" here is part of a long and problematic tendency to associate ambition or individualism with a certain way of being embodied (a tendency that is already rooted in Smiles's text, as I'll suggest in the next section). Sir Keith Joseph, Thatcher's education secretary, also penned an introduction to *Self-Help* in 1986, where he imagines just how horrified Smiles would be by the modern welfare state. Smiles, we learn, "warned us against the illusion that 'help from without'— this time in the form of collective redistribution—could replace individual energy, efficiency, and productiveness."[9] Given how easily *Self-Help* has fit into such a political agenda, Smiles's text can read like propaganda for a Western liberalism and individualism that sees the self as a discrete unit and the nation as merely the "sum"—in short, as the Victorian analogue to Thatcher's "there is no such thing as society."

Considering such origins, it's no wonder that, as Beth Blum notes, the usual response of critics to the self-help genre is to see it "as an instrument of neoliberal governance, a tool of systemic oppression, or an agent of colonial subjection."[10] And yet, as Asa Briggs has put it, "the creed of self-help grew out of radicalism."[11] Smiles was associated with various radical movements in the 1830s and '40s, particularly through his editorial work with the *Leeds Times*, which was known for its middle-class radicalism. In fact, the term "self-help" might have been lifted from the *Leeds Times* editor Robert Nicoll, whose "The Duties of the People" used the expression in 1836.[12] The content of *Self-Help* also has radical beginnings. In the preface, Smiles explains how he delivered a lecture to a group of working men who, "growing ambitious," sought out speakers like Smiles to lecture at their mutual improvement society (7)—one of the many organizations, also including mechanics' institutes and even the Whig-controlled Society for the Diffusion of Useful Knowledge, which sought to develop better educational opportunities for the working and lower-middle classes.[13]

Admittedly, Smiles became less and less interested in radical and public causes as he aged. This has led critics like R. J. Morris to see in Smiles's *Self-Help* a "retreat" that "sublimated the frustrated political ambitions of the petite bourgeoisie radicals of the 1840s."[14] But Smiles never retreated so far as to endorse laissez-faire capitalism and materialism; in fact, he worried that "people had misinterpreted his message and misused his writings" to support the pursuit of mere financial success.[15] Smiles had learned from his earlier association with radicalism, after dabbling in a number of cooperative and combinatory movements, from Owenite experiments in co-ownership to educational schemes. And Smiles praised cooperative movements like the Rochdale Pioneers (a group that similarly embraced the term "self-help"). Here, again, we might see Smiles settling into a sort of middle ground, finding value in, for example, friendly societies that pooled their communities' resources to save money or insure against injury or death but questioning the role of workers' combinations and strikes.[16]

Despite such qualifications, it is telling that some of the foremost Smiles historians have found an echo of his youthful radicalism in his enduring interest in education. Smiles had early imagined how individual self-help could realize a wider political agenda. In 1845 he posited that "education will teach those who suffer how to remove the causes of their sufferings; and it may also make them dissatisfied with an inferiority of social privilege. This, however, is one of the necessary conditions of human progress. If a man be degraded, he must be dissatisfied—discontented, if you will, with that condition of degradation, before he can make the necessary effort to rise out of it." As Alexander Tyrrell argues, Smiles's lectures effectively "urged workingmen to take up a form of education that would create a spirit of dissatisfaction and lead to the admission of 'the mass into the full communion of citizenship.'"[17] From this perspective, the lectures were a "thoroughgoing radical manifesto."[18]

Smiles can also seem radical in the way he held up the average worker. In celebrating what Briggs would call "the gospel of work," Smiles dignified all sorts of labor, praising those who had accomplished something in a range of fields and pursuits. Smiles also cut against class hierarchies by redefining the gentleman in a chapter of *Self-Help*—as a status gained through character and work rather than birth. No wonder then that the socialist Robert Blatchford defended *Self-Help* against charges that "Smiles was the arch-Philistine, and his book the apotheosis of respectability, gigmanity, and selfish grab." Blatchford even recommended the book's "adoption as a reading-book in our schools," noting that "its perusal has often forced me to industry, for very shame," and concluding that "I cannot see how a book which has been food and medicine to one Socialist should be poison to another."[19] Readers beyond Britain and beyond the Victorian era also put Smiles to their own and sometimes radical ends, as Blum has explored. In short, Smiles's text, and the wider genre of self-help, was not intrinsically or necessarily a tool for oppression.

It's telling that this text can yield such opposed readings in the first place. Putting Smiles in his political and historical context, examining how he bridged or moved away from his earlier radical orientation into a middle-class ethos, critics have read *Self-Help* as both a precursor to collective political action, and as a retreat from such politics. Such disagreements point to the need for more attention on Smiles's text and the larger genre of self-help. As much as studies of eighteenth- and nineteenth-century literature have interested themselves in tracing the development of individualism and ideas about the nation, the term and genre of self-help are largely absent.[20] Nor have studies of the self-help genre filled in this gap: despite the ink spilled on Smiles's (and the genre's) politics and the recent interest in how readers responded to such texts,[21] we have little critical work on the stylistic and formal qualities of *Self-Help* itself.

If critics have found room for such opposed interpretations because Smiles resists depicting his individuals interacting through actual social structures or institutions, then the sheer, dizzying number of Smiles's examples also contributes to this room for interpretation. In his introduction to the Oxford World's Classics edition of *Self-Help*, Peter W. Sinnema tallies the number of names mentioned at more than 750. And this crowd is quite a jumble: describing the organizational strategy of *Self-Help*, Christopher Clausen has suggested that "Smiles resembled nothing so much as a vacuum cleaner that rolled from room to room of a large dusty house filling up its bag."[22] The excessiveness and messiness of Smiles's work is all the more striking if we zoom out to imagine the larger literary field in which it participated—the many imitations, translations, and even sequels by Smiles himself. In this genre, repetition seemed to be more virtue than vice. As even Smiles notes in the preface to *Self-Help*, there was "nothing in the slightest degree new or original" in his counsel (7). Nevertheless, readers bought up *Self-Help* across multiple editions, leading Smiles to follow up on his success with *Character*, *Thrift*, *Duty*, and *Life and Labour*. Meanwhile, many other authors tipped a hat to Smiles while putting their own spin on the genre, with Orison Marden's *Pushing to the Front* being a particularly popular example in the United States.[23] Other adaptations were targeted to wider audiences, like Jessie Boucherett's version for women, or the Christian Knowledge Society's version for children, titled *Higher and Higher*. As the genre went on, it seemed to become almost a commonplace to, like Smiles, acknowledge one's own unoriginality. In his *Getting on in the World;*

*or, Hints on Success in Life*, William Matthews admits, "It is, of course, hardly possible to say anything absolutely new; the most that a writer can hope to do is to recombine and present in novel and attractive forms, with fresh illustrations, so as to impress persons who have not been impressed before, thoughts which have substantially been repeated from the days of Solomon to those of Smiles and 'Titcomb.'"[24] The prolific W. H. Davenport Adams echoes this title and sentiment in his *The Secret of Success; or, How to Get On in the World*, noting that his work "follows in the track of worthy predecessors, such as the evergreen 'Pursuit of Knowledge under Difficulties,' by Mr. Craik, and the admirable 'Self-Help,' by Mr. Smiles."[25] Commenting on the output of such texts on both sides of the Atlantic in the nineteenth century, Irvin G. Wyllie observes, "Only a people mad with success could have endured the length and repetitiousness of these manuals."[26]

If Smiles's *Self-Help* gathers great individuals into an analogue of the nation, then being so "mad with success" can seem problematic given the closed system of Britain, where, as explored in the introduction, concerns about population and competition were particularly fraught. As if to ward off such fears of ambition turning outward, Smiles keeps the focus on the individual. Each individual is very much compressed, which is the result of Smiles's stylistic strategies, even as it is also suggestive of the force of a crowd that crushes the biographies, sardine-like, into the text. Smiles's selection strategy was motivated by the need to keep the audience's attention; as he notes, "the lives of individuals, as indeed of nations, often [concentrate] their luster and interest in a few passages" (8).[27] Accordingly, Smiles includes "busts rather than full-length portraits," in many of which "only some striking feature has been noted" (8).

Many texts in the mode of Smiles's *Self-Help* similarly compress their examples. But this compression is particularly important to *Self-Help*. Unlike many other contemporary texts that relied on exemplary biographies, such as his own inspiration, George Lillie Craik's *The Pursuit of Knowledge under Difficulties*, Smiles's *Self-Help* is explicitly organized by characteristics rather than by individual biographies. Thus, the chapter titled "Energy and Courage" provides copious examples of these characteristics, while "Leaders of Industry" collects many types of inventors and industrialists. This emphasis on particular qualities versus full lives is also clear from the way Smiles introduces examples: Augustin Thierry's "entire life presented a striking example of perseverance, diligence, self-culture, and untiring devotion to knowledge" (278); "the career of John Howard was throughout a striking illustration of the same power of patient purpose" (206); and John Hunter furnishes "an illustrious example of the power of patient industry" (120). Smiles wrote in his *Autobiography* that it was these elements that stuck in his own memory after reading Craik's work: "I had been greatly attracted when a boy by Mr Craik's *Pursuit of Knowledge under Difficulties*. I had read it often, and knew its many striking passages almost by heart."[28]

Through the accumulation of these streamlined biographies illustrating the importance of common qualities, an implicit argument forms: a great number of successful people had these qualities, so these qualities must lead to success. The logic behind this is of course dubious (an example of post hoc, ergo propter hoc). It's also strategic. Smiles's Victorian readers couldn't reinvent the steam engine. They could, however, emulate George Stephenson's work ethic— how, for example, he taught himself math in odd moments between tasks. As Smiles writes in *Self-Help*, success comes "by the diligent exercise of qualities in many respects of an ordinary character, but made potent by the force of application and industry" (189). Thus, unlike Thomas Carlyle's concept of the hero, who is extraordinary in a way that sets him apart from other men, the self-help figure makes ordinary qualities, such as perseverance or honesty, extraordinary. This is also a strategy that would seem designed to prevent readers from imagining themselves in competition with others: the goal to become a more hardworking and persevering person or to learn everything one can in odd moments can be achieved by everyone (vs. being the first to invent a combing machine or joining the top 10 percent). As Craik puts it, "in the pursuit of knowledge, it matters not how many be the competitors"—knowledge "multipl[ies] itself to meet the wants of all" (1.286). It is telling that Smiles played such a key role in perpetuating these narratives about individual agency that downplayed the role of competition. When narrativizing his own experiences, Smiles recounts where his career ran up against a too-competitive field, particularly as a young man who had received an education to become a surgeon at a time when "the number of surgeons was greatly in excess of the public demand."[29] The desire to emphasize individual agency clearly overrode even personal experience.

Smiles's emphasis on the individual's power becomes even more specifically a question about effort and work versus ability and talent. Smiles, and the wider genre, insistently reimagines the role of genius and sudden bouts of inspiration. Genius too easily implies not only innate ability but also, as Kant theorized, a sort of leap in thought—a leap suggestive of an instinct or ability that cannot be taught, in distinction to replicable, step-by-step instructions accessible to everyone.[30] In *Self-Help*, even great masterpieces are not produced with the help of any mythic forces; they are produced by men working in an overtly concrete and physical way. Biographies of such figures thus concentrate on how these so-called geniuses had to prepare their minds and bodies to receive their eureka moments or to execute their works of art. Accordingly, in Smiles's telling, geniuses engage in the same repetitive work as the rest of us—to the extent that genius itself becomes an embodied, physicalized quality. This is most explicit in the chapter "Workers in Art," where Titian is an "indefatigable worker" (139) who spent seven years on a single painting, and where we learn that Claude Lorrain was always "closely copying buildings, bits of ground," and even studied the sky, "watching it for whole days from morning till night, and noting the various changes occasioned by the passing clouds and the increasing and waning light" (142). Similarly, Newton relied not on a flash of insight but on a mind "devoted for years to the laborious and patient investigation of the subject of gravitation" (110). Genius is not so much an innate ability as a habit ingrained on the mind and body over years. The emphasis on work over genius became a marked feature of self-help texts. Edwin Paxton Hood quite explicitly links all these ideas in his *Peerage of Poverty*, cautioning against the "mistake" of thinking that "Genius may dispense with labour,"[31] and instead pointing to biographies of "noble-minded persons who make the body obedient to the will of the mind."[32] As Smiles and the larger genre repeated over and over, it is hard, physicalized work—which can also come in the form of "mind work" or "brain work"[33]—that makes for success.

And yet, as much as Smiles and the larger genre insisted on this message, they don't show the slow development of such characteristics and habits—and they actually recreate the problem of innate ability by implying that these exemplary characters had exactly those traits that make for successful self-help from the start. Many of these traits align with the sort of energy or perseverance that are closely associated with ambition. For example, Smiles notes that William Smith's parents were unable to provide him with much of an education (a typical start to self-help stories) but that, even as a youth, "one of his marked characteristics . . . was the accuracy and keenness of his observation" (129). Similarly, when he introduces the missionary William Carey, Smiles observes, "an eminently characteristic anecdote has been told of his perseverance as a boy" (94). And in the case of the abolitionist Sir Thomas Fowell Buxton, Smiles writes that the "power of will, which made him so difficult to deal with as a boy," is the "backbone" of the grown man's character (219). Rather than show a character developing, self-help biographies often start with the same qualities or drives that will come to individuate that character.

These tendencies in Smiles's portrayal of successful men come to the fore in the biography of the Duke of Wellington. Smiles dwells at length on Wellington's character, repeatedly ascribing his success to qualities like his "business faculty amounting to genius" (233), his "perfect honesty" (233), and his "mastery of details" (234). Wellington does not so much develop as repeatedly demonstrate these characteristics. In fact, far from developing, these qualities are already at maximum capacity—"a business faculty *amounting to genius*," a "*perfect* honesty," a "*mastery* of details." Nor do they flag: Wellington's attention to detail "characterized him throughout his Indian career" (234), while his "individual firmness and self-reliance . . . never failed him even in the midst of his greatest discouragements" (235).

The only moments of possible development come when Wellington learns something. This happens both rarely and idiosyncratically, as when Wellington "learns" that bad arrangements can ruin the morale of an army (233). It is presented as a discovery, and yet, the lesson is absurdly self-explanatory. In another instance, Wellington considers how other armies had already fallen to Napoleon: "His clear discernment and strong common sense soon taught him that he must adopt a different policy" (234). Rather than outside forces teaching Wellington something, the syntax suggests, his own qualities teach him. This logic, of one's own qualities teaching oneself, is close to that of pulling oneself up by the bootstraps, of an enclosed system that dissociates the individual into a subject and an object. Smiles syntactically reflects this logic: "Another feature in his character, showing the upright man of business, was his thorough honesty" (236). The dependent clause interrupts an otherwise wordy version of a simple idea ("Another feature in his character was his thorough honesty"). And the dependent clause reveals the circular logic at the root of the sentence, as "upright" is a close synonym for "honest." This circular syntax is the stylistic equivalent of Smiles's characters, whose success is retroactively imagined as predetermined by their hard work.

The logic behind Smiles's biographies is often reminiscent, particularly in the above example, of Calvinism: circumstances do not develop character but reveal it. As Smiles notes in his biography of Wellington, "Shortly after this event the opportunity occurred for exhibiting his admirable practical qualities as an administrator" (233). When Smiles describes Wellington's early attempts to find another position, he notes that, "had he succeeded, no doubt he would have made a first-rate head of a department, as he would have made a first-rate merchant or manufacturer" (233). In Smiles's telling, by sheer force of character and hard work, the individual bends material reality to his will—hence Wellington "transformed an army of raw levies into the best sol-diers in Europe" (236). Although such anecdotes were intended to develop the reader's character, they actually neglect their own character development in interesting ways. This is compounded by the fact that, much like Lukacs's hero in the epic, these individuals go through trials that we already know they will overcome by virtue of their inclusion in Smiles's text.

As Smiles accumulates his examples, he shows, in form as well as explicit argument, that these specific cases from specific contexts actually contain uni-versal lessons. In this way, *Self-Help* aspires to the logic of the maxim: these characteristics are reproducible and predictable, always leading to success—or at least a good character—regardless of context. The form of the maxim is closely bound up with the tradition of self-help. A predecessor to the nineteenth-century self-help genre, Benjamin Franklin's "The Way to Wealth" is structured around maxims, as is the list of virtues in his *Autobiography*. Franklin's texts were a favorite quarry for later writers in the Victorian self-help genre, who lifted anecdotes from Franklin while neglecting to include any of his irony. Smiles heavily relied on the maxim, or, as he defined it, the "proverbial phi-losophy, embodying the hoarded experience of many generations, as to the best means of thriving in the world" (253). And Smiles not only repeated max-ims but also coined some of his own. The reviewer for *Fraser's* was struck by these "peculiarly apt and happy" "similes, sayings, and illustrations" in *Self-Help*, including such strange formulations as "purposes, like eggs, unless they be hatched into action, will run into rottenness."[34] Although questionable in content, this maxim perfectly replicates the syntax of proverbial wisdom, rely-ing on concision, parallelism, and analogy. Such wisdom, Smiles claims, has "stood the test of time" (253). Smiles describes biography in much the same way, as texts that communicate the "grand secret" of past successes, made up of actual experience and qualified to advise present readers "as to the best means of thriving" (253). In its repetition of shortened biographies and advice, Smiles's *Self-Help* transcends the specific case in order to isolate characteristics, which, like the maxim, take on a universal applicability.

As dubious as Smiles's logic may be, there is an impulse here that can seem democratic, even radical, in its desire to see value in everyday, common quali-ties associated with work and labor. This deviates from earlier models of advice literature directed to the upper classes. It also offers a different narrative model and timeline for character development in comparison to what we might read as the novelistic equivalent, the bildungsroman. In contrast, *Self-Help* is less about the organic development of individual psychology in a particular social milieu, and more about the deliberate accumulation of "timeless" characteristics. To motivate and acquire these characteristics seems to require exactly the drive everywhere lurking in the margins but so rarely invoked—ambition, or a desire to improve oneself and one's lot. By sidestepping or redefining these goals, Smiles imagines drives as habits that can be mechanically acquired. As a result of all this, Smiles's exemplary characters seem to verge on a newly identified condition, monomania. Read in this way, *Self-Help* can seem less radical or democratic and more in line with Victorian laissez-faire or twenty-first-century neoliberal thinking, with individuals finding themselves compelled to work at "helping themselves," in ways that overtly dissociate the mind and body.

## "The Ambition Took Possession of Him": Reforming Ambition

So far, I've claimed that Smiles's *Self-Help* aims to inspire readers to cultivate and embody qualities that frequently suggest ambition while avoiding its problematic associations with sin, crime, and selfishness. I've also suggested that Smiles's text elides showing actual character development, instead imagining how the reader can mechanically acquire a set of qualities through repetition. This all means that ambition itself—or energy, perseverance, application—becomes the goal, rather than a means to an end—like wealth, power, fame, and the rest. Smiles is everywhere careful about how he frames his characters' goals. For example, Smiles often notes the immediate aim, whether it's creating porcelain enamel, inventing the steam engine, or discovering sunken treasure. But we don't hear much about what these characters want to do with these inventions or discoveries afterward. This is a particularly tricky case with William Phipps, who, in hunting treasure, is quite literally after wealth. As if trying to sidestep this problem, Smiles claims that it is Phipps's "adventurous spirit" that is "kindled" upon hearing about a sunken ship (178). And Phipps is forgiven for his interest in treasure when he magnanimously shares everything among the crew—this is an ambition that lifts all boats (or at least everyone on this particular boat). Smiles's final word is that Phipps was known for "probity, honesty, patriotism, and courage" (182).

In his hurry to avoid thinking too much about what one would do with recovered treasure or how one might monetize inventions like porcelain or a combing machine, Smiles instead makes the means—perseverance, hard work, energy—into the ultimate goal. As a result, *Self-Help* is strangely full of examples of men who seem to work for the sake of working, as if driven by some instinct or compulsion. In these cases, Smiles's stories and their form most clearly begin to mimic the symptoms of monomania, newly discovered and named in the nineteenth century. This overlap is a side effect of the formal characteristics and rhetorical goals of Smiles's compressed biographies. It's also suggestive of how ambition was imagined as an embodied and potentially dangerous drive in a closed system.

An especially telling example of these tendencies is Smiles's inclusion of William Smith, who discovered the geological time line contained in the strata of the English landscape. Noticing "that each layer of clay, sand, and limestone held its own peculiar classes of fossils" and "pondering much on these things, he at length came to the then unheard-of conclusion, that each distinct deposit . . . marked a distinct epoch of time in the history of the earth" (130–31). In Smiles's version of the story, Smith quickly escalates from "pondering" to obsessing: "This idea took firm possession of his mind, and he could talk and think of nothing else. At canal boards, at sheep-shearings, at county meetings, and at agricultural associations, 'Strata Smith,' as he came to be called, was always running over with the subject that possessed him" (131). Smith sounds like a caricature in the vein of Mr. Dick, substituting strata for King Charles I.

Characters are in fact frequently "possessed" in *Self-Help*. The idea of using rollers "takes possession" of Richard Arkwright (43), the subject of mechanical invention "took complete possession" of Jacques de Vaucanson (62), "the ambition took possession of [John Flaxman]" to sculpt (195), Joshua Heilmann's idea for a combing machine "obtained complete possession of his mind" (66), Bernard Palissy is "possessed by the determination to master the secret of the enamel" (72), and Austen Layard is "possessed with a desire" to explore (97). A carpenter repairing pews learns Hebrew after he becomes "possessed with a desire to read" the Bible in the original (114), Thomas Clarkson is "possessed" by the question of slavery (217), and Dr. Livingstone is "possessed" by the desire to become a missionary (205). Similarly, John Howard's idea of bettering the condition of prisoners "possessed him like a passion" (207), while Thomas Wright's mind was "possessed by the subject" of returning liberated convicts to useful life (254). Sometimes this obsession takes on a religious quality, with characters becoming "devoted" to tasks. "Devoted himself" appears ten times across the text, often with an explicitly religious goal: Josef Wolff reads the *Life of Francis Xavier*, which "fires" "a passion the most sincere and ardent to devote himself" to a missionary career (307), while Ignatius of Loyola reads *Lives of the Saints*, which likewise "inflames" and inspires him "to devote himself to the founding of a religious order" (307).

As these examples demonstrate, another side effect of the cultural uncertainty about the value of ambition is that the drive to do something great often comes *to* the subject, versus arising *from* him. In fact, ambition often seems to reside in the biographies of great men, which, like a calling, will find the right reader. Again, while Smiles provides a useful case study for this phenomenon, it is not unique but a feature of the larger genre. As William Robinson writes in *Self-Education*, to "inspire a noble emulation, we would in the first place urge you to peruse the biographies of eminent and worthy individuals, who have risen from the humbler walks of life."[35] Smiles imagined a chain of self-helping men, with "admiration exciting imitation, and perpetuating the true aristocracy of genius" (308). Smiles often draws attention to how physical, instinctual, and embodied this process can be, as when he claims that "the very recollection of the deeds of the valiant stirs men's blood like the sound of a trumpet" (305). Here the biography or self-help text is itself the active agent, which is in fact one of Smiles's telling grammatical tics. In the space of a single paragraph, Smiles writes that biography "[calls] forth energies whose existence had not before been suspected," that Plutarch's *Lives* draws Vittorio Alfieri "with passion to literature," and that the perusal of *The Lives of the Saints* "inflames" Ignatius of Loyola (307). As Smiles summarizes it, all this is to demonstrate that the "brave and aspiring life of one man lights a flame in the minds of others" (308). This passage echoes the definition of inspiration, which literally means a "breathing or infusion into the mind or soul" from an outside source, "a breathing in or infusion of some idea, purpose, etc. into the mind."[36] Readers and examples of self-help "catch" and embody the drive, which is contained not in some supernatural realm but in the lives of other men. As Paxton puts it, remembering Craik's *The Pursuit of Knowledge under Difficulties*, "it is impossible to read [these biographies] without catching some portion of the inspiration breathed forth from lives so heroic, and many of them so divine" (136). And there is some evidence that this worked, perhaps most immediately among self-help writers themselves, as we can trace direct lines of inspiration from Craik's work to Paxton's and Smiles's, and from Smiles's *Self-Help* to Orison Marden's *Pushing to the Front*.[37] Readers also reported how they took inspiration from these texts, sending letters with thanks and news about their successes—including tributes like naming a store or a child after the author.[38] Such cases confirm this sort of imagined identification—which could trouble underlying assumptions about individualism and to what extent an individual draws out his own innermost qualities versus patterning himself on someone else.

Once Smiles's subjects are inspired and possessed, they come to be defined by their pursuits. Workers find ways to incorporate their passions into their labor, propping a book on a loom or spinning jenny and studying at the forge or out in the fields. Or they simply forgo sleep to pursue their interests. James Sharples would "rise at four o'clock in the morning to read [Burnet] and copy out passages; after which he went to the foundry at six, worked until six and sometimes eight in the evening; and returned home to enter with fresh zest upon the study of Burnet" (166). Craik, who so inspired Smiles, is similarly enthusiastic about single-minded characters. In my favorite example, which comes from the second volume of *The Pursuit of Knowledge under Difficulties*, Craik relates how Herschel ignored bodily needs to study, to the point that he "would not even take his hand from what he was about . . . and the little that he ate on such occasions was put into his mouth by his sister" (2. 288). (This tends to be how women appear in self-help texts not specifically focused on "female examples"—as helpers or, in other cases, as hindrances to male ambitions.) When these obsessions take hold, they supersede the physical needs of the body. As Smiles writes of George Wilson in the later volume *Character*, this early academic's persevering and "cheerful laboriousness" in the face of illness exhibits "the power of the soul to triumph over the body, and almost to set it at defiance."[39] Such language aligns with Paxton's, quoted above, about "[making] the body obedient to the will of the mind."[40] It also aligns with our understanding today of how the "supercrip" narrative has been employed for inspiration. Of course, Craik's and Smiles's examples are not all focused on characters with an illness or disability, but the ease with which such conditions are figured as "obstacles" or "difficulties" to be overcome uncannily dovetails with discussions of how the supercrip narrative relies "on concepts of overcoming, heroism, inspiration, and the extraordinary" while focusing on "individual attitude, work, and perseverance rather than on social barriers, making it seem as if all effects of disability can be erased if one merely works hard enough."[41] No wonder, then, that critiques of the supercrip narrative also overlap with critiques of self-help—that the narrative overemphasizes "personal, individualized attributes such as willpower and determination" in ways that obscure structural and political conditions.[42]

There are also rhetorical reasons behind these overlaps—behind these ways of exaggerating an internalized conflict, often framed as occurring between the mind and body, the individual and some "obstacle." As if compensating for the stories' repetitiveness and lack of suspense—after all, these examples are selected because they all eventually succeed—writers like Smiles and Craik intensify the effort needed for, as well as the duration of, the work. In *Self-Help* we hear about characters who toil "unceasingly" (48), who are "incessantly industrious" (34), or who "labour indefatigably" (216). In fact, "indefatigable" is a favorite narrative shorthand: "indefatigable industry" occurs thirteen times in the text, "indefatigable labour" three, and, as a modifier for other nouns, "indefatigable" makes a further twenty appearances. Although Smiles concentrates on characters who eventually succeed, we occasionally get a glimpse of those who were not so lucky. In explaining John Heathcote's bobbin-net machine, Smiles writes, "Many ingenious Nottingham mechanics had during a long succession of years been labouring at the problem of inventing a machine by which the mesh of threads would be *twisted* round each other on the formation of the net. Some of these men died in poverty, some were driven insane, and all alike failed in the object of their search" (53). While failure can seem the greatest threat haunting *Self-Help*'s margins, another implicit risk, for those who succeed as well as for those who fail, is illness, particularly the risk of being "driven" to insanity. This risk is often acknowledged when self-help texts distinguish between types of ambition. For example, Adams observes that "every healthy soul seeks to rise," and so "we do not desire to discourage an honourable ambition." But, he warns, "we pity those who suffer that ambition to overmaster them."[43] Similarly, William Anderson praises "he who can control and regulate his appetites and passions," while pointing to the cautionary tales of "overweening and insane ambition" that end in "degradation and death."[44]

Such characters who work from morning to night, to the point of forgoing sleep or forgetting to eat, might well have risked being diagnosed with monomania. Jean-Étienne Dominique Esquirol identified and named this condition around 1810 in France, and, by the 1820s, monomania "had already percolated down to the nonmedical French intelligentsia and been incorporated into their language."[45] This concept seemed to respond to a specific and widespread need. In his history of obsessive-compulsive disorder, Lennard J. Davis summarizes the rapid spread of the diagnosis: "After Esquirol invented the term, it became the single most frequently made diagnosis for patients entering the asylum at Charenton between 1826 and 1829 (when statistical records were kept), making up 45 percent of the inmate population. For the other famous asylums—Salpêtrière and Bicêtre—monomania diagnoses were the most common or second most commonly made."[46] The concept proved equally useful across the channel. The first occurrence of "monomania" in English dates to 1815, in J. G. Spurzheim's *The Physiognomical System of Drs Gall and Spurzheim*. It quickly took hold of the British imagination, to the point that Thomas Hood's *New Monthly Magazine* quipped that "monomania has become every man's business, since it has been discovered to be more epidemic than the influenza, and that it would not be too much to change the old maxim of *quot homines tot senteniae*, into *quot homines tot hallucinationes.*"[47]

The symptoms of monomania very much overlap with those of the self-help character. Jan Ellen Goldstein writes that, for Esquirol, "the distinguishing feature of monomania was ... the propensity to garrulousness and energetic activity centered around the preoccupation."[48] An oft-quoted example in British periodicals involved a French watchmaker who was obsessed with perpetual motion. He set to work, in Smilesian fashion, "with indefatigable ardour." And despite other symptoms, it was these ideas that "frequently recurred to him in the midst of his wanderings, and he chalked on all the doors or windows as he passed the various designs by which his wondrous piece of mechanism was to be constructed ... [H]is whole attention was riveted upon his favourite pursuit; he forgot his meals." He apparently went so far as to build various models—and even, after some failures, a version with promise. As the anecdote goes, he then took a victory lap through the hospital, "crying out, like another Archimedes," that he had solved it. But then the "wheels stopped!—the 'perpetual motion' ceased!"[49]

Further justifying such a parallel, the diagnosis of monomania was repeatedly and specifically linked to ambition. The term appears in Esquirol's definition, where he analyzes three case studies of monomanias that "had been rooted in earlier quotidian ambitions and in a high degree of sensitivity to the nuances of social status."[50] In other words, what begins as an ambition to improve one's position and status might become less "quotidian" and develop into pathology. In fact, Goldstein notes that some admissions registers identified a more specific type of monomania: *monomanie ambitieuse*.[51] Edward Charles Spitzka's 1883 *Insanity: Its Classification, Diagnosis, and Treatment* retains the association between monomania and overweening ambition, noting that megalomania is "a term applied by the French to monomania manifesting itself in delusions of a socially ambitious character."[52] Extreme emotions of all sorts were imagined as leading to insanity, but ambition comes in for specific mention—whether it's indulged or disappointed.[53] Such passions "enchain the subordinate faculties of the mind, making the whole of these faculties subservient to one governing and absorbing power."[54]

As perhaps already suggested by this range of manifestations, monomania became a catchall diagnosis, even as it developed a particular association with artists and scientists. In *Monomania: The Flight from Everyday Life in Literature and Art*, Marina van Zuylen argues that "monomania sets in when writing becomes a replacement activity for life itself. Work, friends, and the normal activities that structure the everyday are all staved off and replaced by the all-encompassing, all-excluding act of creating an alternate universe."[55] Davis has further developed this line of argument, demonstrating how frequently the figure of the scientist (Frankenstein, Dr. Jekyll, Freud), the writer (Zola, Flaubert, Freud again), and the visual artist (Max Klinger, Adolf Wölfli, Jay Defeo, and Judith Scott) have been defined by monomaniacal attention and purpose. While such studies have concentrated on those figures (fictional or real) that we associate with genius, it's important to note how the self-help genre's message about the average person and common qualities meant that monomania, too, could be associated with the average worker. Even a writer like Smiles, who disavowed the idea that he was anything more than an everyday writer and who claimed he resisted writing his own autobiography because his life was too humdrum to interest anyone, also pursued an almost monomaniacal writing habit. In his *Autobiography* Smiles offers himself up as an example, recounting how he managed to "write books requiring a good deal of labour and research" while also performing "the secretarial work of a large company" (260). He claimed he "never carried any subject of anxiety, or undone work, home"—not in order to relax, of course, but so that he could then sit down in his study to write on his own account (260). Like so much of Smiles's *Autobiography*, such episodes are then translated into maxim-like advice for readers: "If any one devotes an hour a day, or even half-an-hour to this purpose, it is astonishing what a great amount of literary work may be accomplished" (260).

Even according to Smiles, this habit became dangerous when he worked too late into the night and forgot to eat—since the "the brain weakens under protracted labour, especially at night." He imagines his body and, more specifically, his brain rebelling: "My brain got excited, and refused to lay aside its capacity for thinking." The result of "burning the candle at both ends" (297) was a "sharp attack of paralysis" that resulted in aphasia—a condition that uniquely incapacitated Smiles for writing. Suddenly, the same person who had previously seemed to have hundreds of names and biographies at his fingertips lost his ability to recollect "all proper names," and even words in general (299). As much as Smiles touts hard work and perseverance, such moments reveal the extent to which this depends on the mind and body—and how the desire to exert the mind's power over the body backfires on both, with this dissociation becoming a dangerous narrative employed about the successful individual, and one still very much with us.[56] While Victorians were concerned about the way overworking could backfire on the body—with even "brain work" leading to monomania, brain fevers, strokes, or an early death—today we know all too well how different occupations endanger workers' health, how stress takes a physical toll, and how overwork can lead to mental illness and burnout.

Juxtaposing these examples demonstrates the thin line between committed self-help characters and hardworking monomaniacs in the Victorian imaginary, demonstrating the extent to which these two character types use similar traits or actions to different results. While Spitzka imagines the case study of the inventor who fails—"the projector of some insane invention, who, before being committed to an institution, revels in bright anticipations of the prospective income to be derived from it" (287)—Smiles (as well as the larger genre) takes on the inventor who succeeds. The difficulty of distinguishing hard work from pathology has much to do with the value of ambition in the Victorian era and how self-help narratives tried to reframe this drive. Smiles holds up hard work and perseverance as the ultimate goal. Even if this seems to re-direct ambition to better outlets—versus selfishness, criminality, and competition—it also blurs into overwork and illness. In this way, Smiles could hold up a character whose hard work paid off as an example to emulate, while someone whose work failed might instead appear as a case history outlining the development of monomania. Zooming out, an all-consuming ambition might be good for the progress of science or literature, but it might take its toll on the individual who risks poverty or illness.

In *Obsession: A History*, Davis argues that we might understand the rise of illnesses like monomania and obsessive-compulsive disorder, from the mid-eighteenth century to our present day, as too much of a needful thing—a close attention to detail. Davis goes so far as to suggest, "When an industrial culture evolves to emphasize and rely on a greater sense of precision, repetition, standardization, and mechanization, that same culture will perhaps regard those attributes differently, and members of that society will mime, imitate, embody, internalize, and exaggerate those qualities" (13). Although Davis does not concentrate on ambition as a key term, there are immediate parallels: much as obsession became both "a dreaded disease" and a "noble and necessary endeavor" (3), ambition both makes and possesses the Victorian individual. In cultivating the ambition needed to navigate a rapidly changing economy, individuals develop themselves—and, in Smiles's reading, the nation and empire—but they risk being subsumed by their pursuits. Our neoliberal equivalent is surely Sianne Ngai's "zany" worker, the "hustler" in a precarious gig economy who embodies the spirit of Lyft or Uber as easily as they toggle between the respective apps and glowing dashboard signs—depending on which company is offering the better rate at any given moment.

Suggestive of the extent to which Victorians were aware of how ambition could make or break the individual, even at the height of the use of "monomania" as a medical term, some were suspicious of the line between the successfully ambitious and the dangerously monomaniacal. As the *New Monthly Magazine* noted, "The most of us are the victims of more than one monomania in the course of our lives; and there are not wanting unfortunates, great generals, grave divines, sound lawyers, able mathematicians, or what not, whose existence has been one long succession of various monomaniae, without a single moment of what may fairly be called a lucid interval."[57] Spitzka similarly illustrates how monomania could be seen as a spectrum when he relates a case of monomania that struck him as a "caricature" of normal ambition. Observing a patient in what was then called the New York City Lunatic Asylum, he comments that "the patient's history presented an exaggerated reflection of the social ambitions which characterized the different communities in which he lived; thus strikingly exemplifying the common observation that insane elusions are caricatures of the opinions and aspirations of the time and place where they are developed."[58] We might read Smiles's biographies as structurally caricaturing their examples, both in how Smiles selects for "striking" episodes and in how he compresses these stories.

Smiles's biography of Palissy the sixteenth-century potter is a particularly telling example of how self-help characters verge on monomania, whether in reality or in the telling. Palissy appeared in the second edition of *Self-Help* in 1866, as one of three potters in chapter 3. (Smiles's desire to keep adding examples is perhaps a sign of his own difficulty with knowing when enough is enough.) The Palissy biography closely adheres to the typical self-help storyline (inspiration and desire, work, obstacle, persevering work, success). Smiles traces the origins of Palissy's passion to an "elegant cup of Italian manufacture," the sight of which "disturbed his whole existence; and the determination to discover the enamel with which it was glazed thenceforward possessed him like a passion" (71). What follows is the obstacle-perseverance pattern of self-help iterated to absurdity. Palissy tries to emulate the glaze: "For many successive months and years . . . he burnt more wood, spilled more drugs and pots, and lost more time, until poverty stared him and his family in the face." When his experiments fail, he determines to start again. And so

Smiles restarts the same narrative: "For two more years he went on experimenting without any satisfactory result, until . . . he was reduced to poverty again." This sentence parallels the earlier sentence describing Palissy's work, both in syntax and content: For [block of time], he [experimented unsuccessfully], until [poverty]. And the solution is the same: "He resolved to make a last great effort; and he began by breaking more pots than ever" (72–73).

Finally, one of the three hundred experimental shards is successfully covered with white enamel. Palissy is inspired to build his own furnace, and again Smiles tries to capture the time and suspense invested in the experiment: "The second day passed, and still the enamel did not melt. The sun set, and another night passed. The pale, haggard, unshorn, baffled yet not beaten Palissy sat by his furnace eagerly looking for the melting of the enamel. A third day and night passed—a fourth, a fifth, and even a sixth,—yes, for six long days and nights did the unconquerable Palissy watch and toil, fighting against hope; and still the enamel would not melt" (74). Smiles offers a particular moment, Palissy "eagerly looking" into the furnace, and asks us to imagine this work multiplied over the course of six days and nights. This is a more concentrated version of what every self-help biography attempts: to condense a life into one pursuit and one replicable characteristic. The single encounter with a beautiful cup directs Palissy's calling and the rest of his life. Everything else—the day job, the family on the verge of ruin—is figured as background or more obstacles to be overcome. And when these experiments also largely fail, Palissy embarks on "the last and most desperate experiment of the whole": "But still the enamel did not melt. The fuel began to run short! How to keep up the fire? There were the garden palings: these would burn . . . They were burnt in vain! The enamel had not yet melted. Ten minutes more heat might do it . . . There remained the household furniture and shelving." And of course, on the "verge of ruin," after sacrificing even the household furniture, Palissy finally succeeds (74–75). The closely watched enamel finally melts; the material world bends under the strength of the individual will. But how easily it could have been otherwise if the experiment had failed—like that of the French watchmaker, who lamented when the "wheels stopped!—the 'perpetual motion' ceased!"[59]

If Smiles's *Self-Help* often reads like a collection of cases of successful monomaniacs, it has much to do with the desire to compress years of work into the space of a few "striking" paragraphs or pages and with the desire to ascribe these figures' motivations to the work itself rather than a self-interested goal for a limited resource (like an ambition for money or status). As a result, Smiles holds up characters who restrict their sleep for years on end, or who never tire of learning about the subject that "possesses" them, or who run hundreds of experiments before succeeding. *Self-Help* thus formally mimics the symptoms of monomania—while also gesturing, if only implicitly, to the dangers of the ambitious individualism that the genre celebrated. In this we can see how, as much as self-interest was imagined as a check on more dangerous passions, as Albert O. Hirschman famously argued, the closely associated concept of ambition risked veering into violence or illness that would backfire not only on societies but on individuals themselves. From the examples of *Self-Help* to that of Smiles himself in his *Autobiography*, the limit to ambition is the mind and body—pointing to the many ways in which self-help has assumed what we now call an able-bodied and neurotypical subject, while presenting any deviation as an obstacle to be overcome by yet more hard work.

Such narratives about success, so popularized by texts like Smiles's *Self-Help*, get at key questions for thinking about ambition, individualism, and character in the Victorian era. By concentrating so closely on the individual, Smiles's work elides a clear politics. Even as his work seems to align with the messaging of laissez-faire liberalism and, later, neoliberalism, these narratives also implicitly question the dream of "limitless individual autonomy." Smiles's *Self-Help* itself seems to point to where exactly these limits lie, in the individual mind and body. While historians and literary critics have long been interested in how the eighteenth and nineteenth centuries conceptualized and narrativized individualism, these discussions have usually centered on the novel, from the bildungsroman, to domestic fiction, to realism. As a result, when critics have looked to these novels, they have concluded that ambition and individualism were always circumscribed. For example, from Ian Watt's *Myths of Modern Individualism* to Nancy Armstrong's *Desire and Domestic Fiction: A Political History of the Novel* and *How Novels Think: The Limits of British Individualism from 1719–1900*, protagonists must discipline or compromise their desires to adapt to a wider cultural and economic system. Other recent critics, from Daniel M. Stout to Emily Steinlight, have flipped this equation to think about the tangible ways that the novel actually imagined the collective—in the form of the corporate, the population, and so on. When Victorian fiction is read alongside texts like Smiles's *Self-Help*, where the subject neither collaborates nor competes and where individualistic qualities like perseverance and industry are explicitly cultivated to the point of excess, a different picture of the individual emerges. The limit of individualism in *Self-Help* is one's own body, and the limit case is a loss of physical or psychological integrity.

In managing and redirecting their readers' ambitions, *Self-Help* and the wider genre touted the closely associated trait of perseverance. But the persevering work that creates individuals can also possess and subsume them. Such characters easily veer into monomania, particularly when the point isn't to reach a particular financial or artistic goal but simply to keep working. Importantly, as much as monomania suggests a single-minded purpose, the project of self-help thus dissociates the individual into the object that needs to be helped and the subject that will do the helping. As a result, the self-help figure, that origin point for bootstrapping ambition, encapsulates both the mythology of individualism—of this drive that coalesces the self in order to supersede obstacles and shape the material world to its will—and the risk that one might not be the subject that possesses this individualism but the possessed. As the developing diagnosis of monomania in the nineteenth century implies, ideas about individualism arose against and in tandem with ideas about both physical and mental illness and disability.

The individual and the body thus emerge as the ultimate closed system in texts like *Self-Help*, the sort of competition or zero-sum game that the genre seemed at pains to avoid imagining at the level of society. Reviewers of Smiles also pointed to the way the individual became the site for thinking about such material limits. As one writer at the *Saturday Review* stressed, anyone practicing self-help had to confront the limitations of their time and their energy, both mental and physical: "If every odd and end of time is to be employed in the daytime, the aspirant must have the fortitude to resist all the calls of friends, visitors, love-making, creditors, and other persons who waste or occupy time. Nor is hard work a mere affair of will. The body has to be taxed as well as the mind, and the body is apt to display an ignorant impatience of exertion."[60] The following chapters will take up how this "driven" individual, taxing mind and body, encountered these physical and material limits across the genres of biography, didactic fiction, and the multiplot Victorian novel. These ambitious characters raise further questions about the relation among individualism, ability, and illness, while confronting a different set of material and formal constraints as they meet on a shared playing field—whether as a sum of individuals in the nation and empire or as a jostling crowd of competitors.

# CHAPTER 2

# Expanding the Story of Ambition, Work, and Health in a Limited World

## Harriet Martineau's Economic and Illness Writing

In December 1833, Harriet Martineau fell ill. Although she had suffered from bouts of illness since childhood, she blamed this particular episode on the anxiety and overwork associated with her most recent writing projects. She had just traveled to Newcastle, paying visits and gathering information for a new project, which included firsthand research into a hot and drafty coal pit. She also blamed the "toil and anxiety" of seeking publication for the twenty-five-part *Illustrations of Political Economy* that she was currently wrapping up, a process that had "disordered" her liver and compromised her health ever since.[1] Believing that all this work had finally caught up with her, she wrote to the publisher and printer to notify them that she needed to take a break from her work on the final installment.

The printer responded with bad news. In preparation for the proofs, he had wetted paper—amounting to sixteen guineas—that had to be used now or never. Even more unfortunately, the proofs involved complicated mathematical tables that Martineau had to correct herself (*Autobiography*, 202). But to do this work while ill required the assistance of others. Martineau remembers this scene vividly in her *Autobiography*: "So, I set to work, with dizzy eyes and a quivering brain; propped up with pillows, and my mother and the maid alternately sitting by me with sal volatile, when I believed I could work a little" (202–3). This anecdote was apparently repeated and circulated, contributing to Martineau's reputation for overly ambitious work. As she writes, "I was amused to hear, long afterwards, that it was reported to be my practice to work in this delightful style,—'when exhausted, to be supported in bed by her mother and her maid'" (203). The way this anecdote traveled—and even, perhaps, overwrote the reality—suggests just how pervasive these tropes about hard work proved to be. Martineau's example of physicalized intellectual work "under difficulties" was later included in self-help texts and collections of exemplary biography, from Catherine J. Hamilton's series *Women Writers: Their Works and Ways* (1892–93) to W. A. Davenport Adams's *Woman's Work and Worth in Girlhood, Maidenhood, and Wifehood* (1880). Such anecdotes focus our attention on the successful individual who disciplines and overcomes her body; as Adams puts it, "There was true courage in the calmness with which she persevered in her literary work while suffering from a dangerous illness."[2] At the same time, such passages gesture to the real limits posed by these physical conditions.

Unlike these inspirational anecdotes, Martineau sought to tell a much fuller and more nuanced story about the relationship between work and health. She returned to such issues over and over across her writing career, from her *Life in the Sick-Room*—which has been read as a sort of self-help guide for those living with a chronic illness or disability—to the series she wrote for *Once a Week* on different careers and their impacts on people's health—with topics such as "the maid of all work" and "the policeman." And this attention to the body is apparent across her *Autobiography*, which starts with her earliest memories— memories of illness. Her later poor health and deafness were blamed on malnutrition as a baby, which was attributed to a poor wet nurse but might also have been related to Martineau's apparent milk allergy (39–40). Whatever the cause, Martineau recalls, "my health certainly was very bad till I was nearer thirty than twenty" (39). And she continued to suffer various ailments in later life. In 1839 she was taken seriously ill with a uterine condition and lived as an invalid (her term) for five years. As a last resort, she experimented with mesmerism and made a miraculous recovery (although this led to a distressingly public debate over the exact nature of her condition). Later in her life she was diagnosed with a heart condition, but here, too, the threat of death proved a slow-moving one; she lived with the condition for twenty-one years. As a result, throughout Martineau's *Autobiography*—a text that was itself written out of a fear that she would die before completing what she considered "one of the duties of [her] life" (34)—she is attentive to when her body prevented her work, enabled a different sort of work—such as her writing on illness and deafness—or became the subject of *others'* work.

Martineau was thus uniquely positioned to describe the relationship between ambitious work and physical health. In comparison to the self-help genre's tropes about the successful individual overcoming difficulties, and setting the body at defiance to do so, Martineau painted a richer picture borne of living with chronic conditions. And, importantly, she wrote in similar genres, framing both her autobiography and her work on illness as sources of advice for readers. In explaining her motivation for writing the *Autobiography*, she records how she had "always enjoyed, and derived profit from, reading [the biographies] of other persons" (34), and she repeatedly offered her experiences as lessons for others, particularly in *Life in the Sick-Room*. These texts thus overlap with the nascent self-help genre, with its interest in inspiring readers to learn from examples. They also speak back to the self-help ethos—and its "fantasy of limitless individual autonomy."[3] Martineau imagines her illnesses in nuanced and sometimes even counterintuitive ways, with her conditions allowing as well as preventing certain types of work—particularly as these conditions intersected with her gendered position. As a result, across her *Autobiography* and *Life in the Sick-Room*, Martineau conceptualizes her illnesses and disability through careful attention to her agency as well as the systems of dependence she negotiates as a woman writer.

All this is complicated by another major branch of Martineau's writing career, particularly the series that paved the way for that career. Her *Illustrations of Political Economy* was a popular and influential series, selling approximately ten thousand copies per number and reaching a total readership estimated at 144,000.[4] Such sales numbers meant that Martineau's work sold better than many of Dickens's novels, which, as Elaine Freedgood reminds us for comparison, were considered "highly successful" at two or three thousand per month.[5] The series also attracted the press's attention. As the *Spectator* observed, "The first day of each month is marked by no publication of more importance than Miss Martineau's *Illustrations of Political Economy*."[6] Martineau's didactic narratives about how to navigate the economy put the onus on individuals, who must act first if they want change from nations and governments. As Martineau argues in the preface to her *Illustrations*, "Unless the people will take the pains to learn what it is that goes wrong, and how it should be rectified, they cannot petition intelligently or effectually, and government will regard their complaints as unreasonable and their afflictions as past help."[7] The *Illustrations* provide both these general lessons as well as many examples of particular characters who set better or worse examples. This genre of popular political economy thus dovetails with texts like Smiles's *Self-Help* in managing readers' ambitions (or self-interest) with an eye to the greater good of the nation.

However, as much as Martineau stresses the importance of understanding economic principles in order to be both self-reliant and a good citizen, these lessons are frequently at odds with the realities her characters face, given the wider systems of an increasingly global economy and environment. This tension is most apparent—and acknowledged as such—when Martineau considers Malthus's population principle. Malthus infamously put humans in conflict with the earth, which cannot be made to produce more food as quickly as the human population increases. When she illustrates this principle in *Weal and Woe in Garveloch*, Martineau likewise represents humans at odds with the environment—which plagues the hardworking characters with everything from storms, to unproductive soil, to bad fishing seasons. Taking her illness and economic writing together, we can better see how Martineau represented the scope as well as the limits of individual agency and ambition, whether at the scale of one's own body or of a wider, global system. If, as I suggested in chapter 1, Smiles's *Self-Help* holds up examples that align hard—and typically physicalized and gendered—work with success, even as such examples threaten to blur into case histories of monomania, then Martineau's attention to this intersection of the individual—her ability, health, and work—and the larger system—of the nation, empire, and economy—offers an important counternarrative.

## Disability and Narratives of the Woman Writer

Martineau's attention to the tensions between autonomy and dependency emerges against the backdrop of early industrial capitalism, which, even (or perhaps especially) as it was developing into a huge and complex network of systems, also saw the rise of the mythology of the self-made and self-reliant individual. Martineau's major contributions to the philosophy and practice of living with a chronic condition, as well as the popularization of political economy, gave her a unique position from which to see ambition's dependencies and contingencies. Her vantage point also had much to do with her gendered identity as a writer. As Linda H. Peterson has argued, Martineau tapped into and reshaped the myths that "allowed women writers to claim new territories of endeavor and high achievement for their work"—myths that, she concludes, "were more enabling than disabling."[8]

I want to build on Peterson's important work on nineteenth-century women's authorship by suggesting that Martineau was simultaneously tapping into and reshaping myths about ability and disability. Disability studies has long attended to the specifically gendered aspects of illness and disability, looking back to ancient Greek theories that the female was the "deformed" version of the male. Martineau navigated hearing loss and lived with chronic health conditions while also establishing a long, successful career and striving to support herself even when she was too ill to work. She thus frequently navigated ideas about gender, illness, and ability, in ways that uniquely imagined the individual as part of these wider categories. Such categorization has often been a challenge, for disability studies widely and Victorian applications specifically, because having a disability has only unevenly been imagined as an identity marker that groups people (as opposed, for example, to thinking about gender or race) and because it is a relatively new term (although Victorians and Martineau herself used the word in other contexts, and often to discuss political limitations).[9] Even if the terminology differs, however, Martineau importantly addressed her experience of "afflictions" such as illness, invalidism, and deafness—and imagined herself speaking to people experiencing or caring for others with similar conditions. In her *Autobiography* and *Life in the Sick-Room*, Martineau continually draws attention to the material and embodied conditions of her writing and to where her position as a woman writer or as a person with a chronic illness or disability allowed or obstructed her career.

Martineau was intimately acquainted with the difficulties that were so celebrated by writers like Craik and Smiles, who imagined that obstacles would spur individuals to work harder (with these stories, in turn, inspiring others). But the difficulties they faced were, unsurprisingly, frequently gendered. Being a woman was itself a "difficulty," one that Craik's sequel, *The Pursuit of Knowledge under Difficulties, Illustrated by Female Examples* explored over and over—with young women only gaining access to an education through independent study or male family members (an oft-repeated scenario involves brothers who teach their sisters or share a tutor). In her *Autobiography*, Martineau frames her family's financial crisis with attention to how it affected her writing career. While the sinking family fortunes were of course detrimental to their quality of life, Martineau saw how this opened a door for her. As Freedgood has argued, Martineau was both "victimized and liberated" by her family's financial circumstances: their ruin in the wake of a bad investment actually gave Martineau the "liberty to do my own work in my own way."[10] The need to make one's own living was (and continues to be) a way of justifying a woman's writing. It is a repeated trope, for example, in Craik's "female examples," who justified their careers by explaining that they needed to support themselves and often their children or relatives. (As the next chapter explores, this was also how Dinah Craik, related by marriage to G. L. Craik, rationalized her career.) Martineau was well aware of this phenomenon and explored the scenario in her fiction as well. In *Deerbrook*, as Ann Hobart has shown, Martineau portrays economic problems as *opportunities* for women—female redundancy and market crises allowed women to enter the public space of the economy and support themselves.[11]

Even if Martineau was able to justify her career in these ways, the work involved was still not easy. To the contrary, Martineau emphasizes the physical work involved in writing and how it causes or worsens her illnesses. Thus, although she pokes fun at the idea that anyone would believe she regularly wrote while literally propped up by her mother and maid, such rumors might have gained traction because Martineau already had a reputation for hard, physicalized work. In her *Autobiography*, she remembers the especially difficult time before the success of her *Illustrations*:

> My own heart was often very near sinking,—as were my bodily forces; and with reason. During the daylight hours of that winter, I was poring over fine fancy-work, by which alone I earned any money; and after tea, I went upstairs to my room, for my day's literary labour. The quantity I wrote, at prodigious expenditure of nerve, surprises me now,—after my long breaking-in to hard work. Every night that winter, I believe, I was writing till two, or even three in the morning,—obeying always the rule of the house,—of being present at the breakfast table as the clock struck eight. Many a time I was in such a state of nervous exhaustion and distress that I was obliged to walk to and fro in the room before I could put on paper the last line of a page, or the last half sentence of an essay or review. (129)

This is all overtly physicalized and suggestively parallels the way Smiles imagined his own overwork and ensuing stroke (as explored in chapter 1). Martineau similarly stresses the connection between the mind and body, as well as the very physicality of the mind, with repetitive activity leading to damaged nerves and exhaustion. Martineau was attuned to these connections, as when she recalls other periods of working late: "Night after night, the Brewery clock struck twelve, while the pen was still pushing on in my trembling hand" (141). She similarly remembers the search for a publisher as an overtly physical and exhausting process, detailing how she "trudg[ed] many miles through the clay of the streets, and the fog of the gloomiest December I ever saw" (141). Such passages could easily have appeared as the stuff of an inspirational biography in a self-help book, posing one's body and exhaustion as obstacles to overcome.

Even after such intense bouts of writing, Martineau describes keeping to a strict schedule of disciplined work. She records that "it has always been my practice to devote my best strength to my work; and the morning hours have therefore been sacred to it, from the beginning." In London, she recalls, she would boil coffee at seven or seven-thirty, and then work till two, followed by time for visitors (157). The obituary Martineau wrote for the *Daily News* (and that her friend Maria Weston Chapman edited) recounts this schedule with yet more emphasis on her work: "It was at that time that she formed the habit which she continued for the rest of her life,—of sitting up late, while going on to rise early. She took, on an average, five hours or five and a half of sleep, going to bed at one in the morning, and being at her breakfast at half past seven, to save the precious morning hours for her most serious business. Such was her practice, with few intervals, to the date of her last illness" (664).

Such schedules seemed made to be broken. Across her *Autobiography*, Martineau observes when this productivity veered, even by her standards, into excess. For example, recalling the year 1849, Martineau notes she "found that [she] had been overworking" (551); a few pages later, she remembers that, despite an already busy schedule, the project of her three-volume *History* "could not be delayed." When Dickens wrote inviting her to contribute to *Household Words*, Martineau accepted because its "wide circulation" was too tempting to pass up (557). Later, Martineau again admits she had "too many irons in the fire" (593); a couple dozen pages later she "fancied [she] was going to do what [she] pleased" (622). But, in July 1854, the invitation to write a "Complete Guide to the Lakes" proved an "irresistible appeal," and she was back to a busy writing schedule (622). One has the sense that Martineau had trouble saying no to a new project, which is perhaps one reason that Hartley Coleridge reportedly claimed "she was a *monomaniac* about *everything*."[12]

Martineau worried that all this work took a toll on her health and even caused her second major illness. Around the time of the above-mentioned projects, she recalls some early warning signs, including "odd sensations at the heart" and "hurried and difficult breathing." If she had been "duly attentive" to such signs, she "might have become aware already that there was something wrong" (622–23). The thin line Martineau encounters here between self-reliant work and self-harming overwork was the subject of much wider debate in the period, including, for example, new regulations on women and children's work, the factory workweek, and workplace safety. As noted above, Martineau wrote a series of articles meditating on health in different professions. Taking a similarly focused view on the literary worker as a class, Martineau remembers in her *Autobiography* that she was "always aware of the strong probability that my life would end as the lives of hard literary workers usually end,—in paralysis, with months or years of imbecility" (156). Authors who relied on stimulants were particularly at risk. Martineau recalls hearing that "there was no author or authoress who was free from the habit of taking some pernicious stimulant; either strong green tea, or strong coffee at night, or wine or spirits or laudanum" (158).

Such attention to the embodied conditions of her writing and her long-term health leads to a major difference in how Martineau frames her work (sometimes brought to a fever pitch) as compared to Smiles's inspirational biographies or autobiographies like Trollope's that encourage disciplining the body into hard work. Although Martineau was successful early in her career, she was still concerned about her ability to support herself in the long run, against the vicissitudes of readers' interests and the publishing industry. And so, even with her success, she was determined to live within her means and save money against the future. The example of Sir Walter Scott particularly haunted her:

> It was my fixed resolution never to mortgage my brains. Scott's recent death impressed upon me an awful lesson about that. Such an effort as that of producing my Series was one which could never be repeated. Such a strain was quite enough for one lifetime. I did not receive any thing like what I ought for the Series, owing to the hard terms under which it was published. I had found much to do with my first gains from it; and I was bound in conscience to lay by for a time of sickness or adversity, and for means of recreation, when my task should be done. I therefore steadily refused to countenance any scheme of ambition, or to alter a plan of life which had been settled with deliberation, and with the sanction of the family. (197)

Martineau imagines the economy of her health and her writing in this passage, which creates something of a double bind: Martineau needs to work in case she falls ill and needs the money, but she can't overdo it—she can't indulge any "scheme of ambition"—because that could be what causes an illness.

At the same time, Martineau also highlights how the experience of living with disabilities and illnesses actually enabled some of her writing. Although Martineau elsewhere emphasizes the work involved in having any disability, she also came to imagine her deafness as actually spurring her "self-mastery"—outlining what can seem like a Victorian precursor to today's "supercrip" tropes. Looking back in her *Autobiography*, she writes, "Yet here am I now, on the borders of the grave, at the end of a busy life, confident that this same deafness is about the best thing that ever happened to me;—the best, in a selfish view, as the grandest impulse to self-mastery; and the best in a higher view, as my most peculiar opportunity of helping others, who suffer the same misfortune" (84). Martineau also notes how her deafness actually afforded certain types of multitasking, as when she was traveling with friends and also gathering her thoughts for *Eastern Life*:

My deafness which would, in the opposite case, have imposed a most disabling fatigue, was thus rather an advantage . . . During the ten weeks that we were on the Nile, I could sit on deck and think for hours of every morning; and while we were in the desert, or traversing the varied scenery of Palestine, or winding about in the passes of the Lebanon, I rode alone,—in advance or in the rear of the caravan, . . . without a word spoken, when it was once understood that it was troublesome and difficult to me to listen from the ridge of my camel, or even from my horse. (519)

This ability to retreat into her own thoughts assists Martineau in her writing, even as, elsewhere in the *Autobiography*, she writes that a "deficiency" in the senses is its own sort of work: "Life is a long, hard, unrelieved working-day to us, who hear, or see, only by express effort, or have to make other senses serve the turn of that which is lost" (82–83).

Martineau's attention to such nuances—of how disabilities or illnesses might sometimes limit, complicate, or enable certain types of work—is also apparent in *Life in the Sick-Room*, where she details her experiences of living as, in her terms, an invalid. Most important for Martineau's understanding of work and ambition are the passages where she speaks to the special "insight" that comes with illness:

We see the whole system of human life rising and rising into a higher region and a purer light . . . While we use our new insight to show us how things are done,—and gravely smile to see that it is by every man's overrating the issues of his immediate pursuit, in order that he may devote all his energies to it, (without which nothing would ever be done,) we smile with another feeling presently, on perceiving how an industry and care from above are compensating to every man his mistake by giving him collateral benefits when he misses the direct good he sought,—by giving him and his helpers a wealth of ideas, as often as their schemes turn out, in their professed objects, profitless.[13]

Such passages interestingly fuse Christian imagery with ways of imagining self-interest in early economic thought—the way the individual privileges her particular, "immediate pursuit" and how, even if she is unable to see the whole, this pursuit somehow works according to a larger scheme for the greater good. Building on this logic, Martineau emphasizes compensations or "collateral benefits"—the idea that failure or disadvantages (of illness, wealth, gender, etc.) somehow open a different door. Martineau's *Life in the Sick-Room* teaches the reader that, from her perspective of the sick-room, she can see "the folly of the pursuit of wealth" and "the emptiness of ambition" (78), with these messages interestingly dovetailing with those of Craik, Smiles, and the developing self-help genre, which also, as we've seen, sought to redirect ambition toward compensations in the form of "a wealth of ideas" and the development of character.[14]

Martineau's insight inspires the form and style of her writing, as she was working quickly and against the clock. As Maria Frawley observes in her introduction to *Life in the Sick-Room*, Martineau and Florence Nightingale shared a sense that they were writing against death: Nightingale wrote to Martineau in 1858, agreeing that "I too have 'no future' & must do what I can without delay" (23). In Martineau's case, this sense that she was writing against her own death did not just inspire her to write—and quickly—but also to write out of order. Martineau notes this pattern in her writing process for both *Life in the Sick-Room* and the *Autobiography*. Of the former, she remembers, "I never wrote anything so fast as that book. It went off like sleep. I was hardly conscious of the act, while writing or afterwards,—so strong was the need to speak. I wrote the Essays as the subject pressed, and not in the order in which they stand" (*Autobiography*, 449). Martineau's sense of urgency leads to this practice of writing out of order, with different subjects "pressing" in their turn, even if they may not logically follow one another. In January 1855, when she was diagnosed with a terminal heart disease, Martineau similarly found inspiration to confront a project that, otherwise, would presumably have remained on the back burner—her *Autobiography*. Although she recalls that writing her autobiography had emerged as a "real duty" long before and had been "a weight on [her] mind for some years" (557), it wasn't until this diagnosis that it became a real emergency. As Iain Crawford describes, Martineau "suspended most of her professional commitments and dedicated what she assumed were her final months to writing the *Autobiography*, which she intended to appear after her apparently imminent death."[15] And in this project, as she had with her *Essays*, Martineau decided to write out of order.

In commenting on her writing process, Martineau again and again shows how her health shapes her writing. In one passage, she stands back to observe that she is writing her *Autobiography* with the threat of death looming over her, much as she wrote *The Hour and the Man* many years earlier: "I find, in the sickly handwriting of that spring of 1840, notices of how my subject opened before me . . . I find, by this record, that I wrote the concluding portion of 'The Hour and the Man' first, for the same reason that I am now writing the fifth period of this Memoir before the fourth,—lest I should not live to do the whole" (439). In such passages Martineau purposefully disrupts the illusion that she is telling her life's narrative sequentially, instead drawing attention to the choices she has to make in the face of finite energy and time. The text itself starts to feel like a zero-sum game, where she has only a certain amount of space and time for the words she can write against her failing health.

To occupy this imaginative standpoint outside of her own life, to see it whole and choose which sections most need to be written, invites a certain blurring between one's perspective and the godlike omniscience of a third-person narrator. In constructing this perspective, Martineau used the same tools that served her in the *Illustrations*. Much as she had aspired to reconcile the individual experience of the economy with the bigger picture of its workings, so too does she imagine herself as simply one among many individuals. Rachel Ablow similarly theorizes that Martineau achieved what she terms a writerly "impersonality," specifically through her experience of pain, which enabled her to regard the self "as if it were equivalent to any self." The sufferer becomes "the ideal legislator, albeit one who is prohibited by her condition from acting in the world."[16] Erika Wright reads this phenomenon as an emerging relation between invalidism and omniscience. Drawing on Audrey Jaffe's location of the omniscient narrator "not in presence or absence, but in the tension between the two," Wright argues that "the cultural understanding (and narrative construction) of the invalid's power marks their presence in the narrative as a form of absence, their knowledge as a form of transcendence, their being as 'beyond the ken.'"[17] This positioned Martineau above the fray of individual interests and ambitions, able to see how they interact on a competitive playing field. As much as we associate this moral "impersonality" or emerging omniscient perspective with Martineau's period of invalidism, then, we can see this mode developing long before with her *Illustrations*. These early tales continually adjudicate between the particular and the universal, the individual situation and the general rule—thus questioning the relation between the individual's ambition or agency and a larger system of increasingly global socioeconomic and environmental dependencies.

## Space for Ambition in Harriet Martineau's *Illustrations of Political Economy*

In the preface to her popular *Illustrations of Political Economy* Martineau writes, "If we were to dedicate our work to all whom it may concern, it would be the same thing as appealing to the total population of the empire." True to this sweeping vision, Martineau explains that her tales will employ a "wide . . .

diversity of scenery and characters" to represent "widely different states of advancement in various parts of the world."[18] The first tale, *Life in the Wilds*, opens with a description of the setting in South Africa's Cape Colony:

> There are few climates in the world more delightful to live in than that of the south of Africa. The air of the mountains behind the Cape of Good Hope is pure and wholesome; and the plains which stretch out towards the north at a great height above the sea, are fertile in native plants when uncultivated, and richly repay the toil of the farmer. The woods are remarkable for the variety of trees and shrubs, and there are as many animals which may serve for food or for beasts of burden as in this country.

The narrator imagines this as a setting ripe for ambitious individuals, with land and animals ready to be used. Although these "advantages would lead numbers of our countrymen to settle in southern Africa," there is, the narrator warns, "one great drawback": people already live here, and they periodically raid the colonial settlements for supplies.[19] Martineau's tale follows just such a settlement and raid, with the process of rebuilding serving as the narrative catalyst to learn some political economy.

With this first tale and first passage, Martineau reinforces the preface's emphasis on representing the wider empire. Significantly, Martineau situates many of her tales in the wider empire and beyond—including, in addition to the Cape Colony, Ireland, Australia, America, France, the Netherlands, Siberia, Ceylon, and Demerara—thus representing global and imperial trade networks.[20] Such passages from *Life in the Wilds* mark an enduring concern across the *Illustrations*: Martineau places her subjects in the web of a wider material world, a world already very much inhabited. Across the tales, land is the ultimate source of wealth—a wealth that is frequently appropriated by the empire, by white settlers, and by English landlords. While many of her characters ambitiously seek to improve themselves and their station, others are persecuted or forced to leave their homes and even to emigrate (to places where they often simply encounter different forms of scarcity and competition).[21] But Martineau also depicts the natural world as more than a playing field to move across and to act upon; it frequently resists all her characters' best-laid plans, whether it takes the form of failing crops or natural disasters. By putting her subjects in such overtly physical altercations and competitions among themselves and with the natural world, Martineau depicts economic activity through competitions and zero-sum games, suggesting the sort of "ecological realism" that critics like Elizabeth Miller have associated with the later rise of naturalism.[22] Even in these much earlier tales, across these literal and metaphorical registers, Martineau's *Illustrations of Political Economy* reveals a concern with how the ambitious subject interacts with a limited playing field as well as with her competitors.

Martineau's attention to the environment in her *Illustrations* is all the more interesting because this is an aspect that early political economists—the source of the "principles" Martineau sought to illustrate—often overlooked or took for granted. In this way, we can read Martineau's tales as theorizing beyond their source texts in ways that distort or conflict with their original principles.[23] Significantly, as much as Martineau preaches economic self-reliance, her attention to the material environment that the individual acts upon (or is thwarted by) suggests a wider system of material dependencies. This is fitting given that Martineau contributed to the popularization of the term "environment," with Herbert Spencer likely drawing on its use in her translation of Comte.[24]

Many of Martineau's plots dramatize encounters with the natural world, from colonial settlers in *Life in the Wilds* worrying about lions and poisonous snakes while subsisting by hunting and gathering, to the many depictions of farmers and fishers across tales like *Brooke and Brooke Farm*, *Ella of Garveloch*, and *Ireland*. Natural disasters frequently serve as reminders about the limits to human ambitions, with monsoons, hurricanes, fires, and a flood appearing across the tales, all of which wreak financial disaster (particularly in *Demerara*, *French Wine and Politics*, *Cinnamon and Pearls*, and *Messrs. Vanderput and Snoek*). But the environment is most frequently and explicitly at odds with Martineau's characters when she illustrates Malthus's population principle. Although *Weal and Woe in Garveloch* was Martineau's most focused—and most controversial—tale about the Malthusian principle, the looming sense that the material environment is limited haunts many of her tales, as Ella Dzelzainis has shown.[25] The need to better balance the human population with natural resources is the reason to enclose the commons in *Brooke and Brooke Farm*. It's the reason the English characters emigrate in *Homes Abroad*. It's why Armstrong in *The Hill and the Valley* is scolded for letting his garden rot. And it's the lesson preached by *For Each and for All*: "That multitudes have little ease and no leisure is the fault of overpopulation" (42). Readers clearly got the message, to the point that Martineau pleaded with them in the preface to *Berkeley the Banker* to "give [her] time to show that [she did] not ascribe all our national distresses to overpopulation" (i).

Martineau was right to defend herself: the *Illustrations* do far more than hammer over and over at Malthus's principle. For example, she juxtaposes such messages to other, seemingly contradictory lessons about nature being "inexhaustible" (*Life in the Wilds*). One character in *The Loom and the Lugger* even optimistically imagines that the world might have resources enough to outfit everyone in lace and pearls (51–52). Martineau also echoes Godwin's arguments about human work and intelligence gradually improving to resist any natural limits (particularly in *Life in the Wilds*). And we could read Martineau as ultimately illustrating not the limitations of the material environment as a whole but rather how a sense of scarcity is created by *artificial* restrictions and violence—including imperial power structures that exploit colonies' populations and resources (*Ireland, Cinnamon and Pearls*), the system of slavery (*Demerara*), and aristocratic or class interests that rig the legal system for those in power (the aristocratic privileges that literally trample a vineyard in *French Wines and Politics* or the Corn Laws in *Sowers Not Reapers*). Wherever we imagine Martineau's final critique landing, I would argue that this sense of environmental limitations is key to understanding both her *Illustrations* and why so many readers understood her tales as essentially endorsing Malthus over and over again. To make this point, I want to turn to Martineau's most explicit engagement with Malthus and to the setting that she chose for it—her Garveloch tales.

Martineau's *Ella of Garveloch* and *Weal and Woe in Garveloch* appeared as the fifth and sixth tales of the *Illustrations*. Both take place on an island, reminiscent of *Robinson Crusoe* (a similarity that was not lost on Martineau's reviewers).[26] *Robinson Crusoe* also uses the island setting to isolate the actions of *homo economicus*, providing a microcosm of individualism and capitalism. According to Ian Watt's reading, "Crusoe's island gives him the complete *laissez-faire* which economic man needs to realize his aims." Crusoe is free of the problems that come with a larger market, such as taxation, the labor supply, and exchange rates—in short, the problems that come with other individuals. The fantasy of the supposedly deserted island relies on this sense of uncontested agency—there are no other owners or competitors—but it also relies, as Watt notes, on a version of imperial control: you can build "your personal Empire with the help of a Man Friday who needs no wages and makes it much easier to support the white man's burden."[27]

Martineau's *Ella* takes place in the slightly more populated Scottish Hebrides, but here, too, the land plays a pivotal role. Some of the key "principles" the tale is meant to illustrate involve extrapolating rent prices from the land and soil's qualities:

> Real RENT is that which is paid to the landowner for the use of the original, indestructible powers of the soil.
>
> Land has these powers in different degrees.
>
> The most fertile being all appropriated, and more produce wanted, the next best soil is brought into cultivation; then land of the third degree, and so on, till all is tilled that will repay tillage.[28]

Despite the straightforward list of principles, the tale poses open questions about how much the value of land is under an individual's control, even if that individual is working with good soil. Much like Martineau's predecessor in this didactic genre, Jane Marcet's *Conversations on Political Economy*, many of these principles in *Ella* are made explicit through the educational dialogue between characters. Across *Ella*, the characters debate how to calculate the value of land and goods, and they specifically circle back to questions around how their neighbors' actions might affect them and their land's value. When the ambitious and hardworking Angus hopes to expand operations, the envious Murdochs see him as their competition: they envy him and worry that he wishes to "supplant" their position by taking over their farm (97). In contrast, Angus and his future wife Ella welcome new neighbors for both social and financial reasons. They reason that, although these new workers will increase the demand for lucrative land and thus raise rent prices, these workers will in turn produce more goods. This means that prices will then go back down, finally causing rents to decrease as well. To see this bigger picture of the market, Martineau's story suggests, is to defuse fears of competition.

But in *Weal and Woe in Garveloch*, the big picture is not so reassuring. In this tale, where Martineau illustrates Malthus's principle most explicitly, the action picks up a generation after *Ella* left off. Now the island is *over*populated, and the promise that more people will lead to increased productivity and lower prices no longer holds true—suggesting that some economic principles might be more or less applicable depending on the scale at which one is viewing things. The temporal scale of Malthus's principle also adds to the difficulty of imagining and representing how one will be affected by others' actions. By the end, the culprits in *Weal and Woe* are the families that have children without sufficiently calculating the long-term cycles of cause and effect. But as Martineau's narrative makes clear, such calculations are difficult if not impossible to make. Even those who, gifted with a preternatural foresight, make the "right" choice to abstain from marriage altogether, end up in the same malnourished boat as the rest of the community. Taking these tales together, in translating economic principles into narrative, Martineau's *Illustrations* theorize how the individual becomes further entangled in both environmental and social dependencies. In the process, the *Illustrations* offer an early and important counternarrative to the imagined division between human and natural agencies, questioning assumptions in the era's political economy about the individual economic actor.

It's useful to situate this claim in the context of the era's political economy, its sometimes-paradoxical relationship to ideas about the natural, and its implications for seeing an interdependent system of agencies. On the one hand, political economy tended to assume that "natural" laws govern the economy. As Freedgood writes, both Martineau and the theories she worked to popularize represent economic laws as "counterparts of the natural, immutable, and inevitable laws of the physical sciences, and (for the most part implicitly) of God as their metaphysical author."[29] And some early analogies for the economy, including Montesquieu's *Fable of the Bees*, explicitly naturalized human economic activity. Montesquieu imagined not only a balance "but a strong *web* of inter-dependent relationships" that would cohere communities (at least, that is, human communities), domestically and internationally.[30] Adam Smith similarly suggests such interdependence, from the division of labor that allows one to make so many pins a day, to the flurry of financial interactions that make up the larger economy. Meanwhile, focusing on the natural sciences, Alexander von Humboldt conceptualizes large, interconnected systems, from the isothermal lines explaining climates that span the globe, to the effects of colonizer deforestation in South America on the soil, atmosphere, and insect populations. In seeking to see these bigger pictures, such thinkers also suggested ways of understanding how individual actions ripple across a larger system—and how that system might react. This had implications for thinking about individual actors as collaborating or competing, with texts like Darwin's *On the Origins of Species* feeding into economic thinking that rationalized a competitive mindset. But as Peter Kropotkin argues in *Mutual Aid*, Darwin's work could naturalize cooperation just as readily as competition. The through lines across these fields and concepts is illustrated by how easily Kropotkin jumps between ecological, economic, and social critique, lambasting Western society's "unbridled, narrow-minded individualism."[31]

Even as economic thinking was influenced by and paralleled ideas about the natural, it often ignored or elided the environmental conditions necessary for economic activity—with ramifications that are still with us. Instead, political economy emphasized the individual economic actor and their agency. Martineau was in a unique position to consider the environment alongside political economy and to think across the individual and the wider society—since fiction relies on depicting particular environments and individuals in their communities.[32] In imagining settings, environments, and societies that exert their own unpredictable agency—and that perhaps limit and constrain the subject's actions—Martineau undermines some of the premises of the economic theories she sought to illustrate.

Read in this way, Martineau's *Illustrations* are lessons about not only individual agency but also dependency. And these lessons often come through most clearly when Martineau considers the environment and characters with illnesses or disabilities. This is perhaps not a coincidence, given how both ecocriticism and disability studies have illuminated how the assumptions underlying both political economy and theories of the natural are suggestive of interdependence. For example, the concept of possessive individualism has relied on a tradition going back to Locke and Hobbes that understands embodiment as entailing "property in one's person." According to this view, the individual is "essentially the proprietor of his own person or capacities, owing nothing to society for them."[33] This is immediately problematic when we consider disability. As Emily Russell puts it, "By making one's humanity contingent upon self-determination of one's person, this logic excludes all those who have been constructed as physically dependent."[34] The traditional model of possessive individualism assumes one state—the adult with no disabilities or illnesses—rather than considering how, for example, humans always display a wide spectrum of abilities; or require care in early and later years of life; or are bound up in systems of social, cultural, and economic dependencies. Similarly, recent work in ecocriticism emphasizes dependencies and multiple agencies, from Timothy Morton's theories of interconnection, to Jane Bennett's vision of a web of human and nonhuman forces, to Stacy Alaimo's theory of trans-corporeality. This attention to dependencies seeks to reverse traditional Western assumptions about human agency, where the human is subject and nature is object.[35]

With such background in mind, we can better see how Martineau spoke to ideas about autonomy and dependency, collaboration and competition that developed in the nineteenth century. Martineau is particularly attentive to the dispersal of agency when she engages with Malthus's principle—perhaps because these questions also haunt his work. Malthus's principle presents an inevitable conflict between a growing human population and the limitations of the land (specifically its ability to be improved and cultivated). Throughout the different versions of his *Essay*, Malthus slips between two ways of imagining the earth's role in this conflict: as a material object to be acted upon and as an actor in its own right. On the one hand, Malthus depicts populations roaming across, settling on, cultivating, and fighting over the land. On the other hand, he imagines the earth as a force to be reckoned with that might, like a resistant business partner, "refuse to produce any more."[36] At one point in the revised second edition (1803) Malthus even depicts the earth and the human population taking on the allegorical roles of the tortoise and the hare. He uses this analogy to argue that we must change our population dynamics rather than try to change the earth's production. He reasons that "it would appear to be setting the tortoise to catch the hare. Finding, therefore, that from the laws of nature we could not proportion the food to the population, our next attempt should naturally be to proportion the population to the food. If we can persuade the hare to go to sleep the tortoise may have some chance of overtaking her."[37] With this analogy, Malthus enlivens an abstract principle by turning it into narrative—giving the earth a powerful (if slow) subject position, which forces the human population to act differently.

Martineau confronted these questions about turning principles into narratives in both more direct and more sustained ways. She presents this task in the following terms: "It struck me at once that the principles of the whole science might be advantageously conveyed . . . not by being smothered up in a story, but by being exhibited in their natural workings in selected passages of social life" (*Autobiography*, 124). This interestingly downplays Martineau's own creative agency, suggesting that she is simply exhibiting the "natural workings" of the principles. Far from simply recording the elusive actions of Smith's invisible hand, however, Martineau overtly intervenes with her authorial control. *Weal and Woe* picks up on *Ella of Garveloch* with the story of Ella and Angus, now a long-married couple with nine children. The narrative covers four years. First, we witness two good seasons: good fishing and good crops, young people marrying and starting their own families. Then, of course, in Malthusian fashion, the tides turn. After two years of lackluster and even failing crops and hauls, the island experiences famine and illness—and an increase in interpersonal competition and conflict. The form this story takes is thus incredibly condensed, with much of the action summarized, compressed into dialogue, or skimmed over entirely.

When Martineau does zoom in to dramatize Malthus's principle through particular scenes, she concentrates on how the islanders compete among themselves. This narrative device shifts the dynamics—from the human population versus the earth, to humans against humans. The characters' antagonistic struggles offer a stark contrast to what political economists celebrated about competition, specifically its much-vaunted power to establish and stabilize market values and ultimately lead to greater efficiency. Although Malthus rarely imagines his population directly competing among themselves for material subsistence, this worst-case scenario lurks in the margins of his work. In the 1798 edition, for example, Malthus writes, "The vices of mankind are active and able ministers of depopulation. They are the precursors in the great army of destruction; and often finish the dreadful work themselves. But should they fail in this war of extermination, sickly seasons, epidemics, pestilence, and plague, advance in terrific array, and sweep off their thousands and ten thousands. Should success be still incomplete, gigantic inevitable famine stalks in the rear, and with one mighty blow levels the population with the food of the world."[38] Malthus seems reluctant to imagine his overabundant population competing over resources. Instead, we learn about "sickly seasons," "epidemics," "pestilence," "plague," and "famine." And yet, the abstract "vices of mankind" are suggestively pointed to in the imagery of a "great army of destruction" and a "war of extermination." By the 1803 version, Malthus included a different analogy. Here he imagines a "mighty feast" that is crashed by uninvited guests:

> A man who is born into a world already possessed, if he cannot get subsistence from his parents on whom he has a just demand, and if the society do not want his labour, has no claim of *right* to the smallest portion of food, and, in fact, has no business to be where he is. At nature's mighty feast there is no vacant cover for him. She tells him to be gone, and will quickly execute her own orders, if he do not work upon the compassion of some of her guests. If these guests get up and make room for him, other intruders immediately appear demanding the same favour. The report of a provision for all that come, fills the hall with numerous claimants. The order and harmony of the feast is disturbed, the plenty that before reigned is changed into scarcity; and the happiness of the guests is destroyed by the spectacle of misery and dependence in every part of the hall and by the clamorous importunity of those, who are justly enraged at not finding the provision which they had been taught to expect. The guests learn too late their error, in counteracting those strict orders to all intruders, issued by the great mistress of the feast, who, wishing that all her guests should have plenty, and knowing that she could not provide for unlimited numbers, humanely refused to admit fresh comers when her table was already full.[39]

Part of what makes this passage so tricky is that the analogy isn't very apt: these guests who come crowding, whether they have a "right" or not, presumably have agency in a way that a child being born into the world does not. More importantly and disturbingly, the ethics involved in asking someone to leave a private feast are markedly different from those involved in suggesting that a person doesn't have a right to sustenance. Adding to the confusion, the analogy keeps shifting perspective and, accordingly, sympathy or blame. This strange, extended analogy reveals just how difficult it is to represent, let alone assign agency and responsibility for, a conflict between a population and the environment. It also raises questions about whether the conflict is in fact between people and the environment, or triangulated across the environment, those people in control of the feast, and those who are left out.

This is a central dilemma for Martineau's narrative. Toward the beginning of the story Ella talks with her friend Katie, observing that it is a "rich season" and the best fishing in memory. We learn that a local farmer, Duff, expects "the best harvest he has had since he took the farm."[40] Katie exclaims, "Thank God!" but then she worries: "It almost frightens me sometimes when I see the numbers that are growing up, to think how we are to get oat and barley meal for them all" (68). Even more clearly invoking Malthus's language, Katie argues that "Duff's farm ought to yield double and double for ever, if it is to go on to feed us, for our children will marry and have their little tribes as we have. If you and I live to be like many grandmothers in these islands, we shall see our twenty or thirty grand-children, and perhaps our eighty or ninety great-grand-children" (69). As this passage suggests, it is difficult to turn the slow work of generations into a narrative; the nineteenth-century novel typically relies on scenes and a cast of characters belonging to one or two generations. It can similarly be difficult to turn the actions of the collective—the stuff of political economy and statistics—into narrative. In such passages, the subject becomes a generation rather than an individual. For example, the young people decide, as a generation living in good times, that "their courtship should end in immediate marriage" (93). With wages rising higher and higher, they assume "the only thing at present wanted was a greater number of labourers" and imagine that "when their tribes of children were grown up, all would be right" (94). As expected, the threat of overpopulation is then realized, and Martineau confronts the challenge of finding ways to represent this conflict through particular scenes.

As the island's crops and economy falter, the characters increasingly find themselves in competition. The first sign of trouble in the village is a work of sabotage—someone slashes all of Fergus's fishing nets before a critical trip out to sea. The magistrate is worried that this sort of crime comes with people "jostling" too closely, and he sees this as a harbinger of worse times to come. He notes that the miseries of poverty are fast approaching when "men begin to fancy their interests opposed to each other,—which the interests of men in society can never be. Fair competition leads to the improvement of the state of all; but the jealousy which tempts to injure any interest whatever is the in-fallible token that distress is at hand" (79). This sort of sabotage serves as the tipping point where competition shifts from healthy to destructive—from competition that imagines an abstract marketplace where each acts and is judged fairly, to competition that will break the rules to beat out rivals.

Martineau's most striking scenes illustrate what such interpersonal compe-tition might look like. One disturbing scene describes the famine-stricken crowd competing to collect shellfish at low tide. Ella tells her son that she has kept her children from the beach at these times, "lest they should learn to fight like the hungry people on the shore" (101). Later, when a ship bearing grain approaches the island and people hurry to meet it, we get a montage of literal physical conflict: "Here a poor invalid, putting forth his utmost power to keep up with his competitors, was jostled aside or thrown down by the passers by" (119). Dan arrives late and is upset to see he has little chance of getting any-thing. The narrator notes that it is "the policy of the bystanders to turn their rage upon each other," and, in this spirit, Dan "kick[s], struggle[s], deal[s] his blows right and left," and attacks a former friend (120). If such scenes suggest how competition can stir a lazy character like Dan to exertion, they also cau-tion that such exertion might take the form of pushing others out of the way—particularly someone like the unnamed "poor invalid."

This anxiety seeps into the islanders' psychology. The characters that serve as bad examples repeatedly imagine that the other villagers are trying to take their place. For example, Rob Murdoch, Ella's mean-spirited cousin, revives his hatred of Angus, "having been formerly taught by his father than Angus was a traitor who intended to supplant him" (73). Or, when the malingerer Dan misses an opportunity to work, he imagines "some vagabond or another stept into his shoes" (93). In distinction to the earlier tale (*Ella*), however, now even the most moral and self-sacrificing characters participate in this competitive way of thinking. Rather than fight over scarce resources, these more ethical characters choose a sort of martyrdom. The hardworking Kenneth, Ella and Angus's oldest son, decides to give over his rations of grain so that his younger siblings can eat more. After seeing the worst of the famine, Kenneth signs up with a recruiting party to become a soldier. He justifies the decision to his mother by noting that "there are so many brothers growing up to fill my place; and my going will make room for one of them" (131). Characters like Kenneth no longer have recourse to a rosy big picture that sees more people as (eventually) working to the common good. Instead, the island comes to represent the ultimate closed system, with its inhabitants crowded into a zero-sum game for basic necessities.

Whether one jealously guards one's place or gladly gives it away to the next person, this way of thinking imagines land and resources as fixed—rather like an inverted game of musical chairs at Malthus's "mighty feast," with only so many chairs and ever more players looking for a spot to sit. Much work has been done on the figure of the mob and the city in the nineteenth-century novel, and it seems likely that the rise of crowd scenes was partly inspired by these ideas about overpopulation.[41] What Martineau does in her tales, I would argue, illustrates how this competitive thinking could work at a smaller scale, at the level of individuals interacting with one another. Martineau's *Weal and Woe in Garveloch* thus reveals the interpersonal violence that only lurks around the edges of Malthus's *Essay*. Martineau imagines how this principle could inform the ambitious subject's psychology in an age of (at least perceived) overpopulation: with limited resources, her characters jealously guard what they have or enviously look to steal from others' stock. The only alternative imagined in the story is to actively give one's food or spot away: by the end of *Weal and Woe*, the best thing a character can do is to help decrease the surplus population by leaving the island.

This solution is less helpful if we interpret the story figuratively as well as literally. If the island of Garveloch stands for the larger British Isles, then Kenneth's departure raises questions about wide-scale emigration—one of the recommendations that Malthus as well as his critics suggested as a temporary solution. But, as Martineau's other tales about emigration, like *Life in the Wilds* and *Homes Abroad*, demonstrate, the sites where emigrants might relocate were already populated. As Robert Mayhew has explored, Malthus himself was wary of how his critics—including Southey—cavalierly volunteered foreign lands for Britain's population to bleed into, leading him to theorize the ethics of "legitimate supply."[42]

Whether or not Martineau imagined Kenneth as standing in for British emigrants, she certainly wanted readers to attend to both the particular narrative and the general principle it illustrated. She even voiced this concern when she learned that the young Princess Victoria was reading her *Illustrations* (apparently one of her favorites was *Ella of Garveloch*). Martineau hoped that the princess "did not read for the story only. In her position it really would be a very good thing that she should understand the summaries and trace them in the stories."[43] Martineau reveals a concern here that the general principles won't always shine through clearly, muddled as they are with the details of characters' backgrounds and contexts. As Claudia K. Klaver has pointed out, Martineau's *Illustrations* put the devices of realist fiction—with their focus on the individual—into conflict with economic principles—which tend to theorize widescale and collective forces.[44]

*Weal and Woe* reveals a particularly uneasy narrative balance between illustrating individual agency and larger systemic forces. Unable to tinker with the system, characters can choose to leave or to stay, to sabotage one another or to protect what they have, to marry and have children or to remain single. Often, these principles sit uneasily on particular characters' shoulders. For example, Martineau's reviewers—many of whom were horrified that a woman had taken on Malthus at all—were especially bothered by the character of Ronald, Ella's brother, who decides not to marry Katie. Ronald explains that he has chosen not to marry the woman he loves and who loves him because the island is overpopulated.[45] This decision awkwardly bridges the story and the principle: it is difficult to believe, as Martineau's critics vociferously argued, that anyone would so sacrifice their own happiness for their belief in an economic principle that works at the scale of decades, or for the sake of a community that is so thoroughly oblivious to that sacrifice. Ronald's decision does not make sense in the "natural workings" of the narrative, but only at the level of the principles Martineau illustrates: he literally applies Malthus to redirect his desires.

Although exaggerated in this case, the same theoretical difficulty lies behind all of Martineau's tales: how to imagine individual actions in the context of a larger but ultimately limited socioeconomic landscape and environment. Martineau tends to assume a naturalized system of laws and principles navigated by discrete individuals following their self-interest. But in some tales she also points to how characters are interdependent, both through economic and environmental or ecological systems. While Ronald unconvincingly gestures to such an interdependent system and its ethos to explain his choice, another character in the Garveloch tales more poignantly raises questions about agency and interdependency.

So far, I've neglected to talk about this key character. Ella's brother Archie is at the center of the family's care and love. He seems to have an unnamed intellectual disability and is often on the margins of the tale—in part because he exists outside of the family's discussions about work and money. This exclusion is especially striking because otherwise Martineau insists on the importance of everyone understanding economic principles, and she also bucks nineteenth-century conventions by explicitly bringing women into her tales as fully rational economic agents.[46] However, Archie often wanders away from the house to visit the beach or his favorite cave, and he doesn't knowingly participate in the work of the family. In fact, Ella tries to keep him away from the steward who collects their rent, Mr. Callum, for fear Archie might be sent away. And yet the plot turns on him. Archie sparks the central crisis of the tale when he steals eggs and is consequently detained as a criminal. This crisis has all the trappings of melodrama: Ella worries that Archie will die from the trauma of imprisonment in a strange place; Mr. Callum, in rushing to punish Archie, seems to be channeling an arbitrarily cruel stage villain; and both sides race—by boat!—to get to the laird with their version of the alleged theft first. Archie survives this episode, only to drown trying to rescue his family from a capsized boat. As a result, much like other characters with disabilities across nineteenth century-fiction, Archie is exploited as a key mover in the tale's melodramatic and plot elements—adhering to the patterns identified by theorists like Martha Stoddard Holmes in *Fictions of Affliction* and David T. Mitchell and Sharon L. Snyder in *Narrative Prosthesis*.[47]

But if we read Archie's character as central not only to the narrative elements but also to the economic principles that undergird the plot, Martineau troubles the supposedly natural laws included at the end of each tale. Archie doesn't debate the logic of rent prices with Ella or consider the best way to cultivate the land with Angus. Instead, he suggests a conflict between the natural world and a competitive, capitalist mindset. As much as Martineau seeks to illustrate the supposedly natural workings of the economy, she also suggests the extent to which these laws are actually artificial—by pointing to the alternative laws of Archie and the local ecosystem.

Archie is both what his era would call a "natural" and associated with the natural world. When Archie's brother Ronald suggests that Archie might take turns, like the other siblings, at paying the rent, Ella immediately rejects the idea, arguing that Archie "is not made to hold a money-pouch, nor to have any worldly dealings." When Ronald points out that Archie, too, "brings in what helps fill it," Ella explains the difference:

> And how innocently! It is his love for the things that God made that makes him follow sport. The birds are his playmates while they wheel round his head, and

when he takes them on the nest, he has no thought of gain,—and evil be to him
that first puts the thought into him! He strokes their soft feathers against his
cheek, and watches the white specks wandering through the water like snow-
flakes through the air. He does not look beyond the pleasure to his eyes and to
his heart, and he never shall; and gold and silver are not the things to give pleasure to such an eye and such a heart, and he shall never know them. (41–42)

Archie has no sense of monetary gain or loss, private property, or planning
ahead. Although the rest of the family lives close to the natural world, they
continually look for ways to gain by it—tilling the fields to produce better
crops, collecting peat and kelp to sell, and packing herrings for the market.
And at times they are in direct conflict with the natural world, as when Angus and Fergus kill an eagle that's picking off the poultry.

Archie's character also provides reason for the narrative to pause over different sorts of domestic or familial systems of dependencies. At one point,
Ronald and Ella discuss how she cares for Archie:

> "Then he can never know how much he owes you, Ella, for the care you take of
> him. He little guesses how you have spun half the night to make his plaid, and won
> money hardly to find him a bonnet, and all the toil of your fishing, and grind-
> ing, and baking."
>
> "And why should he? He loves me, and all the better for not knowing why.
> He wears his plaid as the birds do their feathers; he feels it warm, and never
> thinks where it came from. He finds his barley-cakes and fresh water in his cave
> as lambs find clover and springs in their pasture. I see him satisfied, and like that
> he should love me for what costs me no toil,—for singing when he is heavy, and
> for wearing what he brings me when he is merry. When he lays his hot head in
> my lap, or pulls my skirt to make me listen to the wind, I value his love all the
> more for its not being bought." (42)

The siblings echo the language and logic of political economy so familiar to
the tales: Archie will never know how much he "owes" Ella, and, if Archie *did*
know the work she put into keeping him comfortable and well fed, his love
would be "bought"—his ignorance makes Ella "value" his love all the more. In
a series that meditates for many pages on questions about value, currency,
trade, and labor such rhetoric is striking. Of course, the language of reciproc-
ity, of owing and receiving, is not exclusive to discussions of economics—it is
deeply ingrained in social and ethical relations and how we talk about them.
In this passage, Martineau toys with the space between, showing how easily

the logic we use to navigate the capitalist system of values and exchanges can inform even the most private of relationships. She also, through Ella, suggests the dangers of a worldview that sees everything in terms of economic principles. Ultimately, in his way of being with his family and environment, Archie works by a different set of principles that the family clearly values—suggesting that these economic principles aren't entirely natural, intuitive, or sufficient.

The family acknowledges Archie's different relationship to the environment and economy when they mourn his death. In the final pages of the tale, while she is grieving her brother, Ella insists she and Angus put off their marriage. But, paradoxically, Ella argues that the business of the family and the island needs to keep going as if nothing has changed. She justifies this paradoxical set of demands by reasoning, "I must see that Archie is still honored by being kept apart from that in which he had no share. The business of our days went on without him while he lived, and it shall go on now, if it were only to show that he bore no part in it" (141). This is suggestive of how the capitalist economic system relies on assumptions about self-determination and the body that don't apply to Archie. As Rosemarie Garland-Thomson has observed, "Just as the principle of self-government demands a regulated body, the principle of self-determination requires a compliant body to secure a place in the fiercely competitive and dynamic socioeconomic realm."[48] This bodily—and, I would add, intellectual—self-sufficiency is generally assumed in political economy and in the Victorian self-help ethos. The peremptory removal of Archie's character thus signals the difficulty the narrative would have had in imagining a place for him as the island develops and expands its systems of exchange.

To read Martineau's Garveloch tales in this way is to uncover a more radical strand in her economic thought—perhaps it seems to go too far, particularly given recent readings of her as an apologist for capitalism.[49] As Peterson puts it, today "readers rarely treat the *Illustrations of Political Economy* as radical or revolutionary literature." But despite being rooted in the writings of Smith, David Ricardo, James Mill, and Malthus, Martineau's tales were also a "return of the 'little book' to a radical ideology."[50] And, as Klaver has persuasively argued across her work, Martineau can be read as going beyond merely popularizing the political economy of her day—she also adds to it in the process of narrativizing it. To be sure, Martineau would most likely have said she agreed with much of the political economy she was illustrating; it's difficult to know the extent to which she intended to trouble the theoretical waters. She certainly believed in the importance of free trade as a natural, even God-given (while she still believed in God), system. For example, in *The Loom and the Lugger* a character eloquently preaches that God has scattered his gifts around the earth in order to encourage different nations to share and trade that bounty. Martineau was also uncertain of the value of strikes, and tended, in *A Manchester Strike* and *The Hill and the Valley*, to side with the capitalists rather than the workers. A number of her tales also ultimately endorse colonial settlements that appropriated land from Indigenous people, from *Life in the Wilds* to *Homes Abroad*. Indeed, her depiction of parish relief in *Cousin Marshall* includes a character who could easily serve as the prototype for Reagan's welfare queen.

And yet Martineau also took up other more radical causes and frequently looked to defend people who had been victimized by those holding more socioeconomic power. She used her *Illustrations* to argue against slavery (*Demerara*), to raise awareness of how terribly the Russians treated Polish patriots (*The Charmed Sea*), to critique the old French aristocracy (*French Wines and Politics*), and to point to the abuses of imperialism (*Cinnamon and Pearls*). More to my point in this chapter, Martineau includes a number of characters across her *Illustrations* who, like Archie, seem to question the entire premise of economic self-interest. Such characters tend to be children with disabilities or illnesses, like Tim in *Tale of the Tyne*, who is blind but still helps with the work of sorting coal, or like Christian in *Messrs Vanderput and Snoek*, the deeply religious child who suffers from a chronic illness and dies with the close of the tale, but not before questioning the economic reasoning of his family. Others, like Archie, are "simple." One such character, Nicholas in *The Loom and the Lugger*, is merely a sacrificial pawn in the larger debate about duties and smuggling that ultimately leads to his murder. These characters are prone to dying in melodramatic scenes—which is in keeping with the trends identified by Holmes, Mitchell, and Snyder. But first, Martineau does something more with these characters, like Archie, who put the lie to the notion that capitalism works naturally and for the ultimate welfare of all. Such characters hint at other ways of being part of and dependent on a system—not as a burden but as a valued member who points to something beyond capitalist logic, even if that something is not entirely realized in the *Illustrations*.

Archie gestures to an alternative to the possessive individualism assumed in most classical political economy. His reliance on Ella is a model of interdependence that, to borrow Russell's language, "provides an ethical model that can reshape the contours of physical, political, and textual forms."[51] Archie and Ella's relationship resists the logic of buying and selling, working on some deeper sort of mutual appreciation and need. Read yet another way, however, these distinctions between the natural and the economic, and between individualism and interdependence, become blurry. In imagining how Archie is dependent upon others (and, significantly, a female caregiver) to provide his clothes and food—and in naturalizing this dependency to the point that it is not recognized as such—Martineau provides a model for taking the material conditions of life for granted in a way that is reminiscent of exactly the capitalist system he operates outside of.

This reading of Archie's character aligns with Martineau's writing on illness. Both initially use the conditions of an illness or disability to theorize a model for living outside of the capitalist economic system, essentially opting out of the competitive world of ambition and self-interest—as seeing all those pursuits and ambitions as, in fact, empty (to return to Martineau's terms in *Life in the Sick-Room*). Archie's intellectual disability means he is kept apart from the family's economic activity, while Martineau's *Life in the Sick-Room* locates the invalid outside the rhythms of "healthy" life and work. And in both we have models of material dependency. Archie relies (even if unknowingly) on the work of others, while Martineau recognizes the work that goes into living with a chronic illness (her own prior work that allowed her to earn against just such a future illness, the work of her servants, and, more abstractly, the work of performing the part of what she would call an "invalid"). But both models falter in the face of imagining a way entirely off the island. Across Martineau's autobiographical and economic writing, she returns to concerns about how to adjudicate between the individual and the collective: between the shrunken scale of the sick room and the almost omniscient perspective Martineau attains there; between the fishing community on a small island in the Scottish Hebrides and the wider global economy. And across these texts, Martineau seems haunted by the limits of a too-human body, a too-finite earth. Much as Martineau's *Weal and Woe* ultimately suggests that, in a material world of scarce resources, the best thing one can do is sacrifice one's place to another, so too, in Martineau's autobiographical writing, does she figure herself, in death, as giving her place to a successor.

Martineau imagines that her death will make room for others—that she will be "leaving [her] place in the universe to be filled by another." This imagery takes on a more overtly sacrificial tone when she describes death as "the laying down our own life, to yield our place to our successors" (473). Martineau goes on to develop the moral implications of this imagery: "The objective and disinterested contemplation of eternity is, in my apprehension, the sublimest pleasure that human faculties are capable of; and the pleasure is most vivid and real when one's disinterestedness is most necessary and complete,—that is, when our form of its life is about to dissolve, to make way for another" (474). This idea of sacrificing oneself for the good of others could appear to cast Martineau as a Christlike martyr, but, given her turn from religion to positivism, it can also be seen as a way of bowing to universal, scientific, and even economic laws. In this way, Martineau's pragmatic approach could be the result of her thinking about a very material and even Malthusian world, further aligning with her economic writing.

Significantly, in these passages Martineau invokes the limited, material environment through her emphasis on *place*. She claims that she is "vacating my *place* in the universe" and "yielding up my *place*" to another (633, emphases mine). And Martineau means "place" both literally and figuratively. Nearing the end of the *Autobiography*, she describes preparing her beloved home, the Knoll in Ambleside, for its next inhabitant: "It has been my chief amusement, this spring, to set my house and field in complete order for my beloved successor,—to put up a handsome new garden fence, and paint the farming man's cottage, and restore the ceilings of the house, and plan the crops which I do not expect to see gathered" (633). This emphasis on literally giving up one's place to another reveals the importance of setting and environment—as if there were only so many material slots in the world, and, by dying, one generously allows another person to step in.

Martineau's attention to the individual's—and the writer's—material dependencies links her economic and illness writing. In both, a theory of scarcity emerges. In *Weal and Woe*, this scarcity is at the level of the most basic subsistence, as the islanders scramble for the remaining grain and shellfish, turning against one another in an increasingly violent zero-sum game. In Martineau's depiction of her writing—both while ill and while anticipating future illnesses—this scarcity is primarily one of time and energy. But here, too, Martineau was acutely aware of the competitions she engaged in as a writer. Much like Kenneth in *Weal and Woe*, Martineau tried to opt out of a competitive system—specifically, what she saw as an "auction" for literary production: "The way in which authors allowed themselves to be put up to auction, and publishers squabbled at the sale was a real and perpetual grief to me to witness. It reminded me but too often of the stand and the gesticulating man with the hammer, and the crowding competitors whom I had seen jostling each other in the slave-markets of the United States" (*Autobiography*, 398). Such a comparison is of course immediately problematic, and yet Martineau might have recognized this to some extent. She was an outspoken abolitionist who toured the United States and, at one point, found herself so hated by enslavers that her life was threatened. (As she recounts this episode in her *Autobiography*, Martineau claims she was even willing to brave such an attack, if it would draw more attention to the American conflict and the suffering of those people forced into slavery.) The language in this passage is reminiscent of her *Weal and Woe* scenes, with "crowding competitors" jostling for wares. Here, the scarce wares are the very humans that, in *Weal and Woe*, were too many.

Martineau was aware of how, even if she didn't see capitalism as inherently or necessarily damaging, its logic was employed to justify and perpetuate violence. She also offers, even if only implicitly, ways of tracing how such violence works across a larger, interdependent system. As she argues in *Demerara* (the tale that appeared immediately before *Ella*) the entire system of slavery was indefensible, both economically and morally. Two tales later, we learn that the economic boom in Garveloch is due, in large part, to trade with the West Indies. Martineau's narrator explains that Garveloch's prosperity depends on the immediate environment, on other fisheries, and on the diets of enslaved people halfway around the world: "A single bad season, the opening of a few more fishing stations, a change in the diet of the West India slaves,—any one of these, or many other circumstances, might reduce the Garveloch fishery to what it had been" (94). In retrospect, this passage makes one read certain scenes in *Demerara* differently—where the enslavers debate diets and where we see characters sitting down to meals of herring. The fishery on a Scottish island turns out to be linked with the larger British empire and global economy, both of which depended on slavery. In situating individuals and their ambitions in larger economic and environmental networks, Martineau suggests the limits of the principles she sought to illustrate through the "natural" workings of narrative. Far from acting as discrete individuals relying on themselves alone, Martineau's characters are bound to others through systems of both dependency and complicity, figured in their embodiment, their economic activity, and their physical environment.

# CHAPTER 3

# Enabling the Self-Help Narrative in Dinah Craik's *John Halifax, Gentleman*

Dinah Craik is one of the many popular woman writers of the Victorian era who fell out of favor in the twentieth century. When critics have studied her writing, their interests have tended to cluster around three areas. The first is her association with the self-help ethos. Her most enduringly popular novel, *John Halifax, Gentleman*, has often been compared to Samuel Smiles's *Self-Help*.[1] Much like one of Smiles's examples of bootstrapping workers, the eponymous hero starts as a poor orphan, works by day and studies by night, and perseveres to succeed—becoming not only a captain of industry but also, as one chapter puts it, "the true gentleman." In the process, and much like Smiles, Craik updated ideas about nobility and work. Although Craik's novel appeared three years before Smiles's *Self-Help*, the connections between the works are apt, and all the more so considering that Dinah Mulock would go on to marry George Lillie Craik, who shared his name with his uncle, the author of *The Pursuit of Knowledge under Difficulties* (1830–31) and the sequel *Illustrated by Female Examples* (1847–48), the former of which inspired Smiles as a young man and provided a precedent for *Self-Help*. Dinah Craik could herself have been included amongst those inspiring "female examples." The stories told about her literary rise follow the same pattern of hard work and perseverance in the face of obstacles—one of those obstacles being the difficulty of navigating the literary marketplace as a woman. This is the second key strand of critical work on Craik, with critics like Sally Mitchell and Elaine Showalter doing the important work, in the 1970s and '80s, of reviving interest in a figure who had been seen (if she was seen at all) as a woman writer who produced "merely" popular and moralistic novels.

Most recently, Craik has been studied for the way her novels represent and narrativize disability, illness, and the body. Given how Craik popularized and herself became associated with the self-help ethos, it is significant that she was also markedly interested in characters that are ill or disabled. This interest stood out even in a period of literary history that, as many critics have argued, heavily relied on representations of disability.[2] In fact, Henry James criticized Craik's "lively predilection for cripples and invalids," although he conceded that it "is no more than right that the sickly half of humanity should have its chronicler."[3] Craik's characters with illnesses or disabilities often neatly fit the patterns identified by critics like Martha Stoddart Holmes and Karen Bourrier, deepening a story's melodramatic interest or drawing out a more central character.[4] But Craik's overall interest in portraying disability also does something beyond these typical patterns. Many of the main voices and characters in her novels have some sort of disability, from the protagonist of *A Noble Life* to the eponymous heroine of *Olive*. Her novels thus radically depart from the tendency in many Victorian novels (and literature in general) to sideline or flatten such characters. And, through these representations of ability and disability, she questions the paths for and value of ambition. These questions are most strikingly posed in her popular *John Halifax, Gentleman*. The novel is narrated by John's best friend, Phineas Fletcher, who describes himself as an invalid. Phineas cheers John along, from telling him the story of Dick Wittington to later praising his friend's progress from rags to captain of industry. As much as Phineas lays the groundwork for and literally makes the narration possible, Phineas's trajectory starkly contrasts with John's self-help plot: while John ambitiously rises and marries, Phineas is too ill to run the family business and decides he will not marry, explaining that he is both "too feeble and womanish" and worried about "hereditary disease."[5]

This novel, described by Robin Gilmour as "the classic novel of self-help,"[6] thus importantly depends on a character who is typically left out of self-help ideology. In many ways, Phineas's disability in fact enables his friend's rise: John Halifax steps into Phineas's family business, taking on roles that might have been filled by Phineas himself. As I'll argue, Phineas's character suggests a critique of the self-help narrative and how it elides the fuller story about ambition by focusing our attention so closely on the individual's rise. In the process, this chapter connects the three major critical approaches to Craik's work outlined above: her navigation of the literary marketplace as a woman writer, her contribution to developing the self-help figure in popular fiction, and her interest in "the sickly half of humanity" (to borrow James's words). If we read *John Halifax, Gentleman* in light of Craik's complicated thoughts about gender, disability, and ambition, Phineas points to ambition's discontents—suggesting a parallel in how both women and people with disabilities tended to be left out of the Victorian era's self-help ethos. In memorializing and mythologizing his perfect friend, Phineas casts the discourse in a nostalgic mode that counters the novel's (and, writ largely, the Victorian era's) overt narrative of progress and perfectibility.

## Merging Narratives: Craik, "Author of *John Halifax, Gentleman*" and Craik, Woman

Dinah Craik was a literary celebrity across the Victorian era, producing fifty-two books, including immediate and enduring bestsellers.[7] For example, Craik's *A Life for a Life* competed with George Eliot's *Adam Bede*, the two novels most in demand at libraries in 1859.[8] And as Bourrier reminds us in her recent biography, Craik was not only "a Victorian bestseller par excellence" but also an internationally recognized figure, with fans including the former prime minister of France, François Guizot, and Vincent van Gogh.[9] Such reminders are necessary today because of the general lack of critical engagement with Craik's work until just the past few years—a lack that in part resulted from her contemporary reception. By mid-career, Craik was "identified as a woman's novelist and critics began to pay less attention to her books; she was, if mentioned at all, praised for her 'high character' and 'moral influence' rather than for the quality of her work."[10] The rise and plateau of Craik's reputation as a writer—and the stories told about it—are central to the argument of this chapter. As much as Craik capitalized on the narrative of a man's work and ambition with her most popular novel, the arc of her own career suggests a sort of glass ceiling for Victorian women writers. This is complicated, however, by the way Craik frames the story of her career and by her writing on the subject of women's work—where she questions how (and to what extent) women should employ their ambition.

Craik's career and the stories told about it are bound up with the publication of *John Halifax, Gentleman*, which, then and now, serves as a major turning point. Within two years, Hurst and Blackett went through four editions of the immensely popular novel; by 1898, further editions were offered by another ten English publishers. In Britain alone, by 1897, a quarter-million copies had been sold. And it continued to be pirated in the United States, amounting to forty-five editions.[11] After the novel's success, Craik often signed her new works or reprints not with her name but with her reputation: "By the Author of John Halifax, Gentleman." In fact, Craik repeatedly and specifically requested this attribution, even when it was against the publisher's usual practice.[12] No wonder, then, that this novel loomed so large, both for her contemporaries and for later critics. Margaret Oliphant recalled that it was this novel that "finally established [Craik's] reputation, and gave her her definite place in literature."[13] Similarly, the *Academy's* obituary remembers *John Halifax, Gentleman* as Craik's "great hit" and an "instantaneous success." A turn-of-the-century introduction to the novel even claimed that "no work of fiction issued during this period has stimulated [the development of the novel] to such an extent"— with the novel being "in steady and constant demand" (as borne out by reprints in 1906, 1907, 1910, 1912, 1913, 1916, 1917, 1919, and 1925).[14] According to Craik's obituary, the success of *John Halifax* allowed for the purchase and furnishing of Corner House, where Craik and her family lived from 1869 on—"practically out of the proceeds of her most famous book."[15] And even according to recent criticism, the novel meant that Craik's "financial worries were over," and "she could afford to pick and choose among offers" for her literary projects.[16]

The reality, as Bourrier's biography has recently illuminated, was not so rosy. The novel "made her reputation, not her fortune"—and within a few years Craik was again struggling financially and experimenting with different projects.[17] This discrepancy between fact and fiction is telling, suggestive of the extent to which both Craik's contemporaries and recent critics have understood the importance of Craik's *John Halifax, Gentleman*—while also testifying to the sticking power of narratives that tend to simplify success.

This narrative about Craik's career might also have to do with how the popular and critical imagination blended Craik's biography with that of her most famous character. Craik's life indeed shares elements of John Halifax's history: she was poor and had to support herself, she diligently worked her way up in her field, and she died both beloved and successful. Given such parallels, Showalter has argued that Craik "projected her own ambitions and struggles onto male heroes who could more appropriately embody her ideals. Like John, Craik had to make her own way in the world."[18] An early and lengthy introduction by Annie Matheson observes that "it is significant that Miss Mulock, who as a rule wrote with extreme ease and rapidity . . . spent much more than her usual pains over this the most enduring of her novels, and was content to write and rewrite again and again rather than risk a blurred or imperfect impression."[19] Bourrier's biography explicitly draws out the parallels, comparing Craik to John, her "hardworking hero," when she describes how Craik gave up dinners and outings to keep working with, in Craik's words, "steady dogged perseverance"[20] on what she predicted would be "far away the best book I ever wrote."[21]

Also not unlike her "hardworking hero," Craik's story was in fact circulated as an inspiring example of hard work and well-deserved success. In a memorial of Craik's life, Oliphant recalls this past in terms typical of mythologizing self-help stories:

> The young Dinah, in a blaze of love and indignation, carried that ailing and deli-
> cate mother away, and took in her rashness the charge of the whole family, two
> younger brothers, upon her own slender shoulders, working to sustain them in
> every way that presented itself, from stories for the fashion books to graver publi-
> cations. She had gone through some years of this feverish work before her novel,
> *The Ogilvies*, introduced her to a wider medium and to higher possibilities . . . If
> there are any memorials of it left, it would no doubt form a most attractive chapter
> among the many records of early struggles. The young heroic creature writing her
> pretty juvenile nonsense of love and lovers, in swift, unformed style, as fast as the
> pen could fly, to get bread for the boys and a little soup and wine for the invalid
> over whose deathbed she watched with impassioned love and care.[22]

This could be an example pulled from G. L. Craik's *Pursuit of Knowledge under Difficulties, Illustrated by Female Examples*. Craik's history is similarly compressed in a way that asks us to imagine her "feverish work" spread across years, while overtly physicalizing her labor. Oliphant even imagines this history appearing in a collection of such inspirational examples, where it would make "a most attractive chapter among the many records of early struggles."
And the story apparently circulated to much the same effect: Oliphant notes that the history of Craik's early life "was told among her friends, and thrilled the hearer with sympathy and admiration."[23]

These ways of narrating Craik's entrance into the literary world clearly align with the plot of popular self-help narratives. But they also involve the plot complications that many women writers included when they told the story of their careers. As Showalter writes, such earlier generations "needed external events, usually financial or emotional disasters, to push them into print. Writing for money then became a heroic necessity, not merely an assertion of ego."[24] Here, I want to point out, the patterns of two different narratives intersect—the woman writer and the self-help character—which both developed in ways that provided a cover story for ambition. The two quite naturally overlap: when he looked for examples of specifically women pursuing knowl-
edge under difficulties, G. L. Craik included many women writers of the eighteenth and nineteenth centuries, including Hannah More and Anne Macvicar Grant. Many of these women writers—and their biographies—
explicitly addressed why they wrote for publication. A common motivation is the need to support themselves and often a family, particularly in the

absence of a stable husband or other male relative. Sticking more closely to the Victorian era's terms, I would add that, even more specifically than "ego," women writers needed to find a way around ambition—a drive that could turn virtuous or sinful, laudable or prideful, necessary or dangerous. No wonder, then, that Matheson carefully framed Craik's motivations: "working not for fame but in the determination to bear her own burden and the burden of those she cared for"—with the result that "she won the reputation for which there had been no petty struggle or selfish striving."[25] These narratives of the woman writer and the self-helper dovetailed all the easier because they both emphasize steady work over genius—with even Craik's most generous critics stopping short of claiming her "genius." Thus, unlike a more "ambitious effort," Craik's novel "is a pastel sketch in which the colours are translucent and delicate, rather than an elaborate oil-painting on a crowded canvas."[26]

Women writers needed to justify their careers, but, at the same time, they faced pressure to cordon off their private lives—what Linda H. Peterson has termed the "parallel currents" model of women's authorship. As Peterson argues, women frequently separated themselves from their authorial roles, whether through pseudonyms or a division between public and private personas.[27] In her memorial of Craik, Oliphant writes that it was "the fashion of our generation—a fashion perhaps not without drawbacks, though we have been unanimous in it—that whatever our work for the public might be, our own homes and personal lives were to be strictly and jealously private, and our pride to consist, not in our literary reputation, which was a thing apart, but in the household duties and domestic occupations which are the rule of life for most women." And, as Oliphant concludes, "No such invasion of her privacy was ever permitted by Mrs. Craik."[28]

Across her writing, Craik explored the reasons that might push a woman into a career and the public sphere—spurring discussions of ambition. In *Olive*, Craik's narrator insists that the heroine becomes an artist primarily because she needs money: "Though this confession may somewhat lessen the romance of her character—it was from no yearning after fame, no genius-led ambition, but from the mere desire of earning money, that Olive Rothesay first conceived the thought of becoming an artist."[29] Later, Craik throws some doubt on whether a "spark" of ambition is ever likely to grow in a woman: "A Brutus, for that ambition which is misnamed patriotism, can trample on all human ties . . . But there scarcely ever lived the woman who would not rather sit meekly by her own hearth, with her husband at her side, and her children at her knee, than be the crowned Corinne of the Capitol."[30]

In *A Woman's Thoughts about Women*, Craik presents similarly complicated views about ambition and gender. Originally published as a series of essays in *Chambers's Edinburgh Journal*, here Craik takes up the question of the "surplus-woman problem," arguing that, even if the roles of wife and mother are the ultimate calling, single women, too, need useful work.[31] This message parallels the self-help ethos in its celebration of work and self-reliance, even while specifically gendering the drive. Craik asserts that ambition is a stronger drive in men than in women and even cautions that, if a woman is ambitious, this drive should be questioned or redirected. For example, she cautions women who approach the arts: "Let men do as they will—and truly they are often ten times vainer and more ambitious than we!—but I would advise every woman to examine herself and judge herself, morally and intellectually, by the sharpest tests of criticism, before she attempts art or literature, either for abstract fame or as a means of livelihood."[32] Craik distinguishes between levels of ambition in women and in men and warns women against becoming artists without knowing their abilities—as if a discrepancy between abilities and ambitions is that much more egregious if the artist is a woman.

Such sentiments can be difficult to square coming from a woman writer who built a successful—even ambitious—career. Craik did, however, imagine another way of getting around ambition—reimagining the drive by claiming its most lofty and praiseworthy associations. Craik insists that women's lives are founded on "daily, regular, conscientious work: in its essence and results as distinct as any 'business' of men." But, Craik continues, "what [men] expend for wealth and ambition, shall not we offer for duty and love—the love of our fellow creatures, or, far higher, the love of God?"[33] Here Craik offers two paths, the self-interested drive for "wealth and ambition" and the other-oriented drive of love, duty, and religious feeling. This is an interesting twist on William Casey King's history of how ambition was refashioned from entirely sinful to potentially virtuous—when "harnessed" for national and religious ends.[34] In Craik's vision, however, this alternative drive and economy, responding to divine as well as human duties, is explicitly gendered as feminine.

Craik seems to shape John Halifax's ambition with a version of this gendered drive in mind. John is driven by what Craik elsewhere saw as a feminized, rebranded version of ambition—by duty, love, and religion—to improve himself and his community. This led many readers and critics to question the paradox or even hypocrisy suggested by a character who always succeeds without appearing to pursue his success. As one reviewer observed, John's character is a "somewhat paradoxical conception of a provincial citizen of the world, a rich millowner and manufacturer, free from ambition, ostentation, and other vulgar vices of the class—in fact, a commercial Bayard."[35] Or, as an even more blunt reader put it, the novel revolves around "a basic economic hypocrisy; it is a success story in which the hero always insists he cares nothing about money."[36] As the next section explores, such accusations stem from Craik's desire to imagine a "higher" form of ambition, often coded as feminine in her other writings, and closer to a spiritualized aspiration than an individualistic ambition. In short, John Halifax is not driven by a "selfish" ambition to gain wealth and fame but by an aspiration based on duty to and love for others.

## "Out of Every Trial, John Halifax, Gentleman, Rises Sublime": A Perfect Ambition

Many of Craik's reviewers isolated John's unrelenting goodness as a fatal flaw. The *Saturday Review* complained that "we have not a fault to find with him; and here lies the error of the book."[37] The *Athenaeum* similarly cited John's "impossible perfection" as the "mistake of the book," adding that "the authoress has been too anxious to make her hero perfect, and has by so doing thrown a fictitious rose-coloured tint" over the character.[38] As Henry James lamented, "'John Halifax' was an attempt to tell the story of a life perfect in every particular; and to relate, moreover, every particular of it."[39] The exasperated reviewer from the *Examiner* collected these "particulars" of John's egregious goodness into a brief plot summary: he "quells rioters by Christian conduct, and is the best guardian of his master's property. He falls in love, and is the most highminded of lovers; then he becomes a model husband; then a model father; and afterwards, prospering in life, he becomes a model master, model neighbour, model landowner and squire." But "the carrying of such a hero through a lifelong series of trials, and showing him in each heroical, suggests impossible perfection."[40]

Despite such complaints, in the face of the novel's enduring reputation, even James had to concede that John Halifax "is infinite; he outlasts time; he is enshrined in a million innocent breasts"—"before his awful perfection and his eternal durability we respectfully lower our lance" (845). Such characters became a trademark, with Craik securing her place "in a competitive marketplace" by offering novels that could always "be counted on for their goodness."[41] Of course, Craik's characters are by no means the only ones in Victorian literature accused of being too good to be true. It's easy to see *John Halifax, Gentleman* working in the tradition of didactic fiction, which, like the inspirational biographies of the era (and particularly in texts like *The Pursuit of*

*Knowledge* and *Self-Help*), provided models for behavior. In fact, in his review of the novel, R. H. Hutton claimed *John Halifax* "is a fictitious biography, rather than a novel."[42] In short, Craik was certainly not alone in her desire to hold up an example, real or fictional. But given the wider field of didactic novels and inspirational biographies that *John Halifax* circulated in, it is interesting—and, I think, significant—that so many critics hit the limit of their ability to suspend disbelief with John's character.

Much of what makes John Halifax perfect aligns him with the self-help ethos. John repetitively touts the importance of hard work, persistence, and duty. At "odd minutes going along the road," John educates himself, noting that "it's astonishing what a lot of odd minutes one can catch during the day."[43] As an older man, John sprinkles maxims across his conversation: "No man knows how much he can do till he tries" (294); "nothing venture, nothing have" (329). But John is not motivated to accrue money for its own sake. Late in the novel, we learn that John has striven to act like Bayard, much as if he had been following the advice of G. L. Craik and Smiles, to seek out the biographies of great men for inspiration: "If there was one point I was anxious over in my youth, it was to keep up through life a name like the Chevalier Bayard— how folks would smile to hear of a tradesman emulating Bayard—'*Sans peur et sans reproche!*' And so things might be—ought to be" (374).[44] As the *Literary Gazette* pointed out, this character presents something of a paradox: a "commercial Bayard," a successful millowner who is "free from ambition."

Or at least John is free from the negative connotations of ambition. The word is used only twice in this novel but with tellingly opposed moral valences. First, John uses it when he responds to Lord Luxmore's praise of his public speaking: "I have no pretention or ambition of the kind. I merely now and then try to put plain truths, or what I believe to be such, before the people, in a form they are able to understand" (264). It is later used by Phineas, who laments that John has lost his drive in the wake of his daughter's death: "All the high aims which make the glory and charm of life as duties make its strength, all the active energies and noble ambitions which especially belong to the prime of manhood, in him had been, not dead perhaps, but sleeping" (358). These passages encapsulate Craik's attempt to redefine ambition. John does have ambition, but it's the noble kind belonging "to the prime of manhood," not the wealth- and fame-oriented (but also coded as masculine) ambition that Craik criticizes in *A Woman's Thoughts about Women*.

John thus seeks wealth not for its own sake but merely as a by-product of his drive for progress and usefulness. He explains this to his children: "When

I was a young man, before your mother and I were married, indeed before I had ever seen her, I had strongly impressed on my mind the wish to gain influence in the world—riches if I could—but at all events, influence. I thought I could use it well, better than most men; those can best help the poor who understand the poor" (365). John's first object is influence—a term often associated with the middle-class Victorian woman's diffusive morality, and another cue that Craik is inflecting John's ambition with her gendered version of the drive. John's influence is to be used not for his own good, but for that of the poor: in seeking influence John relegates riches to a conditional aside, to an afterthought set off by dashes ("—riches if I could—").

This attitude toward money—as a by-product, not the goal—again aligns with self-help texts that praise good character over good financial fortune. But expanding an example across the many pages of a novel depicting characters and their motivations presents an interesting narrative difficulty, particularly as we see the steps of their upward mobility. When the Halifax family wants money, it is not for a project that will benefit only them. For example, when John converts the cloth mill to steam power, it is because Lord Luxmore has maliciously diverted the stream that previously powered it. John doesn't make the transition simply to trailblaze new technology and earn greater profits; he needs to keep the business going (and employing the many workers). As Phineas explains, the motivation is "not merely the making a fortune, as he still firmly believed it could be made, but the position of useful power, the wide range of influence, the infinite opportunities of doing good" (261). The fortune would "merely" be made, almost as a side effect. In another example, John suggests that the Halifax household should leave the small abode of Longfield for the larger Beechwood Hall. As he puts it to his wife, the question is "whether, now that our children are growing up, and our income is doubling and trebling year by year, we ought to widen our circle of usefulness, or close it up permanently within the quiet bound of little Longfield" (363). And although Ursula finds the latter the "happiest," John replies that this is exactly why they must move: because staying at Longfield "*is* the happiest" (363). It is almost as though the family must continue to double and treble their income and move into grander houses despite themselves.

This sense that the family has a moral and spiritual imperative to improve themselves implies that the ultimate model for John's ambition is not just Bayard or Carlyle's captain of industry but God's perfection. John posits that God means for the world (like all his creations) "gradually to advance toward perfection" (303). The successful conversion to steam energy, or the move to a more "useful" position, is a step closer to such perfection. To choose the useful and the good, John must act not only for himself or his family but also for the wider community (and presumably nation and empire). Or, as Phineas puts it, "He wished—since the higher a man rises, the wider and nobler grows his sphere of usefulness—not only to lift himself, but his sons after him; lift them high enough to help on the ever-advancing tide of human improvement, among their own people first, and thence extending outward in the world whithersoever their talents or circumstances might call them" (366). Here we find more of Craik's key concepts for redefining ambition. Although the useful influence that John hopes to wield starts with him and his family, the ultimate goal is to widen such influence, rippling outward into the world.

The exact details of how John achieves this vision are obscured by Phineas's narration, which, given his illness and self-proclaimed lack of understanding ("I was no man of business, and could assist in nothing" [389]), tend to paint John's career in only the broadest of strokes. Nor does Phineas suggest much change in John's character, from age fourteen to death. Although the novel has many of the markers of a bildungsroman, John is so consistently good that he doesn't leave much room for development. As a result, his success seems tautological in the style of Smiles's self-help stories, which were selected on the very principle that each person eventually succeeded. In fact, the point of the novel is not to build John into a gentleman and captain of industry but to demonstrate that he has always had these qualities. This is reinforced by the fact that, even as a poor orphan, John carries a Greek Testament from his parents, with the word "gentleman" written after his father's name (36).

Perhaps because of John's static character, the plot itself is strangely episodic. Whereas long-term plot complications would offer opportunities for John to change, these episodes provide the chance to reveal qualities John already possesses. For example, to give a quick summary of the plot while illustrating this point, most of the complications are solved in a chapter or two. John rescues men from the river and saves the tanyard from a flood (chapter 4), goes to a play against his employer's wishes (chapter 6), faces the bread riots (chapters 7 and 8), sees Ursula through her father's sickness and health (chapters 11 through 13), falls sick himself because of his seemingly hopeless love (but then gets engaged to Ursula) (chapter 18), confronts the Parliament question and voting day (chapters 23 and 24), deals with an outbreak of smallpox (chapter 25), converts to steam power (chapter 26 and 27), prevents a run on the bank during financial crisis (chapters 30 and 31), and helps his sons when the brothers fall in love with the same girl (chapters 32 to 34). Many of these episodes involve other characters making the mistake of thinking John has the wrong kind of ambition. For example, Abel Fletcher accuses John of social climbing when he attends a dinner ("Why cannot thee keep in thy own rank?" [198]). Although John is not interested in associating with those of higher rank, he is interested in seeing Ursula, who will be in attendance. Ursula's uncle, the debauched Squire, then assumes that John wishes to marry his niece for her money. When the Squire reclaims Ursula's inheritance, however, John still marries her. Whenever the other characters doubt his motives, John is proven innocent of acting out of mere self-interest, or the wrong sort of ambition.

In part, we can attribute these many ways in which John's character is statically perfect to Phineas's retrospective narration. Phineas admits that he might "unwittingly be drawing a little from after-experience" in his description of John as a boy (59). But this tendency to narrate with the benefit of hindsight is more pervasive than Phineas admits here. For example, when Phineas introduces Lady Caroline to the reader, she is already doomed to a poor ending ("Poor Lady Caroline" [205]). And we are so beaten over the head with intimations of Muriel's premature death that at least one critic remarked that, really, "she might have died earlier with advantage to the book."[45] More importantly, this retrospective stance seems uncannily to direct the plot, with John's decisions too perfectly aligning with the right side of history. *John Halifax, Gentleman* spans the years 1794–1834, years that represent much tumultuous change: half of the French Revolution, the Battles of Trafalgar and Waterloo, the Reform Act, the abolition of slavery in the British empire—not to mention much of the Industrial Revolution. Craik pointedly incorporates this historical span in the novel. When smallpox enters a nearby village, we learn that John has previously consulted Dr. Jenner and, unlike many of his neighbors, has vaccinated his children himself. John is eager to convert to steam power when it becomes available, although many such real-life captains of industry were uncertain about the initial costs to convert versus the long-term profits to be made with greater control over production. (In fact, historians are still investigating the slow and uneven transition to steam power, with Andreas Malm questioning not only why it happened when it did, but *"why steam power was adopted at all."*)[46] When John's neighbors suffer in the panic year from investments that had previously "sprung up like fungi, out of dead wood" into "sudden and unhealthy overgrowth," we learn that John has avoided ruin because he chose to buy land rather than stocks (378). In fact, most of the "sunshiny valley . . . was already his own property" (374). As a result, John is aligned with progress. And naturalizing John's decisions, Craik's contemporary readers were already on the side of the progress that the novel's characters are only beginning to undergo. As Mitchell observes, "By the time Craik wrote, most people approved of the things John Halifax espoused." Readers could thus identify with John and enjoy "a delicious satisfaction when—as history makes inevitable—John Halifax and the reader are vindicated."[47]

And yet, even as Phineas's hindsight enables this vision of inevitable progress and improvement, it is also the source of a nostalgic pleasure. Phineas delights in dwelling on the past, despite its imperfections. As I'll argue in the next section, Phineas's backward-looking nostalgia provides a counterbalance to the strict narrative of progress that defines *John Halifax*'s plot as well as the self-help ethos in general. Importantly, Phineas's nostalgia is linked to his role as a narrator with a disability. In framing the story of the "perfect" John Halifax through the nostalgic perspective of his friend, Craik suggests the submerged competition and discontents of the novel's self-help plot. This has echoes in the self-help genre itself, with its insistence on a progressive forward march, inspired by the very streamlined biographies of mostly men, who are mostly long dead—whose stories can, thanks to the "rose-coloured tint" of retrospection, project images of heroes advancing the nation's progress.

## "We Found It Hard to Learn This Easy, Convenient Habit—to Forget": Disability and Nostalgia

Many readers were inspired to make the pilgrimage to Tewkesbury, the town where Craik claimed she first conceived of her most famous novel and the town behind the novel's fictional Norton Bury. This literary tourism continued even after Craik died: four years later, the *Leisure Hour* published an illustrated article, "The Country of John Halifax," describing the buildings and landmarks that were adapted in the novel. As the writer reports, "Hundreds of Americans come to Tewkesbury every year and identify the scenery of that notable book," artists travel to sketch the landscape, and tourists gather to see the house where the author wrote the novel (supposedly "all in a fortnight").[48] According to Matheson's introduction to a 1900 edition, Tewkesbury was second only to Stratford-upon-Avon for literary tourists.[49] Tewkesbury was also the site for a memorial to Craik. After her death, a committee—including such literary figures as Alfred Tennyson, Robert Browning, Matthew Arnold, and Margaret Oliphant—planned a memorial in the form of a marble medallion in Tewkesbury Abbey.[50] Craik's memorial naturally included a quotation from the text of *John Halifax, Gentleman*—a text that, through Phineas's nostalgic narration, teaches the reader how to remember even in the face of inevitable change. As I'll argue, Phineas's nostalgic narrative voice is bound up with his status as a man with a disability and chronic illness. His nostalgia contrasts starkly with John Halifax's story: while John's forward-looking momentum drives his own socioeconomic improvement as well as the valley's industrial progress, Phineas's memory fixates on an idealized past.

Given the tourist industry around *John Halifax, Gentleman* and Tewkesbury, readers seemed to emulate Phineas's nostalgia. Craik's novel shares both thematic and structural elements with the novels that Nicholas Dames's *Amnesiac Selves* argues are most illustrative of the way Victorian nostalgia is represented. The novel is structured to follow the arc of a life, ending with John's death, which is a way of remembering not for desultory memories but "only in the light of an end, a death; a memory that is always only the necessary prehistory of the present."[51] The novel's nostalgia is also inflected through both John's upward mobility and Phineas's disability. Both characters thus experience the sort of dislocation that Dames argues is the root of all nostalgia, a term that originated as a medical diagnosis for homesickness. First, Phineas's life diverges from what was imagined for him by his father, who envisioned his son taking over the family business. And second, John's drastic socioeconomic changes mean he is constantly dislocating himself upward, often into social groups for which he has no sympathy. Indeed, if such a sense of "dislocation is the dilemma nostalgia is invented to solve,"[52] then all self-help narratives can be read as necessarily nostalgic. Ambition and self-help narratives require movement out of one's original condition and sphere, dislocating the subject, even if in the service of bettering one's lot.

As Dames ultimately demonstrates, the Victorian novel is less interested in modeling how to remember than in how to avoid and evade precise memories. This teaches the reader to forget as well as remember. If there is a submerged memory in *John Halifax, Gentleman*, it is how Phineas allows for John's upward mobility. To resuscitate this memory is to see how Phineas's disability is intricately linked with John's rise in the novel. This starts with Abel Fletcher seeking someone to push his son's wheelchair; he hires the orphan John, who is eager to earn a meal in whatever way he can (figure 1). In Alice Barber Stephens's illustration of the scene, John almost replaces Phineas: in the foreground, Abel places his hands on John's shoulders, while Phineas watches, set back and to the side. And John eventually works his way up in the same business that was intended for Phineas to inherit. In adulthood, Phineas adopts the role of "uncle" in John's household, taking on the interests of the family

*Figure 1.* Abel Fletcher gives John Halifax the job of pushing Phineas's chair. Illustration by Alice Barber Stephens for the 1897 New York edition of *John Halifax, Gentleman* (New York: Thomas Y. Crowell, 1897).

even as he remains a step removed from them. Across the novel, his disability and chronic illness position him in opposition to many of the novel's assumptions about self-help and individualism.

In her short but suggestive article on physical disability in Victorian literature, Cindy Lacom argues that ideas about disability developed alongside the ideology of self-help. She observes that "public perceptions of and responses to people with disabilities and to the very concept of disability were shaped by diverse and broad forces: developing capitalist economic theories and an ideology of self-help, a national obsession with empire building, the growth of industrialism, and a variety of legal discourses."[53] In conceptualizing disability, Victorians contrasted it with the ideal of ability—with the ethos of self-help and self-improvement. As David T. Mitchell and Sharon L. Snyder observe, such thinking "rests upon this inversion: rather than simply deviating from widely expressed biological traits, disabilities demonstrate that the ideal cannot exist without its 'deviant' contrast."[54] Just as these concepts develop through contrast, so too do Craik's characters emerge in counterpoint to one another. Phineas's disability contrasts with and gives occasion for John to exhibit his perfections—his physical ability to help Phineas and, as a result, his morality. This aligns with tendencies pointed out in recent criticism about Craik's use of characters with disabilities.[55] In the other direction, as I'll argue, Phineas's inability to work (that is, in ways that the narrative recognizes) offers a compelling if unspoken challenge to the self-help ethos that John embodies. In one of the earliest scenes, John hands Phineas his crutches "with a grave, pitiful look," and Phineas attempts a bad joke about John not needing such things (because Phineas is "ashamed" and not yet "used to" the crutches). John's response— "I hope you will not need them always"—demonstrates how his character insists on a forward momentum that casts the body and its needs as something to be overcome (43).

G. L. Craik and Samuel Smiles's brand of self-help exhorted readers to strive despite all obstacles. In fact, the inspirational biographies they used to illustrate the importance of hard work structurally depended on obstacles that would eventually be overcome. As a result, physical impediments to hard work, like poverty or illness, are posed as temporary or even as catalysts spurring further energetic work. When self-help texts imagine illness as what inspires or is overcome by hard work, they align uneasily with what we recognize now as the "supercrip" narrative. (Although, as the introduction and earlier chapters have argued, it was exactly the hard work that the self-help ethos celebrated that often led to overwork and illness.) There are, historically as well as today, problematic reasons for these associations between self-help— with its emphasis on hard, physicalized work—and the idea of being "able-bodied," which depends on imagining the ill or disabled body as an obstacle to be overcome. As Rosemarie Garland-Thomson observes, the desire to associate "'hard work' and economic and social success" is a long-standing one.[56] This association breaks down, however, when an individual is unable to engage in remunerative work. Then, "if the myth of autonomy and self-determination is to remain intact, those whose situations question it must be split off into a discrete social category governed by different assumptions." As far back as the English Poor Laws of 1388, the state and other institutions "have molded the political and cultural definition of what we now know as 'physical disability' in an effort to distinguish between genuine 'cripples' and malinger-ers, those deemed unable to work and those deemed unwilling to work."[57] Ideas about economic self-determination, individualism, and self-help have been defined against their limit case—the person figured as physically unable to help himself in a society that was structured not to allow for such mobility in the first place.

Phineas's narration is an important site for parsing out such ideas about work and disability in the self-help ethos and for understanding how these concepts were put to formal use in the novel. Phineas does not claim to work in the story's terms, and yet he serves the crucial narrative function of remem-bering and narrating. The entire Halifax household values holding onto their shared past: as Phineas remarks, "in our family we found it hard to learn this easy, convenient habit—to forget" (470). But the task of remembering falls most heavily upon Phineas's shoulders. Phineas's role as narrator is mirrored and enabled by his physical role in the novel. Although we do not know the precise nature of his physical limitations, he is sometimes ill and requires crutches or a wheelchair (as when he first meets John). As it turns out, all of this means that Phineas is well positioned to observe the most important do-mestic spaces of the novel.

Phineas is frequently on the physical margins of the novel's scenes, some-times fading into the background. As a result, he is privy to some intimate conversations and interactions, allowing him to observe as if literally from the position of the third-person, "fly on the wall" narrator—as suggested by Al-ice Barber Stephens's illustration in figure 2. When Phineas hears Lady Caro-line and Ursula talking about love and marriage, he observes, "Probably they thought I was away too—or else they took no notice of me—and went talk-ing on" (234). Similarly, he later witnesses John's private grief over Muriel: "John went to the door and locked it, almost with a sort of impatience; then came back and stood by his darling, alone. Me he never saw—no, nor anything in the world except that little face" (355). He is also privy to moments of par-ticular intimacy between husband and wife: "And once, when the children were out of the room, and I, sitting in a dark corner, was probably thought ab-sent likewise, I saw John take his wife's face between his two hands, and look in it—the fondest, most lingering, saddest look!" (442). Phineas is taken "no notice of," not seen, and "thought absent"—he lives with the sort of invisibility or forgetting that disability activists today point to as a continuing problem.[58] And Phineas often plays along, as when he "slips out" of a scene in order to confirm his own absence: "They had altogether forgotten any one's presence, dear souls! So I kept them in that happy oblivion, by slipping out" (242). As a character with a disability and on the periphery of the family unit, Phineas is frequently treated as invisible, even as this invisibility means that he witnesses events that allow him to tell the fuller story.

Further, because Phineas's condition seems to foreclose both work and marriage in the plot, his interest in the Halifax family, combined with his marginalization in the domestic space, positions him as a quasi-omniscient narrator. This is suggestive of the emerging association Erika Wright identifies between invalidism and omniscience in the Victorian era—an association we also see in Harriet Martineau's work (explored in chapter 2). Drawing on Audrey Jaffe's definition of the omniscient narrator as located "not in presence or absence, but in the tension between the two," Wright argues that "the cultural

*Figure 2.* Phineas observing John Halifax and Miss March (the future Mrs. Halifax). Illustration by Alice Barber Stephens for the 1897 New York edition of *John Halifax, Gentleman* (New York: Thomas Y. Crowell, 1897).

understanding (and narrative construction) of the invalid's power marks their presence in the narrative as a form of absence, their knowledge as a form of transcendence, their being as 'beyond the ken.'"[59] Given such a role—on the margins of the story and yet pivotal to its telling—Phineas appears to fall into exactly the sort of "narrative prosthetic" role that Mitchell and Snyder have identified as a recurring trope for characters with disabilities.

Complicating all this, however, Phineas hints that his chronic illness or disability is not the only reason he does not take over his father's business. The tanyard prompts some of Phineas's bouts of illness, but he also simply hates the trade: "Mentally and physically I alike revolted from my father's trade. I held the tanyard in abhorrence—to enter it made me ill for days; sometimes for months and months I never went near it" (56). We might read this as the equivalent of Phineas "slipping out" of a scene or, in this case, out of a potential competition with John Halifax's upward mobility. It also suggests how having a disability could legitimate some types of roles and agencies that otherwise remain unavailable to characters—and, by extension, to Victorian narratives. In her examination of how disability and narrative form intersect in Craik's *Olive*, Tabitha Sparks has argued that "Olive's deformity allows her to shape-shift into a number of conventionally exclusive destinies, including professional artist and wage earner, wife and mother."[60] Phineas's disability similarly opens as well as forecloses certain narratives: in a gendered inversion of the pattern Sparks identifies in *Olive*, Phineas is able to refuse the world of business and instead to situate himself in feminized, domestic spaces.

Phineas's association with the domestic spaces of the novel has been read as another parallel with Craik's position as a woman writer. Such a reading goes back to Craik's contemporary reviewers, who read Phineas as a woman-like figure. Hutton accused Craik of a "curious inability to conceive of men as they are in relation to each other," to the point that "it is difficult to suppress a fear that Phineas Fletcher will fall hopelessly in love with John Halifax, so hard is it to remember that Phineas is of the male sex."[61] But Phineas's supposed alignment with a "feminine" position does not extend to feminized work. Just as Phineas does not work outside the home, he is also removed from the feminized work of the domestic space, something he draws attention to when describing Ursula's transition from heiress to tradesman's wife, as she adopts her own gendered form of the self-help ethos. Phineas recalls how he used "to lie in their cool parlor, and listen to [Ursula's] voice and step about the house, teaching Jenny, or learning from her . . . she never was idle or dull for a minute. She did a great deal in the house herself. Often she would sit chatting with me, having on her lap a coarse brown pan, shelling peas; slicing beans, picking gooseberries; her fingers . . . looking fairer for the contrast with their unaccustomed work" (248). Although men with disabilities were frequently portrayed as feminine or likened to women in the Victorian era,[62] such passages remind us that Phineas is just as removed from this feminized work as he is from the realm of masculine work. Instead, in this passage, Phineas "listens" and "looks"— apparently collecting scenes for the memorial he will write of John's life.

In other passages, Phineas's acts of remembering are more explicitly made to stand in as an alternative to paid labor. When Phineas accompanies John on a task, he makes no attempt to be a "man of business" but instead stays in the garden to wander, watch, and *remember*:

> I was no man of business, and could assist in nothing. So I thought the best I could do was to pass the time in wandering up and down the familiar garden, idly watching the hoar-frost on the arbutus leaves, and on the dry stems of what had been little dear Mrs. Jessop's favorite roses—the same roses I had seen her among on that momentous evening—the evening when Ursula's bent neck flushed more crimson than the sunset itself, as I told her John Halifax was "too noble to die for any woman's love." (389)

While John works to divert an economic crisis, Phineas remembers an emotional crisis. Phineas is not fixated on future goals—he "wanders," "idly watches," and conjures up memories in the "familiar garden." To traverse known territory to kill time—and to enjoy doing it—flies in the face of the ambitious self-help ethos that drives headlong into progress. Phineas models a different sort of work, ignoring the garden's present state, with its cover of hoarfrost, instead choosing to remember the bushes in full bloom. His memory then fixes on that earlier scene's minute details, on Ursula's neck bent and flushed, and on a single, isolated line from his speech to her. The first time we saw this scene it was already narrated as a memory, since Phineas is supposed to be telling the history of John's life in retrospect. In this passage Craik exposes the layers of Phineas's memory (remembering the story in order to narrate it and then, within the story, remembering how he remembered earlier times). This passage thus models how a reader might remember the earlier scene by similarly refining and encapsulating it into a single image. Phineas's narration frequently does this work for the reader—reminding us of major plot points and contrasting earlier situations with later developments.

The most prominent examples of this nostalgic mode cluster around Muriel, John and Ursula's blind daughter who dies in childhood. As painful as remembering Muriel is for the family, they are loath to leave the landscapes of their intense nostalgia (this is part of the problem with moving from Longfield to Beechwood). These old places give Muriel a ghostly presence. As Phineas notes, "Ay, even then I thought I saw [John's] eyes turn to the spot where a little pale figure used to sit on the doorsill, listening and waiting for him, with her dove in her bosom. We never kept doves now" (368). A few pages after the doorsill memory, Phineas is again watching John and imagining how he misses Muriel as he traverses a landscape he associates with her: John "walked thoughtfully along, almost in the same footprints where he had been used to carry his darling up the hill-side to the brow of Enderley Flat. He seemed in fancy to bear her in his arms still—this little one, whom as I have before said, Heaven, in its compensating mercy, year by year, through all changes, had made one treasure that none could take away—the only child left to be a child forever" (372). Such passages demonstrate how intensely Muriel focuses Phineas's nostalgic narration and how Phineas does this by imagining John's emotions. In both of the above passages, Phineas senses John's feelings of loss: Phineas "thought [he] saw [John's] eyes turn to the spot" (368), and he later describes John as "[seeming] in fancy to bear her in his arms still" (372). When a character returns to the town, Phineas interprets John's silence: "I saw that this sudden meeting had brought back, with a cruel tide of memory, the last time they met—by the small nursery bed, in that upper chamber at Enderley" (392). Phineas is not content to be a mere fly-on-the-wall observer here. His own ambition, a sort of narrative ambition, aspires to see from the perspective of an omniscient narrator, able to read the internal "tide of memory."

Muriel's death can of course be read as yet one more way that John's rise is affectively managed by the novel, reminding us of the family's, and especially John's, values and religious feeling. It also does something more (after all, as we've seen, the novel has plenty of other strategies for reminding us of John's goodness and worthiness). The narration's nostalgia, particularly when focused on the loss of Muriel, suggests a resistance to a forward momentum that reads all looking backward as, in Dames's terms, "necessarily a looking-forward—a dilution and disconnection of the past in the service of an encroaching future."[63] The imagined compensation in the passage above, the "treasure" of remembering Muriel as "a child forever," rings hollow. In spite of his stated intentions, Phineas demonstrates the mental gymnastics required—

and the discontent that results from trying—to reframe all changes and losses as necessarily "in the service of an encroaching future."

Even if only implicitly, Phineas's concentration on the past resists the forward march of the novel's plot, which insists on change, improvement, and progress. In this way, Phineas echoes the discontents around the nineteenth century's political, technological, and cultural changes—from the Luddites' destruction of the signs of industrial progress, to the revived interest in medieval subjects. In *John Halifax, Gentleman*, this tension between memory and progress is made most explicit when Phineas remembers a scene that comes to stand in for John's self-help narrative. When the young John first meets Phineas, the two boys explore the Fletchers' lawn, encircled by a yew hedge. Phineas asks John what he would do if he were stuck in the lawn, trapped within the hedge. John responds, "I'll tell you what I'd do—I'd begin and break it, twig by twig, till I forced my way through, and got out safe at the other side" (46). This response signals John's persistence and offers another analogy for individual self-help—like "climbing the ladder" or "pulling one's self up by the bootstraps"—another way of reimagining upward mobility as entirely centered on the individual. John confirms the metaphorical implications many pages later, when he alludes to the story while speaking to Phineas and Ursula: "No, love; I shall never be 'patriarch of the valley,' as Phineas used to call it. The yew hedge is too thick for me, eh, Phineas?" (261). John invokes this memory in the middle of the novel. And when he again alludes to this memory in the final chapter, it serves to link the beginning, middle, and end of the narrative (and his life) with this image of the yew hedge. In his last conversation with Phineas before he peacefully dies in his sleep, John wonders whether the new tenants "keep the yew hedge clipped as round as ever" (494). By this point, the yew hedge is a memory wrapped in memory, layered within different contexts and over determined. A symbol already associated in Celtic and British tradition with death and churchyards, Craik's yew hedge interestingly provides both an analogy for John's ambitions and a way of symbolically focusing nostalgia.

At first glance, such an overlap between these forward- and backward-looking tendencies promises to stitch together the novel's dislocations, bridging the contrasts between poverty and wealth, ability and disability. But this nostalgia over the yew hedge implicates John and the reader in Phineas's desire for the past, which proves to be an unresolved tension. To make sense of this, it's important to note how Craik elsewhere pits the desire for the past against the heavenly injunction to progress toward perfection. In a passage that clarifies how elements of nostalgia and perfectionism conflict in the novel, Phineas reveals a sense of guilt when he gives way to memories:

> It was a scene—glowing almost as those evening pictures at Longfield. Those pictures, photographed on memory by the summer sun of our lives, and which no paler after-sun could have power to reproduce. Nothing earthly is ever reproduced in the same form. I suppose heaven meant it to be so; that in the perpetual progression of our existence, we should be reconciled to loss, and taught that change itself is but another form for aspiration. Aspiration, which never can rest, or ought to rest, in anything short of the One absolute Perfection—the One all-satisfying Good, "in whom is no variableness, neither shadow of turning." (395)

Phineas begins to describe the scene at Beechwood, but, in an inversion of Dames's model for Victorian nostalgia, these memories are merely the "paler after-sun" of the longer past and more perfectly captured memories—and it is "those pictures" that hijack the paragraph. The distant past—as crisply remembered as if it were "photographed"—thus distracts Phineas from remembering a more recent past. But the second sentence of the passage derails both grammatically and logically as the subject of "those pictures" is described in two dependent clauses, with the sentence then dropping off abruptly. Phineas's argument is marked by similarly muddled logic. He claims that nothing is ever reproduced in quite the same form but reassures us that this is part of the heavenly plan for how we experience the progression of our existence. "Progression" here shifts meaning from "progress" as movement in a particular direction to "progress" as improvement. The word "change" is even more explicitly redefined in this passage: Phineas claims it is simply another word ("another form") for aspiration. And aspiration, finally, is defined as looking toward "the One absolute Perfection." Slipping down this slope of equivocating definitions, Phineas comes close to aligning change with God. In such passages, the narration conflates John's earthly and heavenly aspirations, spiritualizing his ambition.

Such aspirations toward the heavenly neatly align with the tenets of perfectionism. This worldview ultimately sought to recreate everything in God's perfect image, which, as Andrew H. Miller argues in *The Burdens of Perfection*, in the nineteenth century means improving oneself according to a biblical injunction. If Phineas conflates the passage of time with change, change with aspiration, and aspiration with a heavenly endpoint, then his backward-looking nostalgia assumes a heretical tinge. His desire—for things to *return* to the way they were—conflicts with perfectionism, or the aspiration to become closer to God. In short, nostalgia seems sinful when it longs for things past rather than a future communion with God.

This conflict is made explicit with the final appearance of the yew hedge. In the final pages, John echoes Phineas's thoughts on perfectionism:

> "Do you remember how we used to lie on the grass in your father's garden, and how we never could catch the sunset except in fragments between the abbey trees? I wonder if they keep the yew hedge clipped as round as ever."
>
> I told him, Edwin had said today that some strange tenants were going to make an inn of the old house, and turn the lawn into a bowling-green.
>
> "What a shame! I wish I could prevent it. And yet, perhaps not," he added, after a silence. "Ought we not rather to recognize and submit to the universal law of change? How each in his place is fulfilling his day, and passing away, just as that sun is passing. Only we know not whither he passes; while whither we go we know, and the way we know—the same yesterday, today, and forever."
>
> Almost before he had done speaking—(God grant that in the Kingdom I may hear that voice, not a tone altered—I would not wish it altered even there)—a whole troop of young people came out of Mrs. Tod's cottage. (494)

This passage again brings nostalgia into conflict with perfectionism, with John quite explicitly resisting nostalgia in the name of God. But John's acquiescence to the law of change—like Phineas's claim that the memory of Muriel, frozen as a child forever, is a compensatory "treasure"—is not entirely convincing. Phineas does not immediately or explicitly agree with John. In fact, by dwelling on John's voice, Phineas implicitly disagrees with him: he wishes for things to stay the same and for John's voice to sound the same in heaven as it does on earth.

This passage is a fitting endpoint for the novel, encapsulating the tension between the progressive momentum of John's plot and the backward gaze of Phineas's nostalgia. It is telling that John's nostalgia in his final moments rests on the yew hedge, that symbolic obstacle in his self-help narrative and, in the wider culture, the symbol of the final barrier before reaching God's perfection. John's last words interpret his own self-help story as part of God's change, linking his earthly ambition for influence in the valley with his aspirations toward heaven—a link Craik worked to forge by redefining ambition as a drive that serves Christian love and duty. And by setting John's death on the day that Britain abolished slavery in its colonies, Craik implies that such perfectionism is at work both in the novel and in the nation's and larger empire's history. This scene thus offers itself as a self-reflexive end point for the novel: John remembers his childhood vision of the yew hedge while dying amid Britain's celebrations of progress. The scene also encapsulates how the narrative discourse has worked to remind us of this counterbalancing way of understanding the "progress" of time, through Phineas's nostalgic narration and the reader's resulting emotional response. Phineas's desire to experience again those times "photographed on memory by the summer sun of our lives" or to hear John's voice as it was subtly pits him against the self-help story that he tells. It is only in his nostalgia that Phineas questions the self-help ethos that, with its insistence upon both literal and metaphorical mobility (always upward, always into the future), excludes him. Much as chapter 2 explored in the context of Martineau's autobiographical writing, the experiences of illness and disability—and the narrative structures and perspectives they offer—are uniquely able to question the Victorian self-help ethos and its associated ideas about ability, ambition, and individualism. As Martineau puts it in her *Life in the Sick-Room*, for people with these experiences, it is all the harder to sympathize with "those states of mind, and those classes of interests which involve ambition, or any kind of personal regard for the future."[64]

In so directly pairing the characters of John Halifax and Phineas Fletcher, Craik's novel dramatizes these tensions between dependence and independence, women's and men's ambitions, ideas of perfection and disability, progress and nostalgia. The novel's resulting dislocations find expression in Phineas's nostalgic style, which registers ambition's discontents even as it apparently smooths them over—much as Phineas avoids competing with John in the family business or "slips out" when other characters fail to notice him. In choosing to dramatize these tensions through the characters of John and Phineas, Craik resolves some of the cultural anxieties around ambition. Rather than pitting an ambitious character against rivals—in the style of Dickens—Craik instead manages to fashion a novel out of the sort of life that G. L. Craik or Smiles would have compressed into a brief, inspirational biography. This "fictitious biography," as Hutton's review would have it, thus explores the narrative potential in aspiration, a drive that looks upward and, if it imagines others at all, sees them not as competition but as subjects to lift, all together.

But John's aspiration is enabled by Phineas, who not only remembers and narrates the novel, but also structurally allows for John's career. Phineas's intense love for John forestalls a reader's realization that Phineas's disability is what enables John's rise—to borrow Dames's terminology once more, it is perhaps what the text wants to teach us to forget. Similarly, Phineas's nostalgia, in longing for a happier past, only implicitly gives the lie to progress, which works by way of dislocating changes. Ultimately, *John Halifax, Gentleman* suggests that, as much as the self-help narrative relies on a certain conception of ambitious individualism, it was culturally enabled by the cover story of an aspiration to religious feeling, duty, and influence, rippling far beyond the individual. Craik's decision to narrate this novel through Phineas can serve, like the deus ex machina that removes any competition from John Halifax's path, to obscure the implicit violence behind even the most high-minded of ambitions. In the next chapter, I turn to the multiplot Victorian novel and to perhaps the most famous, or infamous, example of competitive ambition that turns to violence—where one character's success depends on another's failure and where everyone is very much aware of the competitive socioeconomic stakes. But although *Vanity Fair* is certainly William Makepeace Thackeray's best-known critique of ambition, the danger of this drive haunts much of his writing, as he experimented with how, exactly, one would know whether one's ambition was justified.

# CHAPTER 4

# "At What Point This Ambition Transgresses the Boundary of Virtue"

### From Thackeray's *Barry Lyndon* to *Vanity Fair*

Taking up the phrase "all claret would be port if it could" in one of his *Roundabout Papers* for the *Cornhill*, Thackeray reflects that "a desire to excel, a desire to be hearty, fruity, generous, strength-imparting—is a virtuous and noble ambition; and it is most difficult for a man in his own case, or his neighbour's, to say at what point this ambition transgresses the boundary of virtue, and becomes vanity, pretence, and self-seeking."[1] Thackeray returned over and over to questions about where exactly ambition "transgresses" that boundary— and what ramifications this might have for the artist as well as the average individual and the wider socioeconomic system. These questions seemed particularly pressing in the first half of his career: Thackeray addressed excessive ambitions in his reviews of artists and paintings; in his shorter novels and sketch work, including *The Luck of Barry Lyndon*, about an unscrupulous fortune hunter; in *The Book of Snobs*, with his newly coined term, "snob," poking fun at those who aspire to a higher socioeconomic class; and in his first long novel, *Vanity Fair*. Taking these works together, we can see how Thackeray explicitly linked discussions about artistic ambition—how ambitious writers and artists should be, how to assess one's own abilities, how an ambition could produce or mar a work of art, and so on—with discussions about the ethics of ambition. As I'll argue in this chapter, Thackeray's aesthetic and ethical questions point to a concern with the distribution as well as the calibration of ambition. In his art reviews, he stresses that there is only so much genius in the world, meaning that there should also be only so many ambitious artists. Translating such concerns into fictional narratives, Thackeray implies that the zero-sum logic of the socioeconomic system, as well as the structures of these narratives themselves, will cut ambitious characters down to size.

In questioning where ambition crosses into vanity or selfishness, Thackeray gestures to his own ambitions, as if toying with how much to claim or disavow them. This results in a sort of self-reflexivity, with the narrator hovering between omniscience and embodiment. We can see this style emerging across the development of Thackeray's narrator in the *Punch* series titled *The Snobs of England*, which was later collected into *The Book of Snobs*. The subtitle (to both the series and the book) immediately announces the self-reflexivity that informs the text's—and much of Thackeray's—stylistics: the work is not just about snobs; it is also written "by one of themselves." The narrator confesses to his own authorial ambition, noting he has "a conviction on my mind that I had a work to do" and "a Purpose to fulfil," in the midst of a passage that also disavows that ambition by locating it in a "Voice" that urges him to write: "the Little Sedulous Voice Came To Me and Said, 'Smith, or Jones' (The Writer's Name is Neither Here nor There), 'Smith or Jones, my fine fellow, this is all very well, but you ought to be at home writing your great work on SNOBS.'"[2]

Despite this initial coyness about his motivation and identity, the narrator takes on an increasingly fleshed-out and consistent character as the series proceeds. He turns out to be neither a Smith nor a Jones, but a "Mr. Snob." However, Thackeray still plays with the persona and perspective, as when Mr. Snob is the addressee ("you") who approaches a young woman ("You go up [with your usual easy elegance of manner] and talk to Miss Smith in a corner" [73]). Even when the narrator applies it to himself consistently, it's still difficult to determine exactly where he stands. For example, in chapter 42, "Snobs and Marriage," the narrator shifts between third- and first-person perspectives:

> Punctual, I say, to the hour of five, which Mr. and Mrs. Raymond Gray had appointed, a youth of an elegant appearance, in a neat evening-dress, whose trim whiskers indicated neatness, whose light step denoted activity (for in sooth he was hungry, and always is at the dinner hour, whatsoever that hour may be), and whose rich golden hair, curling down his shoulders, was set off by a perfectly new four-and-ninepenny silk hat, was seen wending his way down Bittlestone Street, Bittlestone Square, Gray's Inn. The person in question, I need not say, was Mr. Snob. HE was never late when invited to dine. But to proceed my narrative:—
>
> Mr. Snob may have flattered himself that he made a sensation as he strutted down Bittlestone with his richly gilt knobbed cane (and indeed I vow I saw heads looking at me from Miss Squilsby's, the brass-plated milliner opposite Raymond Gray's, who has three silver-paper bonnets, and two fly-blown prints of fashion in the window), yet what was the emotion produced by my arrival, compared to that which the little street thrilled, when at five minutes past five the floss-wigged coachman, the yellow hammer-cloth and

flunkeys, the black horses and blazing silver harness of Mr. Goldmore whirled down the street! (123)

This passage starts with "a youth" who turns out to be Mr. Snob, as described by a seemingly omniscient narrator. Then we realize that this narration is coming from Mr. Snob himself, which becomes clear only when he parenthetically defends his tongue-in-cheek brag ("I vow I saw heads looking at me"). Even before Mr. Snob outs himself as the narrator, the description hovers between third-person modes: the "may" implies a limit to the narrator's omniscience, while the details about Mr. Snob signal a fuller knowledge (which of course the narrator has, because he is describing himself). Finally, Mr. Snob coalesces when, deflating all his pretensions, he notes that any sensation he made is nothing compared to the stir created by Mr. Goldmore's arrival.

This sometimes dizzyingly self-reflexive process—of the narrator joking from a critical distance and then reorienting from the embodied perspective of a central character who is aware of his own foibles—allows the narrator simultaneously to poke fun at, implicate, and distance himself from his own snobbish ambitions. This "hovering" is a hallmark of Thackeray's style. Kent Puckett has pinpointed how Thackeray uses this "hover[ing] between embodiment and omniscience" specifically around social blunders, creating distance between the narrator and the blunder.[3] I want, with this chapter, to suggest that there's an even larger motivation behind this stylistic tic—Thackeray's interest in questioning and moderating ambition. Thackeray was especially attuned to the double nature of ambition in the Victorian era and in the popular self-help narrative. While he clearly found ambition compelling and generative across his career—a career that this chapter will loosely trace from Thackeray's early sketch work to *Vanity Fair*—he also worried about where ambition crosses over into ridiculous or even dangerous self-seeking. In his repeated efforts to achieve a perspective from which to accurately judge this line, Thackeray develops a critical stance that, like the above description of Mr. Snob, aspires to hover somewhere between an embodied presence and a critically distanced omniscience.

## Variations on a Theme: *The Book of Snobs* and the Genre of the Sketch

Throughout Thackeray's work, the sketch emerges as a symbol and metric for gauging and moderating ambition. Given that Thackeray practiced the sketch as both a writer and a visual artist, this mode offered a bridge for thinking about how creators test out their ambitions. The written sketch lent itself as a testing ground for fiction writers in the early nineteenth century: as Amanpal Garcha has shown, the sketch played much the same role as short stories do today, offering authors "a form in which to practice and refine the craft of fiction and with which to get into print."[4] We can see this trajectory in Thackeray's own career, from sketches and short narratives to long, baggy novels. Similarly, for visual artists, the sketch functions as a sort of litmus test for ambition: it might be quickly dashed off to capture an ephemeral impression or it might be the precursor to a grander work. But even the quick sketch carries the risk of appearing too ambitious. As Alison Byerly has argued, the sketch can be, paradoxically, an "ostentatiously unpretentious mode."[5] At the same time, the idea of the sketch is intimately bound up with questions of perspective—as sketches of buildings or models, for example, could be used to imagine a single material object or body from various angles, often in service of a larger project. Fittingly, then, across Thackeray's art reviews and novels, the sketch invites different perspectives from which to judge whether an artist has shown too little, too much, or just the right amount of ambition.

Thackeray's series encapsulates the paradoxical tendencies of the mode, with the work going from the serialized sketches—which his contemporaries referred to as "The Snob Papers"—to a collected work, *The Book of Snobs*. More importantly, the structure itself alternates between stand-alone sketches and sequences that seem to aspire to a longer form. This tendency becomes more pronounced as the series proceeds and as some episodes begin to generate longer narratives. For example, in chapter 31 Thackeray's narrator visits his friend Major Ponto, ostensibly to observe the "Country Snob" in his natural habitat. He ends up staying a full eight sketches—acclimating himself to country life, learning about the rival families in the neighborhood, and attending a party full of those "related to the Peerage or the Baronetage" (109). While at Major Ponto's, the narrator also meets the governess, Miss Wirt, whose piano playing inspires a lengthy description that suggests how a series of variations can begin to generate a more complex narrative. First, she plays the "original" version, then a variation: "She spun up stairs; she whirled up stairs: she galloped up stairs; she rattled up stairs; and then having got the tune to the top landing, as it were, she hurled it down again shrieking to the bottom floor, where it sank in a crash as if exhausted by the breathless rapidity of the descent" (94). Then she performs a version with "pathetic and ravishing solemnity: plaintive moans and sobs issued from the keys—you wept and trembled as you were gettin' up stairs" (94). This scene—which goes on at length, much like Miss Wirt's performance—comments on the very form that *The Book of Snobs* will take: a series of sketches or renditions on a single theme that aspires to a longer form.

It is telling that this passage, with its self-referential meditation on ambition, takes shape around that recurring figure in Thackeray's work—the upstart governess. Although the comedy here takes aim at the excesses of Miss Wirt's ambitious performance—as *The Snob Papers* ridicule all such pretension—Thackeray's narrator uniquely enjoys Miss Wirt's powers. When Mrs. Major Ponto praises Miss Wirt to the narrator, he notes that he has "been accustomed to see governesses bullied in the world" and "was delighted to find this one ruling the roost" (95). Much like Becky Sharp in *Vanity Fair*, Miss Wirt's hard-won and overtly feminized ambition wins the admiration of the male narrator. And much like both Becky Sharp and the narrator, Miss Wirt (a name Thackeray will recycle in *Vanity Fair*, with the Osborne sisters' governess) continually wields her power while disavowing it, calling herself a "poor little governess" (95) and a "poor ignorant female" (96).

Thackeray's narrator might well have sympathized with Miss Wirt's virtuosic performance given *The Snob Papers'* own narrative ambition—to accumulate example after example across the weekly installments. Thackeray was similarly accused of taking his variations on a theme a bit too far. As the weekly sketches appeared—with clerical snobs, university snobs, military snobs—it seemed that everyone was a snob. By the fifth chapter, the narrator admits this is a problem, suggesting that "it is impossible for *any* Briton, perhaps, not to be a Snob in some degree" (16). In the last installment, rather than suggesting that the definitive work on snobbery is now complete, he claims the "labour is endless. No single man could complete it" (156): even if we were to "live for a hundred years more, I believe there is plenty of subject for conversation in the enormous theme of Snobs" (157). Anthony Trollope later critiqued this excessiveness in his study of Thackeray, writing that the sketches "were more charming, more piquant, more apparently true, when they came out one after another in the periodical, than they are now as collected together"; in short, "there are too many of them."[6] According to Trollope, Thackeray's series falls short as a narrative (as *The Book of Snobs*) but works as sketches trickled out across installments (as *The Snob Papers*).[7] Still, the series clearly held generative potential. In sustaining the narrative thread of the sketches, Thackeray varies the performance, multiplies his examples, and keeps his narrator hanging on at the Country Snob's house.

It is significant that these ideas about ambition, generating material, and building narrative out of variation come together in *The Snob Papers*, whose serialization briefly overlapped with the appearance of *Vanity Fair* (which began in January 1847). The two works mark a transition: from sketches and periodical work signed under pen names to Thackeray's first novel in twenty numbers. As Trollope imagined, it was Thackeray's ambition "to do something larger, something greater, something, perhaps, less ephemeral" that led him to write *Vanity Fair*.[8] And Peter S. Shillingsburg reminds us of what a dramatic moment this was for Thackeray: "The composition, production, and financial success of *Vanity Fair* mark the watershed of Thackeray's career as a businessman."[9] This success, as M. G. Sundell observes, transformed Thackeray "from one among the horde of skilled London literary men known only in the trade into a recognized major writer."[10] Written on the cusp of this transition, *The Book of Snobs* straddles two writerly modes. As Puckett argues, the narration is "caught between two competing styles: the embodied, parasitic form characteristic of *Punch's* house style and a recognizably omniscient narration that combines in *The Book of Snobs* a masterful view of a whole social world with the ability to be anywhere and everywhere at once."[11] Puckett marks the development of this "masterful view" in that moment when the snob both identifies with and disavows "another snob's mistake."[12]

The dynamic Puckett identifies—of calling out in someone else the same quality one is worried about in oneself—is part of a larger self-reflexive pattern between ambition and narration in Thackeray's work. While Thackeray's self-reflexive style manifests itself in various ways throughout his writing, it is particularly apparent in the way these narratives use ambition to generate material even as they criticize that ambition. This style arises when Thackeray's narrators comment on upstart characters who are overtly embodied and caricatured, with the critical voice hovering in the space between the diegetic and extradiegetic world, disavowing its own ambitions. Shifting across and hovering in the space between embodiment and omniscience, Thackeray's narrators cultivate a self-reflexive, critical distance from close quarters. This stance bridges much of Thackeray's writing, from his *Snob Papers* to his review work and his novels, and particularly *Barry Lyndon* and *Vanity Fair*.

In his reviews and criticism, Thackeray posits that ambition is a necessary drive for the artist, but that it can also mar the work—as if, like the snob who reveals that he does not belong because he tries to belong, the ambitious artist gives away that he is not a genius because of his ambition. Rather than have such strivers give up practicing art because they are not geniuses, Thackeray instead calls for an aesthetic that is more accessible and more embodied. Some critics have argued that, in the process of doing this, Thackeray defends the mediocre as a specific aesthetic or avoids the relationship between art and the marketplace.[13] But I'm interested in how Thackeray uses these reviews to rehearse some of his own anxieties as an ambitious writer. By specifically implicating the same work that he engaged in, Thackeray develops a self-reflexive critical voice that finds a parallel in his simultaneously embodied and disembodied narrators.

Thackeray tended to imagine artists as having limits to their abilities—what we'd think of now as a "fixed" rather than a "growth" mindset. This view comes through particularly clearly in a piece Thackeray wrote after Samuel Laman Blanchard's death, in March 1846, and while *Snobs* was appearing monthly. Thackeray's essay for *Fraser's* announced itself as both "the History of a Literary Man, Laman Blanchard" and a commentary on "the Chances of the Literary Profession." It also turns out to be a critical review of an earlier memorial by Edward Bulwer-Lytton. Thackeray takes Lytton to task for his depiction of Blanchard as a man who had gone "resolutely through the author's hardening ordeal of narrow circumstance, of daily labour, and of that disappointment in the higher aims of ambition."[14] Thackeray, via his Titmarsh persona, questions Lytton's tendency to pity Blanchard because his ambition was circumscribed by economic and material necessities. Instead, Titmarsh insists, "I have said before, his calling was not thankless; his career, in the main, pleasant; his disappointment, if he had one of the higher aims of ambition, one that might not uneasily be borne. If every man is disappointed because he cannot reach supreme excellence, what a mad misanthropical world ours would be! Why should men of letters aim higher than they can hit, or be 'disappointed' with the share of brains God has given them?" Instead of indulging the premise that every writer should or even wants to have a higher ambition, Titmarsh distinguishes between genius and "everyday" writers: "Let such fall into rank and file, and shoulder their weapons, and load, and fire cheerfully. An everyday writer has no more right to repine because he loses the great prizes, and can't write like Shakespeare, than he has to be envious of Sir Robert Peel, or Wellington, or King Hudson, or Taglioni."[15]

Thackeray's art reviews repeatedly advise tamping down one's ambitions and instead aiming for what one can confidently hit. As another of his reviews, also under Titmarsh, puts it, "I deny the merit of failing greatly in pictures— the great merit is to succeed. There is no greater error, surely, than that received dictum of the ambitious, to aim at high things; it is best to do what you mean to do; better to kill a crow than to miss an eagle."[16] Or, as another review laments, "Why the deuce will men make light of that golden gift of mediocrity which for the most part they possess, and strive so absurdly at the sublime?"[17] Titmarsh aligns himself with these everyday writers, drawing attention to the work he performs in the very article we read. As he argues, "A man who writes (Tennyson's) 'Ulysses,' or 'Comus,' *may* put in his claim for fame if you will, and demand and deserve it: but it requires no vast power of intellect to write most sets of words, and have them printed in a book:—To write this article, for instance."[18] Across his writing, Thackeray includes such critiques that implicate the speaker—from being a snob who accuses other snobs, to pointing out the vices of his characters in *Vanity Fair* while suggesting that these same vices are to be found in everyone (including the narrator). This strategy is common to satire, which, in holding a mirror up to society, implicitly or explicitly includes the writer. Thackeray adds another interpretive twist when, writing under a pen name, he uses this strategy to voice his theories of artistic production and appreciation.

Across these reviews, Thackeray associates mediocrity with an embodied, earthy position, while genius takes on a disembodied, ethereal quality. As he writes in the *Paris Sketch-Book*, "Let us thank heaven, my dear sir, for according to us the power to taste and appreciate the pleasures of mediocrity. I have never heard that we were great geniuses. Earthy are we, and of the earth; glimpses of the sublime are but rare to us."[19] Instead of waiting around for the rare glimpse of the sublime, Thackeray asserts the easy enjoyment of "tasting" mediocrity. As Denise Gigante has shown, the modern alignment of the bodily sense of taste with aesthetic taste emerged in distinction to classical aesthetics, "which were primarily linked to the higher senses of sight and hearing."[20] Thackeray asserts the value of this common, easier sense and aesthetic, which is associated with the viewer's embodiment and which resists the philosophy that we ought to most value what is most rare and most difficult.

This is not to say that Thackeray doesn't appreciate genius—in fact, he suggests that we appreciate genius when it emerges against a background of everyday art. This dynamic comes through in another review of an art exhibition that turned out to have been a mixed bag: "There may be a couple of works of genius, half-a-dozen very clever performances, a hundred or so of good ones, fifteen hundred very decent, good, or bad pictures, and the remainder atrocious." But Titmarsh finds this unevenness to be a point in the exhibit's favor: "What a comfort it is, as I have often thought, that they are not all masterpieces, and that there is a good stock of mediocrity in this world, and that we only light upon genius now and then, at rare angel intervals, handed round like tokay at dessert, in a few houses, and in very small quantities only! Fancy how sick one would grow of it, if one had no other drink."[21] Titmarsh's theory finds comfort in a "good stock of mediocrity" because that is the everyday, earthly stuff that sustains us. His analogy relates taste, genius, and art, aligning the mediocre with the everyday physical needs of the body. This passage also signals how easily Thackeray equates art and commodities, with the pictures handed around as if they were the tokay with the "seal of genius stamped on the cork."[22] What bothers Thackeray here is not the price tags or seals—not the commodification of art—but the paintings that try too hard to give themselves a high price.

Despite (or because of) living in the midst of the age that preached self-help and that lauded the ambition to improve one's abilities and position, Thackeray's narrators question such desires. Titmarsh complains that the overly ambitious paintings mentioned above are "absurd"—a term that often crops up when Thackeray addresses ambition.[23] By way of introduction to the above review, Titmarsh recalls an art student with the suggestively similar name of Harry Tidbody who perversely labors away at his art despite a lack of talent. Initially, Titmarsh's description of Tidbody's work ethic could be a page out of George Lillie Craik's *The Pursuit of Knowledge under Difficulties* or Samuel Smiles's *Self-Help*: "But he rose early of mornings, and scrubbed away all day with his macgilps and varnishes; he worked away through cold and through sunshine; when other men were warming their fingers at the stoves, or wisely lounging on the Boulevard, he worked away, and thought he was cultivating art in the purest fashion" (98). But all this repetitive work does not lead to progress. Instead, "at the end of his second year of academical studies Harry Tidbody could draw exactly as well as he could eight years after. He had visited Florence, and Rome, and Venice, in the interval; but there he was as he had begun without one single farther idea, and not an inch nearer the goal at which he aimed" (98). Tidbody doesn't improve so much as repeat himself— sometimes quite literally. He "spent at least three thousand nights in copying the model . . . He had piles upon piles of grey paper at his lodgings, covered with worthless nudities in black and white chalk" (98). The same model appears over and over, the thousands of nights of labor result in worthless chalk sketches. Tidbody marks the point at which hard work stops paying off and where only artistic genius can show the next step—and this point takes the form of the sketch.

Titmarsh implicates himself—and Thackeray—in these critiques. He recalls seeing Tidbody "perched upon a high stool, and copying with perfect complacency a Correggio in the gallery, which he thought he had imitated to a nicety. No misgivings ever entered into the man's mind that he was making an ass of himself; he never once paused to consider that his copy was as much like the Correggio as my nose is like the Apollo's" (101). Thackeray aligns himself with Titmarsh here; his nose was famously broken in a fight and did not heal well—and was thus notably not at all like Apollo's. In critiquing artistic ambition, Thackeray suggests his own mediocrity, either in Titmarsh's writing or in his own physical appearance. Such passages put Thackeray in an ambiguous position as he draws attention to how he is both in and outside the narrative, like and unlike his narrators and the objects of his critique.

Tidbody presents a morbid echo of Thackeray's own work: a dozen years of turning out sketches and novellas before turning his hand to a long novel, all to regain the financial security he had lost through failed investments. In *Novels behind Glass*, Andrew H. Miller points to two of Thackeray's letters where he measures his success against the patrimony he lost in 1833 at the age of twenty-one. In Miller's reading, the lost patrimony "taught Thackeray about the meager endurance of possessions and supported the cycle of acquisition and loss that he obsessively repeated in the fiction." This is also, I would suggest, a source of Thackeray's interest in ambition and its moderation, about how much work he needed to do so that "at 50, I shall be as I was at 21."[24] In fact, around the age of twenty-one Thackeray was imagining his own abilities and weighing his talents against the literary competition. In a May 1832 diary entry, Thackeray recounts his reactions to Lytton's *Eugene Aram*, declaring, "The book is in fact humbug." He then swerves into a comparison—because, as he notes, "I always find myself competing with him"—and hopefully asserts that "when my novel is written it will be something better I trust." But in this digressive passage Thackeray also starts doubting his own abilities: "How can a man know his own capabilities or his inferiority?" A few months later, in another entry, Thackeray laments his lack of perseverance: "I wish to God I could settle myself into a little steady reading were it but for an hour a day . . . I think I could write a good comedy—I wish I had perseverance to try—"[25] In this light, Thackeray's movement from shorter and more ephemeral work to the novel is all the more significant. Unlike Dickens, who quickly transitioned from *Sketches by Boz* to *The Pickwick Papers*, Thackeray, also publishing in 1837, did not sign his name to a long novel until *Vanity Fair* began serialization ten years later.

This context helps get at why Thackeray might have seen a double bind in the genre of the sketch. Titmarsh explores this dilemma while discussing the different affordances of watercolors and oils. At first each seems to have its own powers and limits, but, as the passage develops, Titmarsh suggests how a good watercolor or sketch produces a sort of longing for the more ambitious version:

> You cannot produce by any combination of water-colours such effects as may be had from oil, such richness and depth of tone, such pleasing variety of texture, as gums and varnishes will give; but, on the other hand, there are many beauties peculiar to the art, which the oil-painter cannot arrive at,—such as air, brightness, coolness, and flatness of surface . . . Why will the practitioners, then, be so ambitious? Why strive after effects that are only to be got imperfectly at best, and at the expense of qualities far more valuable and pleasing? There are some aspiring individuals who will strive to play a whole band of music off a guitar, to perform the broadsword exercise with a rapier,—monstrous attempts, that the moral critic must lift up his voice to reprehend . . . I have seldom seen the works of a skilful water-colour painter of figures, without regretting that he had not taken to oil, which would allow him to put forth all the vigour of which he was capable. For works, however, like that of Mr. Haghe, which are not finished pictures, but admirable finished sketches, water is best; and we wish that his brethren followed his manner of using it.[26]

Titmarsh aligns the watercolor with the sketch: Haghe's watercolors are "admirable finished sketches," with the medium conveying "air, brightness, coolness, and flatness." In contrast, oil lends depth and variety of texture. It is the desire to move from sketch to oils—while still using the tools of the sketch artist—that marks "ambitious" and "aspiring individuals."[27] The trouble with being "so ambitious" is that one cannot correctly gauge one's own weapons or instruments (depending on the analogy at hand) to match them to the work to be done. Far from driving improvement, ambition both marks the creation with its shortcomings and prevents the artist from taking on the sort of work they actually have the tools to accomplish. At the same time, as much as the sketch initially offers a way around the pitfalls of an "ambitious picture," it too can backfire: a good sketch, in settling for what it can do well, gestures to an unfulfilled ambition. As Titmarsh puts it, a skillful watercolor makes him regret the artist had not taken to oil, "which would allow him to put forth all the vigour of which he was capable." In such reviews, the artist's sketch also offers, by analogy, a testing ground for writerly ambitions (as well as, perhaps, the accompanying double bind). In describing oils and watercolors, Titmarsh uses language inflected with the literary equivalents: a multiplot novel like *Vanity Fair* also allows for a "richness" and "depth," a "pleasing variety of texture," whereas the sketches can be airy, bright, cool, and flat. Much as oils can literally be built upon one another, so too can chapters accumulate and create depth.

In his later novels, Thackeray dramatizes the matching of ambition with ability. He repeatedly plots the careers of young men finding their way as artists. For example, the eponymous hero of *Pendennis* takes on a writing career amid literary hacks, while Clive in *The Newcomes* trains and tests his abilities as a painter and sketcher. Clive might remind us of the overly ambitious artist when Thackeray's narrator notes that "of course our young man commenced as a historical painter, deeming that the highest branch of art; and declining (except for preparatory studies) to operate on any but the largest canvasses." The ambitious Clive paints the "prodigious" *Battle of Assaye*, which the Royal Academy Exhibition rejects, and which Clive subsequently declares "rubbish" and destroys.[28] However, Clive eventually settles into modest sketch work, where he meets with more success. In these later novels the artist tests his ability and learns to be critical of his own talents and ambitions.

But Thackeray's early work is most interested in exaggerated ambitions in subjects who lack self-awareness—a situation that calls out for society (or an editor or narrator) to cut these ambitions down to size. Such exaggeration, especially when it's ridiculed or belittled, is suggestive of caricature and parody. We could understand Thackeray's sketch and parody work in the 1840s as having much to do with both letting loose and critiquing his own ambitions as a writer. Thackeray's *Catherine* parodies the popular Newgate novel, and, after the installments of *The Snobs of England* had run their course, Thackeray took on an entire series of such parodies with Punch's Prize Novelists. The design of this series was to imitate popular authors and poke fun at their excesses— from Lytton's pomposity to Catherine Gore's many fashionable references. It is significant that here, too, Thackeray includes himself as a target, recognizing that he also had a marked style. The authors he parodied still understandably took offense, to the point that Thackeray abandoned the series before he took on Dickens. In overdoing all these styles, Thackeray flaunted his ability to recreate the qualities that made other authors' styles unique, even as he marked them out as foibles. Parody provided Thackeray with an ambiguous position both in and outside the judgment, pointing to flaws by reproducing them in more egregious, self-aware form.

With this intense self-reflexivity, Thackeray's style practices much of what twentieth- and twenty-first-century criticism has aspired to. As Rita Felski argues, "Self-reflexivity is the holy grail of contemporary thinking: widely hailed as an unconditional good."[29] But to critique is generally to maintain one's distance: the critic who observes a text suspiciously and from the sidelines has become, in Felski's argument, a ruling paradigm, putting the critic in the role of a detective sniffing out a text's hidden agendas and complicities (much like Thackeray's snob hunter).[30] Unlike Felski's detective-critic, in his development of personas that implicate him in the same foibles—whether the snob hunter or the everyday writer—Thackeray insists on implicating the narrator as an embodied actor in the diegetic world. This insistence, that the critic has an embodied as well as an intellectual stance, is something that Thackeray's style still importantly offers us.

Read in this way, Thackeray's narrator illustrates the quandary between what Amanda Anderson identifies in *The Powers of Distance* as two opposed attitudes toward the pursuit of objectivity in criticism today: "Within much materialist, feminist, poststructuralist, and identity-based criticism, claims to objectivity or reflective reason are seen as illusory, pretentious, hierarchical, and even violent." They are set against the "opposing ideals of avowed situatedness, embodiedness, particularity, and contingency." At the same time, "within some of these same bodies of criticism, detachment simultaneously and often surreptitiously operates as the negative freedom that permits critique, exposure, irony, or parody."[31] Thackeray's narrators notoriously shift between embodied and seemingly disembodied, objective perspectives, while suggesting the powers and limits of both. I'm thinking especially of the moments when we get at the objective truth—for example, that Mr. Snob is indeed flattering himself that he is making a sensation as he arrives for dinner. This isn't achieved by either omniscience or first-person description but through their combination. Far from taking what Anderson critiques as an "all-or-nothing" approach to objective distance, Thackeray demonstrates that critical distance and objectivity are not a permanent stance but, to borrow from Anderson, a "temporary vantage" and an "unstable achievement."[32] And this temporary and unstable vantage point is not reached through distance alone but also through embodiment and proximity—a critical closeness.

As the rest of this chapter takes up, Thackeray used satire in his early novels to similar ends. In *Barry Lyndon* and *Vanity Fair* he exaggerates the ambitions of his protagonists, while his narrator or editor belittles these ambitions from the critical distance of the sidelines—generating novelistic material while taking an ambiguous position within and against such ambitions. Victorian novels obsessively return to plots that suggest felt and formal limits on the ambitious subject, relying on zero-sum games to create interest in who will marry the most eligible young person, or inherit an estate, or win or lose a court case. Thackeray amplifies this sense in his novels about ambitious upstarts, like Barry Lyndon and Becky Sharp, who navigate socioeconomic systems that hold a fixed number of positions of wealth and power. In the process, Thackeray complicates the aesthetic and ethical questions he raised about ambition in his early sketch and periodical work, where he imagines artists working in a world of limited genius, with the viewer sorting between the works that are mediocre (but still satisfying!) and the works of genius. In his novels about upstart characters, Thackeray also experiments with taking different perspectives to critique ambitions, but here, these ambitions overtly seek to acquire power and money in a limited system by seizing it from others.

## Undercutting and Belittling Ambition in *Barry Lyndon* and *Vanity Fair*

Barry Lyndon and Becky Sharp stand out as unscrupulously ambitious characters in Thackeray's work—and characters that highlight how Thackeray imagined ambition across genders. In comparing these characters, I'm participating in a long-standing interest in tracing Becky's character type and structural role across Thackeray's writing. For example, John Carey has argued that "Amelia and Becky, the good and evil angels of *Vanity Fair*, were originally the same person" in *Ravenswing*, the character of Morgiana Crump. Carey sees little of Becky Sharp in the later novels, instead arguing that "not until the end of his career do we get a faint reflection of Becky in Elizabeth Prior, the ballet-dancer turned governess of *Lovel the Widower*."[33] Meanwhile, Katharine Rogers has explored Thackeray's tendency to include opposing female types—like Becky and Amelia Sedley—across his novels.[34] Such readings are suggestive for thinking about how Thackeray uses these ambitious character types and how he stuffs these energies into a single character or splits them up and counterbalances them across a character system. By limiting the field of comparison to female characters, these arguments have neglected to compare Becky Sharp to Thackeray's other ambitious upstarts and thus to the ways ambition is differently gendered and embodied. Indeed, Rogers draws attention to this fact in a footnote: "*Barry Lyndon* and *Denis Duval* have been omitted from this discussion of Thackeray's novels because neither has important female characters: *Barry Lyndon* does not really have a heroine."[35] But comparing these characters across gendered lines suggests how Thackeray uses different subject positions to imagine ambition and its tendency to manifest in competitive or even violent self-seeking.

On the surface, Thackeray's two novels about ambitious upstarts do indeed appear irreconcilably different. *Barry Lyndon* of course showcases a male character's voice, it is in first person rather than third, and it is only a fourth the length of *Vanity Fair*. Although we might assume that Barry's and Becky's paths will take disparate courses according to their genders, their narratives parallel one another in significant ways. Both novels are set in the past during Continental wars, and both feature ambitious characters that begin life poor and under the care of an opposite-sex parent. Both characters thus capitalize on the interest and narrative potential of an underdog.[36] Compounding this, they are "othered" via their nationality (Becky's mother is French, Barry is Irish) even as they attempt to reimagine their heritage (none too accurately) as springing from aristocratic connections. Across their respective novels, both rise through advantageous marriages, engage in potentially or outright criminal acts to pursue money and power—usually by taking it from others—and subsequently fall from grace. These differences and similarities across the two novels suggest Thackeray's interest in tracing the forms that ambition can take when embodied in men or women, and what these forms can do in the space of a longer or shorter novel, as narrated from different perspectives. Taken together, these novels suggest how the socioeconomic world, with its many pursuits of fortune and fashion, function like zero-sum games, with scarce titles and inheritances to go around. Thackeray's narrator in *Vanity Fair* overtly draws attention to how this logic works even within families, asking, "If you were heir to a dukedom and a thousand pounds a day, do you mean to say you would not wish for possession? Pooh! And it stands to reason that every great man, having experienced this feeling towards his father, must be aware that his son entertains it towards himself" (468).

*The Luck of Barry Lyndon* announces itself to be Barry's autobiography, edited by Thackeray's recurring character George Savage Fitz-Boodle. Barry narrates how he lies and cheats his way into power and money, whether by impersonating others or by marrying (and bullying) his way into fortunes. But he claims, repeatedly, to deserve his success, having risen "by my own genius and energy," and to have "won my way from poverty and obscurity to competence and splendor."[37] As if unable to let such exaggerations stand, the editor intervenes, commenting eighteen times in the 1844 text. Thackeray was uncertain as to whether he needed this outside corrective to Barry's first-person voice. Edgar F. Harden notes that, in revising the text for its 1856 publication in the authorized *Miscellanies*, Thackeray particularly edited around Fitz-Boodle. Thackeray removed explicit mention of the editorial role, nine (of fifteen) footnotes, two sections of Fitz-Boodle's commentary, and part of the conclusion. Although Thackeray removed much of the editorial presence, there are, as Harden notes, inconsistencies that "defy explanation." Thackeray retained an allusion to the imagined editor of *Fraser's Magazine*, Oliver Yorke, but removed the attribution "O.Y." He also retained a footnote attributed in 1844 to "ED." but left another. As Harden concludes, "One assumes that [Thackeray] intended to remove Fitz-Boodle and to change the main title and the chapter titles, but one still has difficulty in determining precisely why a fictional editorial presence was partly diminished, partly continued, and inconsistently identified."[38] I rehearse this confusing textual history because I think it points to an ongoing concern for Thackeray: how to portray exaggerated ambition while simultaneously disavowing it. Perhaps one reason Thackeray struggled to write and revise this text is because the power struggle between Barry's voice and that of the editor is not only staged across footnotes but also seeps into Barry's narration.

The editor's commentary in the original text initially offers some comically tentative corrections, observing that "Mr. Barry's story *may* be correct" (38) or noting that he "cannot help pointing out here a truth which seems to have escaped the notice of the amiable autobiographer" (42). In one footnote the editor ventures to question the sheer number of duels Barry supposedly engages in: "May we be allowed to hint a doubt as to a great number of these combats? It will be observed, in one or two other parts of his Memoirs, that whenever he is at an awkward pass, or does what the world does not usually consider respectable, a duel, in which he is victorious, is sure to ensue; from which he argues that he is a man of undoubted honour" (81). The editor does not comment only on the particular instance but also gestures to others—as if training the audience to read Barry's narration more critically. The editor also takes an increasingly aggressive position, emphasizing the distance between Barry and him. At one point he observes that, while a passage might be "allowed" to remain, it is not "because we admire the autobiographer's principles or professions" (79). Later, the editorial voice is so concerned with Barry's maltreatment of Lady Lyndon that he goes on for nearly half a page in a footnote before deciding that "this is a subject for an essay, not a note" (179–80). By the end, the editorial presence reigns supreme: the editor declares in one of the last footnotes that he has "taken the liberty to expunge numerous passages" (201), and he concludes the novel with a final three pages of narrative and commentary, as if shielding us from Barry's voice.

Or, read another way, the editor has taken a lesson from Barry's own playbook. Barry's ambition is everywhere about power, space, and resources. When he tries to scare off his romantic rival Lord George, Barry threatens:

> You are forty years younger than I am in experience. I have passed through every grade of life. With my own skill and daring I have made my own fortune. I have been in fourteen pitched battles as a private soldier, and I have been twenty-three times on the ground, and never was touched but once, and it was by the sword of a French *maître-d'armes*, whom I killed. I started in life at seventeen, a beggar, and am now at seven-and-twenty, with 20,000 guineas. Do you suppose a man of my courage and energy can't attain any thing that he dares, and that, having claims upon the widow, I will not press them? (155–56)

Amplifying the stakes of these power struggles, Barry's exaggerations are associated with recounting or threatening acts of physical violence. The editorial takeover similarly suggests a physicalized contest. As noted above, the editor begins to "expunge" entire passages, while the final comments seem to enjoy lingering on Barry's squalid living conditions in Fleet Prison and on his eventual death of delirium tremens. Stanley Kubrick's adaptation could be read as picking up on this narrative desire by quite literally undercutting Barry's character: in a duel with his stepson, Barry's left leg is shot and has to be amputated.

Barry's violent and physicalized ambition is wrapped up in the narrative's style, its energy and bravado. In Trollope's description, this style takes on an embodied dimension, a lively, springing motion: "As one reads, one sometimes is struck by a conviction that this or the other writer has thoroughly liked the work on which he is engaged. There is a gusto about his passages, a liveliness in the language, a spring in the motion of the words, an eagerness of description, a lilt, if I may so call it, in the progress of the narrative, which makes the reader feel that the author has himself greatly enjoyed what he has written . . . So it has been with Barry Lyndon."[39] But this "liveliness" and "lilt" are qualities of the style, not its creation. Thackeray's notebook suggests a labored writing process: on January 12, 1844, he writes that he is beginning "to flag"; a few days later, he gets through chapter 4 with "a great deal of dullness, unwillingness, and labour"; on February 17, he notes he has been reading for *Barry Lyndon* and writing "with extreme difficulty, a sheet"; four days later he complains of being "very tired"; and by August 12 *Barry Lyndon* is "lying like a nightmare on my mind."[40] Much as the novel conveys the sense of a limited playing field, Thackeray's notes suggest that he understood his own writerly energies to be a finite resource.

In comparison, Thackeray appears to have found Becky Sharp's ambition more generative. Whereas *Barry Lyndon* clearly divides Barry's voice and the editor's, *Vanity Fair* returns to something like the ambiguous perspective wielded in *The Snob Papers*. Here the "hovering" works in a number of ways. First, the narrator flip-flops on whether he is omniscient or a character in the same world. Second, whatever designation we give this narrator, he leaves much space for ambiguity, thus complicating any critiques he might make of Becky and just how far she'll go to climb the social ladder (does she cross a line with Lord Steyne or not? Does she kill Jos or not?).[41] As Nora Gilbert has shown, *Vanity Fair* uses a logic of scandal that doesn't suppress so much as capitalize on the subversive, resulting in a "moral ambiguity that has been, and continues to be, one of its greatest attractions."[42] Third, stemming from and adding to this ambiguous narratorial position and "logic of scandal," the novel problematizes questions about agency. If we imagine the characters as puppets, then the narrator is pulling the strings. But of course, the narrator also suggests he is an embodied, diegetic character, from the occasional suggestion that he is a bachelor in one chapter, or, paradoxically, a married man with his "Julia" in another, to his explicit entrance on the scene at the eleventh hour in chapter 62.

Such ambiguity is especially interesting in a novel that, as Eleanor Courtemanche has shown, portrays the diffusive effects of social, economic, and political complexity—as if attempting to track the actual workings of an "invisible hand."[43] As Courtemanche argues, the plot works as a perverse version of such an invisible hand, with "ironic benefits flow[ing] to selfish agents." Significantly, the novel sets up the sense that Becky and Amelia succeed at one another's expense even when they aren't competing for the same things.[44] With her ability to navigate the diffusive power structures she finds herself in, Becky's character suggests the extent to which the ambitious individual can in fact overcome disadvantageous social and economic systems (although it comes at the expense of others). At the same time, the difficulty of locating the narrator inside or outside the story world, as the observer within a system or the puppet master pulling the strings of that system, complicates any conclusions we might come to about the efficacy of Becky Sharp's ambitious individualism versus the agency of a more or less generous invisible (or authorial) hand.

The socioeconomic landscapes of *Vanity Fair* present limited systems with few paths for advancement—and Becky Sharp is everywhere more circumscribed than Barry Lyndon. She advances from one closed and claustrophobic system to another, with the very limitations of these systems spurring her ambition (and our interest in seeing her overcome them). First, determining to get free of Miss Pinkerton's establishment and its strict socioeconomic hierarchy, Becky practices music "incessantly" and instructs fellow students in both French and music. Negotiating her way out, she next pivots to "the noble ambition of matrimony" (19). But while visiting Amelia, Becky is exposed to only a small circle of eligible young men to choose from. And as an orphan, Becky has "all this work to do for herself" (26), resolving "I must be my own Mamma" (92). Thackeray's narrator emphasizes this self-helping ethos: when she meets Jos Sedley, her "modest eyes gazed so perseveringly on the carpets that it was a wonder how she should have found an opportunity to see him" (18). When Mr. Sedley makes his jokes, "Rebecca [laughs] at them with a cordiality and perseverance" (25). When her plots with Jos fall through because of his rack-punch hangover, Becky does not settle into mere governess work. Instead, even in the limited social circle of the Crawley family, she escapes being a governess, soliciting two marriage proposals.

After her marriage to Rawdon Crawley, Becky faces a different set of material and gendered limitations. She makes the most of the couple's limited resources—selling the horses for a tidy profit during the war, putting off creditors, and storing extra money away for her own use. She also runs a household on nothing a year—nothing, that is, paid by the couple—and can offer her own dinners from the assorted gifts of game from Queen's Crawley and wine from Lord Steyne's cellars. When she settles Rawdon's debts, she functions just as effectively in the public, male-dominated realm of business: the creditors "complimented his lady upon the brilliant way in which she did business, and declared that there was no professional man who could beat her" (369). But even as Becky Sharp maneuvers within and across gendered roles, she does everything *as a woman*. When she makes a successful play against their creditors, her victory is accomplished as "[Rawdon's] lady." We can also see this pattern at work in the passage where Becky instructs Rawdon to "be a good boy, and obey your schoolmistress in every thing she tells you to do . . . While there is life, there is hope, my dear, and I intend to make a man of you yet" (374). Even while promising to "make a man" of her husband, she places herself explicitly in the feminine role of "schoolmistress." Such an ambition succeeds in these contexts by implying its own gendered limitations.

Becky Sharp thus negotiates her way through limited systems and strict power structures by fluidly moving across gendered roles under cover of her overt femininity. Lisa Jadwin reads her mimicry and role playing as typically feminine, the "female double-discourse" that allows women to work around social norms.[45] Similarly, Miller argues that Becky mimics because "she is removed from the powers that determine discursive norms, and parody, as many feminists have emphasized, can be an especially powerful habit of discourse available to those—especially women—who must speak from the margin and in a language they did not design themselves."[46] But Miller also suggests that Thackeray uses this gendered alienation to get at something more universal: Becky Sharp becomes "the emblem for [Thackeray's] own alienation," generalizing Becky's position into "a human condition." In the process, Miller suggests, "the identification and generalization of Becky's position into a human condition eradicates the specifically female character of that threat."[47] But as much as the narrator identifies with Becky Sharp and even holds her up as a universal underdog, he insists that we remember she is a "little lady." I would argue, then, that far from her gender increasing the potential threat of her ambition, it defuses the real sense of danger. Instead, the way her character is feminized tends to signal that her ambition is working at a diminutive scale—more comedy than tragedy. To be sure, Becky gets away with things, from people's money to their happiness. However, as Gilbert has shown, the novel's "logic of scandal" prevents a full assessment of Becky's crimes, obscuring whether, most importantly, she had any hand in Jos's death. (It also obscures whether Becky Sharp is herself a victim of sexual violence or death threats at the hands of Lord Steyne.)[48] And then, even if the narration were clear on these points, Becky is not operating here at the level of the ambition that haunts the historical backdrop of *Vanity Fair*—that of, say, a Napoleon.

In fact, Thackeray repeatedly and comically contrasts Becky Sharp with Napoleon in ways that draw out how Becky's ambition is gendered and belittled, and thus sometimes able to fly under the radar and succeed. The narrator, other characters, and Becky herself compare the "little upstart" with the also physically small but historically larger-than-life figure of Napoleon—transferring "the mythic resonance of Napoleon to Becky Sharp."[49] Becky initiates this association early in the novel when she leaves Chiswick, exulting in having leveled her fluent French against the uncomprehending Miss Pinkerton: "Thank Heaven for French. Vive la France, Vive l'Empereur, *Vive Bonaparte!*" (10). Ideologically Becky Sharp is clearly linked to Napoleon, with her ambition and her belief in merit. Napoleon's Grand Armée famously promoted according to ability, as opposed to the British system, where many of the novel's characters receive their position in exchange for money, including Rawdon Crawley and George Osborne. Becky is associated with the word "merit" across the novel, as when Miss Crawley tells Becky that "if merit had its reward you ought to be a Duchess" (112). Napoleon and Becky are also both repeatedly referred to as upstarts: Napoleon is the "Corsican upstart" (177, 336) and a "wretched upstart and swindler" (263), while Becky is "a little upstart governess" (60) and "parvenue" (362). Becky has a similar power of inspiring followers, as we learn that Rawdon believes in his wife "as much as the French soldiers in Napoleon" (348). But the most "striking comparison," as Robert Polhemus has observed, is "Thackeray's drawing of Becky as Napoleon wearing a three-cornered hat" at the start of chapter 64. Much as Becky's gendered ambition generates the comedy of the comparisons with Napoleon, it is the pettiness of her goals that invites us to laugh when all her best-laid schemes fail—even as that comedy also implicitly critiques the system that allows so few outlets for women's ambitions.

We can see this critique at work in the way Thackeray draws on the rhetoric of self-help and competition to describe Becky Sharp's "pursuit of fashion." As if in an echo of the novel's competitive business world, the fashionable world similarly functions to produce clear winners and losers. After her fall, Becky scrambles to regain her earlier ascendency: "She saw people avoiding her, and still laboriously smiled upon them" (641). And when she encounters obstacles, she perseveres to build "a little circle for herself with incredible toils and labour" (642). Much like the marriage market, the social world is easily portrayed as a zero-sum game (even if it's often for small stakes, especially when compared with the war going on in the background). Social competitions are immediate and visible—who shines in a ballroom, for instance, and who, next to such a bright light, fades into the background. We learn that Becky "of course, quite outshone poor Emmy" (245) in Brighton. In Brussels, when Amelia's appearance at a ball is "an utter failure," the narrator notes that "Mrs. Rawdon Crawley's *debut* was, on the contrary, very brilliant": "She arrived very late. Her face was radiant; her dress perfection" (288). Later in the novel, Becky's much-celebrated performance in charades means that the "twice as handsome" "black-eyed Houri" from an earlier scene is "eclipsed" and "poor Mrs. Winkworth" is "nowhere in the race," while, instead, "all voices were for [Becky]" (515). Each party sets up a race for attention, with one clear winner by the end of the night.

Across such passages, Thackeray self-consciously re-genders the typically masculine narrative of self-help and self-improvement. As his narrator remarks:

You hear how pitilessly many ladies of seeming rank and wealth are excluded from this "society." The frantic efforts which they make to enter this circle, the meannesses to which they submit, the insults which they undergo, are matters of wonder to those who take human or womankind for a study; and the pursuit of fashion under difficulties would be a fine theme for any very great person who had the wit, the leisure, and the knowledge of the English language necessary for the compiling of such a history. (373–74)

Thackeray's "pursuit of fashion" pokes fun at the Society for the Diffusion of Useful Knowledge's most popular publication, Craik's *The Pursuit of Knowledge under Difficulties*. While *Vanity Fair* was being issued serially, Craik published a continuation of his *Pursuit of Knowledge under Difficulties*: in 1847 he took the concept across gender lines and issued a volume "illustrated by female examples." Thackeray's ambitious female character thus appeared exactly as the self-help ethos was expanding to include examples of female self-improvement—with both comparing women's ambitions with men's and imagining women's working on a smaller scale.

Indeed, unlike Barry Lyndon, who is physically large and overpowering (and often violently so), Becky Sharp, for all her ambitions, is repeatedly represented as a diminutive figure. The narrator first describes her as "small and slight in person: pale, sandy-haired and with eyes habitually cast down" (12). Although Thackeray is everywhere fond of using "little" in his descriptions—one of the "critical epithets that recur constantly" according to Geoffrey Tillotson[50]—he is particularly heavy handed with this word when describing Becky Sharp and everything belonging to her. She has "the prettiest little foot in the prettiest little sandal in the finest silk stocking in the world" (377), a "little drawing-room in May Fair" (419), a "dashing little carriage and ponies" (412), and a "little house in Curazon Street" (504). She is called "the little woman" (seventeen times), "the indefatigable little woman" (417), "that brilliant little Becky" (441), or "this artless little creature" (440). When she appropriates finery from Queen's Crawley, it is to suit them to "her own little person" (477). And when Becky or the narrator takes on the self-pitying tone, Becky is "poor little Becky" (490) or the "friendless little woman" (490). Significantly, she is the only adult female character in *Vanity Fair* called "the little woman" until chapter 66 (when Amelia also gets the epithet). Although all the characters are supposed to be puppets, these repeated reminders of Becky Sharp's smallness make her seem all the more puppetlike. The way "little" further signals "female" in the descriptions of Becky Sharp is clearest when she is compared to men: "No man in the British army which has marched away, not the great duke himself, could be more cool or collected in the presence of doubts and difficulties, than the indomitable little aide-de-camp's wife" (299). She may out-cool and out-collect any man in the army, but she is little and someone's wife.

What I think is most interesting about this descriptive tic, however, is the way it works to lessen the severity of moral rebukes against Becky Sharp. When "little" is applied to less-than-flattering descriptions, it effectively softens the blow—as when she is called a "silly little fibster" and a "silly little fool" (480). Elsewhere, she is "that little audacious Mrs. Rawdon" (454) and "the little schemer" (523). Whereas Barry Lyndon is accused of being an Irish upstart or adventurer, Becky Sharp is a "little adventuress" (four times) and a "little upstart" (twice). Lord Steyne, in particular, repeatedly remarks on Becky Sharp's deviousness while belittling her in a way that lets her off the moral hook. When she wheedles more money out of Steyne and he catches her in the lies she uses to do so, he is amused and admiring rather than outraged:

> "What an accomplished little devil it is!" thought he. "What a splendid actress and manager! She had almost got a second supply out of me the other day; with her coaxing ways. She beats all the women I have ever seen in the course of all my well-spent life. They are babies compared to her. I am a greenhorn myself, and a fool in her hands—an old fool. She is unsurpassable in lies." His lordship's admiration for Becky rose immeasurably at this proof of her cleverness. Getting the money was nothing—but getting double the sum she wanted, and paying nobody—it was a magnificent stroke. (524)

As exaggerated as Becky Sharp's abilities are, Steyne compares her first to "all the women" he knows and then only to himself (not to all the men he knows). And, of course, it is clear that even if Becky had asked for double the sum, it would not be enough to make Lord Steyne balk. She is merely a "little devil": her badness is contained, feminine, "little." In fact, she actually inspires Lord Steyne's further admiration—he does not need to compete with or outwit her but only to watch her antics, secure in his position and fortune. And when he wants to be rid of Becky, there is no question that he has the money and power to do so—whether or not he threatens her life in the final chapters, Becky appears to believe the risk is credible given that she doesn't risk hanging around for clearer proof. When applied to Becky, then, the adjective "little" functions, like "cute" in today's discourse, as a way of signaling vulnerability.[51]

Becky Sharp freely invokes her unthreatening figure to escape censure. By exaggerating Becky in the opposite direction of Barry Lyndon's voice—by having her claim to be helpless rather than violently powerful—Thackeray provides an embodied "cover" for her ambition: "You need not be jealous about me, my dear Miss Briggs. I am a poor little girl without any friends, or any harm in me" (139). When Lady Grizzle compliments Becky on her French, she receives a humble reply: "'I ought to know it,' Becky modestly said, casting down her eyes. 'I taught it in a school, and my mother was a Frenchwoman.'" Lady Grizzle is "won by her humility" and "mollified towards the little woman" (505). As the narrator notes, when "attacked," "Becky had a knack of adopting a demure ingenue air, under which she was most dangerous" (505). Such strategies work especially reliably when Becky Sharp confronts men, as she reminds them of how they use their gendered advantage unfairly. Thus she rebukes George: "'Joke away, Mr. George; there's nobody to defend *me.*' And George Osborne, as she walked away—and Amelia looked reprovingly at him—felt some little manly compunction for having inflicted any unnecessary unkindness upon this helpless creature" (61). Or keeping Jos in line: "'I shall take care how I let *you* choose for me another time,' said Rebecca, as they went down again to dinner. 'I didn't think men were fond of putting poor harmless girls to pain'" (26). Becky Sharp disavows her motives and ambitions, asserting that she has no power in these interactions owing to her low socioeconomic origins and her gender, even as we see her directing their course. And the strategy of claiming her underdog status often works—at least, that is, when those in power don't actually perceive her as a threat on their own level.

Like Barry Lyndon, Becky Sharp's energy and sprightliness translate into language overloaded with exaggerations, emphases, and repetitions—a style that is not allowed free rein for long. When the narrator satirizes Becky Sharp, he frequently targets what we sympathize or enjoy most against her, her "vivacity and sense of humour," which is also of course Thackeray's style. Some of the longest passages of Becky's direct speech appear in the form of letters to Amelia and Rawdon. These showcase her exaggerated style, beginning with her salutation to the "dearest, sweetest Amelia" (75). Describing her new situation in this letter, Becky claims the groom behaved "most rudely and insolently" to her and that she "did not sleep one single wink the whole night" (76). Such exaggerations enter her repetitive sentence structures. Although she has just arrived, Becky proclaims that Lady Crawley is "always knitting the worsted," Sir Pitt is "always tipsy every night," and Mr. Crawley "always reads sermons in the evening" (82).

These exaggerations spill over into the narrator's language, as if the narrator, too, delights in playing the mimic. When Becky Sharp works to conciliate

Lady Southdown, Becky Sharp claims that "her views were very much changed by circumstances and misfortunes; and how she hoped that a past life spent in worldliness and error might not incapacitate her from *more serious* thought for the future" (417). Although the narrator takes on the duty of indirectly summarizing Becky Sharp's conversations, we still find the exaggerations and emphases of the original style. The narrator not only holds her language up for judgment; he also amplifies it (and the humor). These echoes of her voice muddle the line between the narrator and Becky Sharp—which is exactly the point of both empathetic and ironic use of free indirect discourse.[52] But this also distances Becky from her own language, as if diffusing her responsibility for the lies and exaggerations.

Of course, the narrator always frames Becky Sharp's exaggerated voice, even if only by selecting which letters or conversations to report. This stylistic pattern finds its corollary in the way the novel generates and checks Becky's ambitions, given her structural position as an underdog—as a young woman and orphan without position or fortune who is compelled to navigate a limited socioeconomic landscape where any prizes come at another's expense. As this chapter has argued, Becky Sharp's ambition often succeeds exactly because it is belittled and circumscribed: she gets away with more of Lord Steyne's money and the reader's sympathy than she would if she posed a more direct or overt threat. In again taking up the problem of ambition with *Vanity Fair*—with his first lengthy novel in a career that, as Miller observes, can sometimes appear "as Thackeray's attempt to restore his inheritance . . . to make him at 50, as he says in [a] letter, what he was at 21" (27)—Thackeray uses a little, feminized puppet to embody ambition.

Many critics have noted an affinity between the narrator and Becky Sharp—to the extent that David Kurnick terms it a "staple of Thackeray criticism."[53] But I think it's worth returning to the gendered stakes of such an affinity. Feminizing ambition to lessen the threat of this potentially dangerous drive is not an immediately intuitive strategy. To the contrary, Nancy Armstrong has argued that ambitious women in Victorian fiction typically serve as a sort of scapegoat. In Armstrong's reading, ambitious women become "a means of simultaneously establishing and disavowing the competition, aggression, and domination that were well on their way to becoming necessary and natural properties of male individuals alone." As she concludes, after mentioning *Vanity Fair* among representative examples, "Victorian fiction portrayed the despicable qualities of ruling-class masculinity as truly despicable *only* when those qualities appear to animate women."[54] And yet, as I have suggested here,

Thackeray was an equal opportunity satirist, ready to question or disavow all forms of ambition, whether artistic or socioeconomic, and whether they were wielded by women or by men. As much as Thackeray might seem, according to Armstrong's reading, to criminalize and exile Becky Sharp for the qualities that we would forgive in her male equivalent, Thackeray's larger preoccupation with ambition suggests he was perhaps more attentive to the gendering of ambition than many of his fellow Victorian writers. After all, he certainly doesn't let Barry Lyndon end happily.

Thackeray was critical of how women were "kept down." In a letter to his mother dated June 1, 1840, Thackeray questioned, "Why is it that one does not like women to be too smart?—jealousy I suppose: a pretty selfish race we are truly. And Lady Morgan has shown how cruelly the ladies are kept down."[55] Lady Morgan, the Irish novelist who wrote *The Wild Irish Girl* and *Woman and Her Master*, came under fire for her politics—particularly her views on Ireland and her praise for the French Revolution. She has also repeatedly been suggested as prototype for Becky Sharp's character.[56] As Micael M. Clarke suggests, "If Lady Morgan is in any way Becky's prototype, then her feminist views would certainly add an extratextual dimension to Thackeray's representation."[57] It would add an especially intriguing dimension to Becky Sharp's ambition and her relation to the self-help narrative—to how Thackeray experimented with fashioning this character who played on the line of being too ambitious, "too smart," even as her underdog position allows room for readers to like and even root for her. The potential connection with Lady Morgan is also interesting for how this real example was put to use in the self-help tradition. Lady Morgan was later featured in collections of exemplary biography and on the title page of Jessie Boucherett's *Hints on Self-Help: A Book for Young Women* (which adapts and quotes at length from Smiles's *Self-Help*). Boucherett's epigraph comes from Lady Morgan's prefatory address to her *Memoirs*: "I would wish to impress on young people who are beginning life, as I did, dependent on their own exertions, the absolute need of concentrated industry; a definite purpose, and, above all, conduct dictated by common sense."[58]

If all ambitious self-help walks a fine line in the Victorian era between laudable aspiration and selfish ambition, then it might be perfectly poised in the representation of an ambitious woman, one who initially invites us to root for her exactly because of her disadvantages but then challenges that sympathy as she plays for higher and higher stakes. As we know all too well after the 2016 US presidential election, ambitious women still concentrate these cultural anxieties in twenty-first-century America. Women might take contemporary self-help's advice to "lean in" at work, but they already put in more hours than their male counterparts when accounting for both paid and unpaid work, and the gender pay gap stubbornly persists.[59] Across career paths, women continue to navigate strange double binds, like being told not to smile too much if they want to be taken seriously but also to smile more, lest they be seen as cold or bitchy.[60] Even gendered qualities that are generally seen as positive—such as empathy—produce a quandary. Emote empathy, and it will be taken for granted because it's expected; fail to do so, and its lack will immediately be felt and commented upon.[61] Equally paradoxically, the American population is critical of women running for positions of power,[62] but generally sanguine once those same women are on the job—if Hillary Clinton's approval ratings as a senator and secretary of state are any indication. It seems that, even more than a woman in power, a woman ambitiously pursuing something is the problem. And so, Clinton could be both one of the most truthful and qualified candidates to run for president and the locus of fears about conspiracies, hypocrisy, and "crooked" politicians. The concerns about Clinton's "likability" quite easily transferred to the next presidential election cycle, where Elizabeth Warren's name needed only to be copied and pasted into the same hand wringing.

Becky Sharp's character still offers us a sort of cultural litmus test, not only in Thackeray's text but also in the many adaptations that have sought to reclaim her as a feminist hero—often, in fact, reading her selfish ambitions as a feminist act.[63] Given how ambitious women heighten cultural anxieties over this drive, it is fitting that Thackeray leaves so much ambiguity in the final scene that would condemn Becky's ambition by fully criminalizing it—as if there is no way to fairly judge this character, even from the narrator's shifting and self-reflexive vantage point. This crystallizes a larger tendency in Thackeray's work. He repeatedly returned in content and style to the question of how one judges ambition, in others as well as oneself. Such questions underlie a number of stylistic and formal tendencies—the confusion over how closely he identified with his pseudonyms, the doubling or trebling of undercutting voices, and the use of narrators who criticize from a distance even as they reveal themselves to be part of the diegetic world. These questions also give form to his novels, which imagine the economic and social worlds as closed systems that may or may not be directed by an invisible hand pulling strings—with characters competing for limited favors, fortunes, and marriage partners. Thackeray's characters embody their various allotted amounts of talent or ambition or goodness, while the self-reflexive style that describes them hovers between embodiment and godlike omniscience, claiming and disavow-ing its own ambitions. Given Thackeray's interest, across his writing, in rep-resenting and critiquing ambition—in experimenting with positions from which to judge when ambition becomes absurd or selfish as it strives after art or riches—it is appropriate that he reached his own writerly ambitions through a novel that dramatizes the double bind of women's ambitions, across Becky Sharp, who is too ambitious, and Amelia Sedley, who is not ambitious enough. And that he has so enduringly been identified with this upstart who invites us to sympathize with a woman's exaggerated ambition.

In the introduction and chapter 1, I traced how self-help texts like Craik's *The Pursuit of Knowledge under Difficulties* and Smiles's *Self-Help* capitalized on the inherent interest and narrativity contained in the successful individual—particularly when that individual starts as an underdog and works so hard that we come to root for their well-deserved success. In fiction, as we've seen, authors complicated this narrative by widening the scope and the stakes. A common plotline would feature two rivals competing—whether the conflict is explicit (as the introduction examined in the case of Dickens), implicit (as in Thackeray's *Vanity Fair*), or disavowed (as in Craik's *John Halifax, Gentleman*). In the next chapter I turn to the structural challenge that multiplot Victorian novels took on when they attempted to account for not one or two ambitious characters but a small crowd. In the process, Anthony Trollope's *The Three Clerks* thematizes competition by invoking two opposed assumptions: that competition is ultimately productive of individuals as well as the common good, and that competition in fact produces winners and losers in a zero-sum game.

# CHAPTER 5

# Individuating Ambitions in a Competitive System

## Trollope's *Autobiography* and *The Three Clerks*

In Anthony Trollope's *The Three Clerks,* two of the titular characters compete for the same promotion in the Office of Weight and Measures. As they prepare for the examination that will determine who gets the promotion, their friends debate the merits of such competitions. Mrs. Woodward, defending the old system—of patronage and knowing the right people—worries about what the exam will do to what we might now call office morale: "There will be three or four men with broken hearts, and there will be one triumphant jackanapes."[1] Her daughter, Gertrude, defends the new competitive system:

> "I would have a competitive examination in every service," said Gertrude. "It would make young men ambitious. They would not be so idle and empty as they now are, if they had to contend in this way for every step upwards in the world."
>
> "The world," said Mrs. Woodward, "will soon be like a fishpond, very full of fish, but with very little food for them. Every one is scrambling for the others' prey, and they will end at last by eating one another." (121)

At stake here are two different ways of imagining the value and uses of competition. Gertrude and her mother use analogies that gesture to debates about how competition functions in a free market—debates that were current in the era's political economy and that seep into the structure of Trollope's novel. From Gertrude's perspective, the exam functions as part of a system that rewards merit, based on assumptions of liberalism and individualism, and ultimately fostering healthy ambitions that benefit society at large—as if channeling Adam Smith's view of competition as an enlivening and ultimately diffusively beneficial force. In contrast, Mrs. Woodward imagines a sort of Malthusian fishpond, where a lack of resources and opportunities turns self-interest into ruthless destruction. While we have seen both ways of imagining the ambitious individual in previous chapters—from Samuel Smiles's self-helpers who lift the entire nation up with their persevering work, to the implicitly or explicitly zero-sum games staged in Victorian fiction—Trollope thematizes these as a cultural and narrative tension. As I'll argue, the tension between these two ways of understanding the ambitious individual in competition is essential not only to *The Three Clerks* but also to Trollope's broader strategies for characterization and narrative. These strategies are still prevalent today, given the intense interest in narratives that follow a set of aspiring subjects who are gradually individuated through their interactions and rivalries (from reality television competitions to dramas following cohorts entering a career together, whether as surgeons, police, lawyers, etc.).

Critics have recently paid new attention to how Trollope's novels engage with the concept of liberalism and the ambitious individualism associated with it. Trollope was everywhere concerned with how the individual "makes his way" in the world, and he was clearly drawn to plotting how the individual climbs, whether in the church, Parliament, or the marriage market. Although Trollope has often been read as a conservative thinker, recent criticism locates where he takes a potentially progressive and critical stance. In *Bleak Liberalism* Amanda Anderson uncovers this potential in the ethos of characters that align with liberal values, while Daniel Wright has pointed to the way some of Trollope's female characters use tautologies to express desires that trouble the assumptions of both the marriage market and rationalism.[2] I want to build on this work by concentrating, in this chapter, on how Trollope repeatedly represents his characters and their choices as emerging through a competitive process. The concepts of individualism and liberalism are thus bound up, for Trollope, with the idea of competition. Across his writing career, Trollope returned again and again to characters making their way in crowded careers and marriage plots. These competitive logics structure his novels, requiring his characters to individuate themselves through the choices they make and the rivalries they engage in. If, as Anderson argues, "character is a key site for elaborating aspirational ideals and for mediating between differing values or perspectives in the text," then Trollope's character systems are particularly interesting because he so self-consciously set out to create characters that would inspire his readers to improve themselves. Trollope repeatedly confronted the problem of ambition: a quality that was necessary for making one's way in the (competitive) world but also a quality that could grow to excess or veer into criminality. With *The Three Clerks*, whose title suggests a fairy-tale like structure, Trollope created characters who have too much, too little, and just the right amount of ambition.[3]

On the one hand, Trollope's novels capitalize on the interest generated by setting characters out to compete (Who will win the exam? Who will Gertrude marry?). On the other hand, as these competitions manifest themselves through a series of zero-sum games, they trouble our more diffusive readerly sympathies—pointing to how the plot and our interest in it depends on creating not only winners but also losers. Both clerks wish for a promotion, but there is only one spot; both fall in love with Gertrude, but they can't both marry her. This tension is always at work in what has been termed Trollope's vacillation plot, with characters waffling as they make decisions about whom to marry, what risks to take, which career to choose.[4] Across these plots, Trollope both employs and critiques the assumptions of Western liberalism and individualism. To make choices about one's life, according to liberal and neoliberal thought, is also to make the individual. But this process is of course in tension with and dependent on material constraints. Both the plots and the narrative discourse of Trollope's novels are structured by the competitions and comparisons the characters enter into, and both emphasize the limitations of resources and space.

Adding to this sense of scarcity, Trollope implies that his characters rarely have all that many options after all. Initially, his plots seem to offer the characters a range of paths to choose from, providing the chance to consider present and future utility, competing values, and so on. But in vacillating between what turns out, most often, to be just two options, Trollope's characters face conflicts similar to those of the reader, trying to fit "more or less" preferences into binary decisions. As this chapter will argue, these strategies take particularly interesting forms in Trollope's most autobiographical works, *An Autobiography* and *The Three Clerks*. Trollope imagines himself as well as his characters individuating themselves through competitions in a materially limited world, presenting a challenge for building a "good" character.

To make this argument, I start by considering how Trollope's *Autobiography* functions like a self-help text in the style of George Lillie Craik's *The Pursuit of Knowledge under Difficulties* and Samuel Smiles's *Self-Help*. Trollope similarly holds up his career as an example to follow, emphasizing hard work and perseverance over genius. And he draws out how this logic tends to lead to *outdoing* one's own work ethic (reminiscent of the way Smiles's examples often read like cases of monomania, as explored in chapter 1). As a result, Trollope appears less concerned about how he competes with others in a literary marketplace, and more concerned about how he competes with himself. But when this logic enters the space of the novel, the competitions turn outward, with many ambitious subjects entering the same playing field and pursuing limited prizes. In *The Three Clerks* Trollope is at his most explicit with this plotting strategy: the eponymous three clerks enter into rivalry for promotions and love interests, the three sisters they eventually marry compete for suitors, and the end of the novel hinges on the result of a different sort of competition, a legal contest. These competitions start in and are complicated by Trollope's descriptions of his characters, which rely on comparisons with one another—with characters emerging as more or less handsome, honest, brave, when compared to others in the fictional universe. Ultimately, I consider how these two autobiographical narratives dramatize the ambitious individual as part of a limited socioeconomic system, while shifting between portraying competition as something that builds individuals or, in pitting people against one another, destroys them, like so many fish "eating one another."

## Trollope versus Trollope: Self-Help and Competition

Trollope claims in his *Autobiography* that it had been "a matter of deep conscience" how he "handle[d]" his characters across his career (201). As he explains it, he wanted to create realistic characters who would also (and as a result of their realistic depiction) inspire a certain moral feeling: "If I could do this [create realistic, human characters], then I thought I might succeed in impregnating the mind of the novel-reader with a feeling that honesty is the best policy; that truth prevails while falsehood fails; that a girl will be loved as she is pure, and sweet, and unselfish; that a man will be honoured as he is true, and honest, and brave of heart" (133–34). If Trollope was always worried about the question of how to present characters as examples for his readers, then this question becomes especially fraught when his own life was the stuff in need of "handling." Trollope's approach in the *Autobiography* is closely aligned with that of the self-help genre, with its reliance on biographies that are meant to be inspiring in how they emphasize hard, replicable work that leads to well-deserved success. And indeed Trollope's *Autobiography* has been read, popularly and critically, as a self-help book—as "an aid to self-reliance, and a supplement to Samuel Smiles's" work.[5] These texts and genres are thus uniquely positioned for understanding how Trollope, in particular, handled the problem of ambition—as a drive that motivates plots and that pushes characters to distinguish and individuate themselves but that also manifests in the sort of competitions that can turn to selfishness and even criminality.

*The Three Clerks* has long been acknowledged as Trollope's most autobiographical novel. Trollope particularly channeled his experiences into the character of Charley. Both Trollope and Charley begin careers in the Civil Service; neither shows much promise. As Trollope remembers, "The first seven years of my official life were neither creditable to myself nor useful to the public service"—in short, he was "always in trouble."[6] Much like Charley, Trollope had an admirer, whose mother, much like Norah's guardian, visited the post office to ask when he would marry her daughter. And Trollope is similarly haunted by a moneylender who admonishes him to be punctual. The most noteworthy parallel, however, is Charley's interest in becoming an author: he begins writing for the *Daily Delight*, with its many rules about starting in medias res, including an incident in every other paragraph, and incorporating a "slap at some of the iniquities of the times" (such as "the adulteration of food," "the want of education for the poor," and the "miscellaneous sale of poisons") (213).

Trollope also lends something of himself to the character of Alaric. Tony Bareham notes the many biographical parallels Alaric Tudor shares with Trollope—from "emotional deprivation" and a "broken domestic circle" to the "false start in life in Europe." And as he jokes, "Goodness knows whether the identical initials are conscious or not."[7] Given that Trollope was an irrepressible fox hunter, there might also be a parallel in Alaric's repetition of an analogy about hunting—though his boots be muddy, his bag is full of game—a pep talk he gives himself whenever he makes a morally dubious decision. Alaric's ambition is a particularly striking similarity. Much as we might read Charley and Alaric as competing versions of Trollope's experience in the Civil Service, we might read *The Three Clerks* as a competing version of Trollope's *Autobiography*. And I would suggest that the imagined splitting of Trollope across Charley and Alaric in *The Three Clerks* is even more apt if we consider how Trollope represents himself in *An Autobiography*—in competition both with a field of other civil servants and writers and with himself.

Trollope's *Autobiography* is not at all what one would expect from the title, as readers and critics have observed since its publication. There are no shocking revelations or artistic or spiritual epiphanies, but the reader does learn the nitty-gritty financial details of Trollope's dual careers, such as which publisher took which manuscript for how many pounds. Trollope warns in his first paragraph that this will be a book not about the "little details of my private life" but rather about his literary career: "what I, and perhaps others round me, have done in literature; of my failures and successes such as they have been, and their causes; and of the opening which a literary career offers to men and women for the earning of their bread" (1). Trollope essentially relates a self-help story: his life follows the rags-to-respectability trajectory of so many of Smiles's biographies of successful men, while he repeatedly calls attention to himself as an example of what others might likewise accomplish in literature. In this he agrees with one of *Self-Help*'s key maxims, that "any man can do what any other man has done."[8] Far from claiming to be a literary genius, Trollope emphasizes his hard work—which further justifies his success while also inviting readerly sympathy. Trollope quite explicitly sets himself up as a model: "By my example may be seen what prospect there is that a man devoting himself to literature with industry, perseverance, certain necessary aptitudes, and fair average talents, may succeed in gaining a livelihood, as another man does in another profession" (98). Read in this way, we can better understand why James Kincaid's description of *An Autobiography* as a "mildly personalized how-to-do-it manual" rings so true.[9] Trollope's *Autobiography* seems modeled not after the Victorian tradition of introspective autobiography—particularly the tradition in which John Stuart Mill and John Henry Newman participated—but rather, after the model of the inspirational self-help biography.[10] Further justifying such a reading, Samuel Smiles was himself inspired to write his *Autobiography* after Trollope's appeared.[11]

Some of the most striking and oft-quoted passages of the *Autobiography* are those detailing Trollope's work ethic. Trollope repeatedly returns to time management, with its requisite language of disciplining the body. He attributes his ability to lead a full life across two careers to "the virtue of early hours": "It was my practice to be at my table every morning at 5:30 AM; and it was also my practice to allow myself no mercy" (248). Trollope becomes his own taskmaster in these passages, describing how it became his custom "to write with my watch before me, and to require from myself 250 words every quarter of an hour. I have found that the 250 words have been forthcoming as regularly as my watch went." Trollope zooms out to quantify how this "division of time allowed [him] to produce over ten pages of an ordinary novel volume a day, and if kept up through ten months, would have given as its results three novels of three volumes each in the year" (249). This language is reminiscent of Smiles's praise of the "careful employment of those invaluable fragments of time, called 'odd moments,'" which, when collected, result in self-help figures producing similarly capacious volumes of writing (including Henri François Daguesseau, who regularly wrote while waiting for dinner, and Madame de Genlis, who composed "while waiting for the princess to whom she gave her daily lessons").[12] Much like Smiles, Trollope emphasizes what is apparently recreatable about his success—the physical actions of rising early, setting aside time for work, and writing a certain number of words per day.

As if taking a page from self-help characters who prop books on plows or spinning jennies, Trollope put the "down time" afforded by his day job to good use. In another oft-quoted passage from his *Autobiography*, Trollope describes how, whenever he traveled for work, he managed to turn "these hours to more account": "I made for myself therefore a little tablet, and found after a few days' exercise that I could write as quickly in a railway-carriage as I could at my desk" (94). Trollope maintained this habit of writing during his travels regardless of the conveyance. On his voyage to the Continent, he wrote aboard ships: "As I journeyed across France to Marseilles, and made thence a terribly rough voyage to Alexandria, I wrote my allotted number of pages every day. On this occasion more than once I left my paper on the cabin table, rushing away to be sick in the privacy of my state room. It was February and the weather was miserable; but still I did my work. Labor omnia vincit improbus" (108). As charmingly Trollopian as these anecdotes can be, they play into a logic common to self-help texts—that recreatable actions lead to similar success. It is worth noting that Trollope's example indeed inspired others, including Henry James, who admired Trollope's "magnificent example of plain persistence" on a transatlantic journey—as he "drove his pen as steadily on the tumbling ocean as in Montague Square." This was, for James, an example of mastery and self-command.[13] Much more recently, the critic R. H. Super recounts following the *Autobiography*'s advice while writing a biography of Walter Savage Landor, remaining at his desk "without cocktails or dinner until the day's stint of pages had been typed."[14]

Emphasizing what is repeatable about his example leads Trollope, like Smiles, to employ maxims. In explaining how he willed himself to work across two careers, Trollope writes that "nothing surely is so potent as a law that may not be disobeyed. It has the force of the water-drop that hollows the stone." Invoking classical allusions, Trollope reminds us that "a small daily task, if it be really daily, will beat the labours of a spasmodic Hercules. It is the tortoise which always catches the hare" (110). And in Latin, "Mens sana in corpore sano. The author wants that as does every other workman,—that and a habit of industry" (111). The frequent recitation of maxims suggests just how fully Trollope fashioned his *Autobiography* to inspire others to emulate his habits, and thus his success. In summing up his own work and translating it into a principle for action, Trollope agrees in spirit and rhetoric with Smiles: "I have been constant,—and constancy in labour will conquer all difficulties" (334).

Trollope kept proof of his constancy in the form of work logs. As if recreating the logic of the Civil Service, Trollope tracked his progress in his "second profession" in a diary, measuring not time but work product, or the number of pages written. Rather like Benjamin Franklin's description of the "little Book in which I allotted a Page for each of the Virtues," each ruled with "seven Columns, one for each Day of the Week, marking each Column with a Letter for the Day,"[15] Trollope describes his diary:

> But as I had made up my mind to undertake this second profession, I found it to be expedient to bind myself by certain self-imposed laws. When I have commenced to a new book, I have always prepared a diary, divided into weeks, and carried it on for the period which I have allowed myself for the completion of the work. In this I have entered, day by day, the number of pages I have written, so that if at any time I have slipped into idleness for a day or two, the record of that idleness has been there, staring me in the face, and demanding of me increased labour, so that the deficiency might be supplied. According to the circumstances of the time,—whether my other business might be then heavy or light, or whether the book which I was writing was or was not wanted with speed,—I have allotted myself so many pages a week. The average number has been about 40. It has been placed as low as 20, and has risen to 112. And as a page is an ambiguous term, my page has been made to contain 250 words; and as words, if not watched, will have a tendency to straggle, I have had every word counted as I went . . . and I have never put a book out of hand short of the number by a single word. (108–9)

Trollope's decision to discuss his writing in terms of pages produced and guineas earned—which emphasizes quantity versus aesthetic quality and invites more attention to his work ethic than to his ability or genius—has long fascinated his readers and critics. Robert D. Aguirre has argued that Trollope's "tabulative mentality," which is reminiscent of both Crusoe and Franklin, "demystif[ies] the labor of writing for pay."[16] At the same time, Trollope materializes the writing process, locating intellectual work in the time spent and pages written. He also, importantly, enters into competition with himself. As explored in the introduction and chapter 1, self-help texts similarly elide the competitive playing field, instead focusing on the exceptional individual who, in persevering despite every obstacle, outdoes himself. Likewise narrowing the focus, Trollope worries not about stacking up against other writers, but about keeping up or exceeding what we might think of as his "personal best." If he falls behind in his daily production, "the record of that idleness has been there, staring me in the face, and demanding of me increased labour."

Keeping his pace poses another risk, one that haunts *An Autobiography*: overproduction. In a repeated anecdote that a Freudian analyst would surely make much of, Trollope recounts the story of an author who wrote so much that he "disgusted the publisher in Paternoster Row" (159), "[spawning] upon [him] three novels a year" (100). Although self-help texts insist that more is more— that more industry and work will pay off either in money or at least in a better character—Trollope worries about how authors might undermine their own successes by offering too much of their writing and thus crowding the market. In describing these scenarios, Trollope gestures to a wider literary marketplace, but, rather than considering how he competes with other writers, he focuses on—or projects such worries onto—how he competes with himself.

Trollope readily confesses to being guilty of such "crowding": "I quite admit that I crowded my wares into the market too quickly, because the reading world could not want such a quantity of matter from the hands of one author in so short a space of time. I had not been quite so fertile as the unfortunate gentleman who disgusted the publisher in Paternoster Row . . . but I had probably done enough to make both publishers and readers think that I was coming too often beneath their notice" (158–59). Trollope thus poses another way of understanding the value of literary "wares," imagining that they might work like any other good in the marketplace, gaining value through their brand name or scarcity. Trollope's solution isn't to produce less but simply to give the appearance of doing so by delaying publication. In fact, when he sails for Australia he notes that, if the ship went down, he had "so provided that there would be new novels ready to come out under my name for some years to come. This consideration, however, did not keep me idle while I was at sea" (315). In presenting his work habits, Trollope sets up a paradox: he is driven to maintain (or even out-Trollope) his writerly output, but this means he risks overproducing and driving down the demand for his work.

As if trying to get around this paradox, Trollope also experimented with publishing anonymously.[17] In the *Autobiography*, he imagines this as a "test" of his ability:

> I indeed had never reached a height to which praise was awarded as a matter of
> course; but there were others who sat on higher seats to whom the critics brought
> unmeasured incense and adulation, even when they wrote, as they sometimes

did write, trash which from a beginner would not have been thought worthy of the slightest notice. I hope no one will think that in saying this I am actuated by jealousy of others. Though I never reached that height, still I had so far progressed that that which I wrote was received with too much favour. The injustice which struck me did not consist in that which was withheld from me, but in that which was given to me. I felt that aspirants coming up below me might do work as good as mine, and probably much better work, and yet fail to have it appreciated. In order to test this, I determined to be such an aspirant myself, and to begin a course of novels anonymously, in order that I might see whether I could obtain a second identity,—whether as I had made one mark by such literary ability as I possessed, I might succeed in doing so again. In 1865 I began a short tale called *Nina Balatka* . . . (185–86)

To test the relative justice of the critics' favor, Trollope replays his early career, becoming "an aspirant" testing the literary waters, which requires taking on a "second identity." And this is no mere figure of speech: Trollope set about developing a new style to fit this second writerly persona. He "endeavoured to change not only my manner of language, but my manner of story-telling also . . . English life in [the two stories] there was none. There was more of romance proper than had been usual with me. And I made an attempt at local colouring, at descriptions of scenes and places, which has not been usual with me" (187). The publisher, Blackwood, thought the piece would "not from its style be discovered" (186). But R. H. Hutton of the *Spectator* did find identifying traces of Trollope's style while reviewing the anonymous *Nina Balatka* in 1867—fittingly, Hutton was tipped off by the phrase "making one's way." After producing two works anonymously, Trollope ran into a setback when Blackwood declined a third attempt. But Trollope optimistically adds, in Smilesian spirit, that this failure did not mean that he "might not have succeeded a second time as I succeeded before, had I gone on with the same dogged perseverance. Mr. Blackwood, had I still further reduced my price, would probably have continued the experiment" (187–88).

After all the depictions of Trollope haggling with publishers, this is a strange episode. As Judith Knelman notes, and as Trollope's mention of "reduced" prices suggests, the purpose of this experiment cannot have been financial: "For *The Claverings* Trollope received £2,800; *Nina* and *Linda* brought him only £450 each."[18] Trollope's desire to compete against his own record overcomes his usual desire to get a good price for his work. Even if the anonymous persona was not entirely successful, this episode in Trollope's career and

*Autobiography* intriguingly functions as a way to imagine individuation through comparison. Trollope's distinctive style is set into relief when he tries to imagine a different sort of tale and style—more romance, more far-flung settings, and more interest in description. And this comparison happens first with his own work.

Moving from Trollope's *Autobiography* to his most autobiographical novel, *The Three Clerks*, the difficulties of staging competitions in the realist novel emerge in new form. With its ever-widening cast of characters and plotlines, the Victorian novel necessarily contrasts different perspectives, interrogating itself to ask, "But why always Dorothea?" As if amplifying this concern with small crowds and varying perspectives, Trollope announces three central characters, with *The Three Clerks* uniquely confronting such questions about how to divvy up attention. Whereas the *Autobiography* avoids thinking too much about the larger literary marketplace by focusing on the individual who outdoes himself, *The Three Clerks* reveals how Trollope's narrative strategies encourage readers to put their sympathies in competition across a cast of characters who individuate themselves via comparisons.

## "She Liked Alaric So Much the Better of the Two": Comparing and Competing in *The Three Clerks*

*The Three Clerks*, much like the *Autobiography*, has endured a rocky reception history. Michael Sadleir early on deemed it a "bad novel"; Kincaid dismissed it as "only another false start."[19] And yet, among his early novels, it was Trollope's own favorite, and Elizabeth Barrett Browning considered it the best of his early works, telling Trollope's sister-in-law that she was "wrung to tears by the third volume," and that Robert Browning, "who can seldom get a novel to hold him," had been "held by all three [of Trollope's novels] and by this the strongest."[20] Fortunately, this text has gotten more critical interest recently, as a novel that takes up ideas about careers, bureaucracy, and competitive examinations.[21] This early novel posed important aesthetic questions in Trollope's development as a novelist, between such realistic elements from his own life, and the plot elements that came to underlie the structure of so many of his novels. Trollope builds a central tension into the form of *The Three Clerks*: instead of tracing the trajectory of one or even two characters, Trollope offers us a crowd—three young men "making their way" in the world, frequently at one another's expense. *The Three Clerks* is preoccupied with zero-sum games that suggest parallels across the socioeconomic field (the Civil Service exam), the realm of feeling and sympathy (the marriage plots), and the legal arena (the trial). But while accumulating these common plots, Trollope's narrator undermines the all-or-nothing decisions that these structures demand. Instead, characters reason and feel in gradations—comparing and sympathizing with one another in ways that rarely align with declaring a clear winner and loser. Trollope is self-admittedly an author who favored character over plot;[22] if we imagine plot and character as themselves in competition for Trollope's writerly attention, then *The Three Clerks* suggests the extent to which Trollope's mode of characterization is at odds with the zero-sum game so frequently used to create interest in the Victorian novel.

The most apparent of these zero-sum games is the Civil Service exam that both Alaric and Norman take in hopes of a promotion at work. Trollope was preoccupied with bureaucracy and examinations—concerns that reverberate through and chime with our own moment—and with how institutions (specifically, the Civil Service) could structure their hiring and promotion practices to better attract and reward ambition. Although cut from the first single-volume edition, chapter 12 in volume 2 of *The Three Clerks* is an extended reflection on the problems that plagued the Civil Service: "The Crown had greatly lamented that the aspiring, energetic, and ambitious among British youths do not flock into its Civil Service. As regards the service this is to be lamented; but as regards the British youths, we hardly think that it is ground for grief. Why should they do so? By what hopes actuated should energy and ambition seek the Civil Service? Ambition climbs. What is there in the Civil Service for her to climb to?" (561). Trollope, in both style and argument, is close here to his various other essays on the topic, including two entitled "The Civil Service" (one of which appeared in the *Dublin University Magazine* in 1855, the other in the *Fortnightly Review* in 1865) and "The Civil Service as a Profession" (which appeared in the *Cornhill Magazine* in 1861). Trollope was especially critical of the Northcote-Trevelyan reforms, which aimed to attract more ambitious young men into the Civil Service and to do away with the patronage system. Trollope disagreed with the means by which such ambition should be attracted—particularly the idea of using a competitive entrance exam. He sarcastically observed that "Sir Charles Trevelyan looks forward to alluring the ambitious, the gifted, and the educated, into his service, by a mere proclamation of the difficulty they are to encounter on their entrance."[23] Trollope also had other reservations about the exam system. In the *Autobiography* he confesses, "As what I now write will certainly never be read till I am dead, I may dare to say what no one now does dare to say in print"—"there are places in life which can hardly be well filled except by 'Gentlemen.'" The system of competitive examination implies that "there are no gates, no barrier, no difference" (36). In fact, these gates were kept closely guarded long after Trollope's death: even by the time of the 1968 Fulton Report, the Civil Service exam still rewarded those with an Oxbridge background, while misogyny and racism have meant women and people of color rarely advanced from low-paying positions.[24]

Although Trollope disagreed with Trevelyan about how to attract ambition and, more problematically, about whose ambition should be fulfilled, he agreed that it was a needful thing in the Civil Service. Instead of entrance exams, Trollope proposed a clear hierarchy for promotions: if "men were confident that they could rise in the Civil Service to be secretaries, under-secretaries, and commissioners; that they or their brethren in the Civil Service must so rise; that, by the law of the service, no one else could so rise—I think we may say that a sufficient amount of competency would be found."[25] Admonishing the reformers specifically for their attitudes toward ambition, Trollope hoped that "we may hear no more of the want of ambition on the part of the clerks, till we also hear of the rewards for which ambition is to struggle."[26] I recount these debates here to show that Trollope clearly valued ambition in the Civil Service. The fact that Trollope addressed this need repeatedly, and in the very novel that uses Alaric Tudor's excessive ambition as his tragic flaw, prevents any easy conclusions about ambition's value. It's not that ambition is always dangerous or morally suspect—in fact, Trollope sees ambition as a needful thing in the Civil Service as in the novel—but that excessive ambition can go awry without sufficient structure and outlets.[27]

Trollope was more amenable to the idea of using competitive exams when it came to promotions. But here, too, he had reservations. He was particularly concerned about the quandary over how to weigh ability versus time in service: "Shall the promotion be given to the most worthy man, or to the first man who is worthy?"[28] In *The Three Clerks*, this question is dramatized by asking what should happen when many worthy candidates apply for a single promotion. As Cathy Shuman has observed, this exam "sets up trajectories, pits protagonists against each other, and invites comparison," all "important structural devices for the multiplot novel."[29] Trollope uses these structural devices, but he simultaneously questions the logic behind such zero-sum games by showing where this logic comes into conflict with our more diffusive readerly sympathies. Both Alaric and Harry are worthy candidates for the promotion, but there is only one promotion. As Charley hopefully if illogically concludes, "Well, lads, I hope you'll both win" (124).

These exams and competitions individuate the characters, who, when stacked up in comparison with one another, emerge as "winners" and "losers" (and as better or worse at winning or losing with grace). But these sorts of competitions start at a much smaller scale. I'm thinking, for example, of the way that Trollope's narrators and characters compare different qualities and behaviors. In distinction to the plot's competitions, there is more room for nuance here—for the "more or less" thinking that distinguishes between shades of qualities. When the narrator introduces Alaric Tudor and Harry Norman in the first chapters, he individuates them not by essential characteristics but by their comparative embodiment of them. As a result, Alaric and Harry already seem to be in a competition for our readerly attention—as if suggesting that from the titular three clerks, a single protagonist must emerge:

> Alaric Tudor when he entered the office was by no means *so handsome* a youth as Harry Norman; but yet there was that in his face which was *more* expressive, and perhaps *more* attractive. He was a much *slighter* man, though *equally* tall. He could boast no adventitious capillary graces, *whereas* young Norman had a pair of black curling whiskers, which almost surrounded his face, and had been the delight and wonder of the maidservants ... Tudor was perhaps *not superior to* Norman in point of intellect; but he was *infinitely his superior* in having early acquired a knowledge how best to use such intellect as he had. (emphasis mine, 7–8)

The passage above emphasizes the extent to which Trollope's descriptions in *The Three Clerks* rely upon comparative language (italicized). The narrator's language is overridden with "more"s and "superior"s, as if neither character is distinctive enough to describe on his own terms, but only in comparison to others. The comparisons extend beyond what is easily tracked by a simple word search for terms like "more" or "less." And subtler still, Trollope relies on parallel structures that suggest rather than announce a comparison.

In tracking such comparisons, we might also consider the amount of description each character comes in for. Taking the above passage, Norman's whiskers get so much attention from both the maidservants and the narrator that they (and their bearer) become the new subject. The third clerk, Charley, enters the novel later, but also by way of comparisons: Charley is "some few years younger than his cousin Alaric," and although his examination at the Internal Navigation "was certainly not to be so much dreaded as that at the Weights and Measures ... Charley, who had not been the most diligent of schoolboys, approached it with great dread" (12). By introducing these characters in relation to one another (and, briefly, to the "schoolboys" in the backstory), Trollope's narrator avoids assigning too many absolute characteristics, instead differentiating the three clerks by their degree of intelligence or attractiveness as compared to others.

Much like a group of self-help characters—or like variations on Trollope himself—the three clerks, without substantial inheritances to fall back on, must all make their own way in the world. As we learn in their introductions, however, it is clear that the young men start with varying degrees of ambition. Alaric is ambitious from the beginning, while Harry is "steady, sober, and discreet" (273) rather than overreaching, even dropping out of the exam when he decides it is more important to Alaric than to him. In contrast, Charley starts as a young ne'er-do-well—the sort of "hobbledehoy" that appears over and over as a type in Trollope's fiction. While Harry, true to form, remains steady throughout the novel, Charley and Alaric are nudged and disciplined into changing. Charley finds his ambition through his love for the youngest Woodward sister and (rather miraculously) becomes a successful author. The ambitious Alaric emerges as the focal point for the drive's dangers, rising through ability and promotion, risking money in the stock market, and eventually being exiled to Australia after making bad investments with his ward's fortune.

It is the ambitious Alaric who takes "Excelsior" or "Ever Higher" as his motto when he considers his career: "That is £1,200 a year. So far, so good. And now what must be the next step? Excelsior! It is very nice to be a Commissioner, and sit at a Board at Sir Gregory's right hand: *much nicer than* being a junior clerk at the Weights and Measures, like Harry Norman. But there are *nicer* things even than that; there are *greater* men even than Sir Gregory; *richer* figures than even £1,200 a year!" (327, emphasis mine). Alaric reveals how ambition is rooted in making comparisons between one's current state and a hypothetical future state. By looking up toward the next rung of the ladder and imagining further promotions, Alaric follows Nicholas Dames's examples of careerism in Trollope.[30] But unlike many of Dames's examples, Alaric is willing to cheat the system; in fact, Alaric is the counterexample to the sort of "domestication" that the career path is supposed to provide in Dames's analysis. In the following passage we see Alaric jumping onto an entirely different career ladder, as well as an entirely different set of metaphorical associations: "If the sportsman returned from the field laden with game, who would scrutinize the mud on his gaiters? 'Excelsior!' said Alaric to himself with a proud ambition; and so he attempted to rise by the purchase and sale of mining shares" (169). As the most ambitious clerk, Alaric reveals that ambition is not so easily domesticated and limited to a single career trajectory. In fact, in Alaric's character Trollope demonstrates that ambition risks overflowing its outlets, whether in the structure of a career or a novel.

Trollope uses the same comparative language to introduce the three sisters who will eventually become the wives of the three clerks, implicitly drawing parallels across the career and marriage plots. The two older sisters are

> *both* pretty—but Gertrude, the *elder*, was *by far the more strikingly so*. They were, nevertheless, *much alike*; they *both* had rich brown hair, which they, *like* their mother, wore simply parted over the forehead. They were *both* somewhat *taller* than her, and were *nearly of a* height. But in appearance, as in disposition, Gertrude carried by far *the greater air of command*. She was the *handsomer* of the two, and the *cleverer*. She could write French and nearly speak it, *while* her sister could only read it. She could play difficult pieces from sight, which it took her sister a morning's pain to practise. She could fill in and finish a drawing, *while* her sister was still struggling, and struggling in vain, with the first principles of the art.
>
> But there was a softness about Linda, for such was the name of the second Miss Woodward, which in the eyes of many men made up both for the *superior* beauty and *superior* talent of Gertrude. Gertrude was, perhaps, *hardly so* soft as so young a girl should be. In her had been magnified that spirit of gentle rail-lery which made so attractive a part of her mother's character. She enjoyed and *emulated* her mother's quick sharp sayings, but she *hardly did so with her mother's grace*, and sometimes attempted it with *much more than* her mother's severity. (23–24, emphasis mine)

Trollope's narrator introduces Surbiton Cottage's eligible women by insisting that we imagine them against one another. But even as these descriptions stage various competitions, they ultimately trouble any easy overall assessment of which sister is the "best." We may think that Gertrude has the greater abilities and therefore is the most eligible sister, but then we learn that she lacks Linda's softness, and that her wit is not accompanied by her mother's grace. (Although Gertrude in fact emerges as both her mother's and her uncle's favorite, and the one sought by both Harry and Alaric.) The third sister, Katie, is introduced much as Charley is—almost as an afterthought. Of Katie, "it is not necessary at present to say much . . . She gave fair promise to be at any rate equal to her sisters in beauty, and in mind was quick and intelligent" (24). As their introductory passages suggest, the three clerks and the three sisters will find themselves competing with one another throughout the novel, taking and waiting for turns as the novel's subject.

This pattern of competing for narrative space aligns with Alex Woloch's argument in *The One vs the Many*. I'm thinking particularly of Woloch's description of "characters who jostle for limited space within the same fictive universe" and how such jostling works in a novel that features "dual (and sometimes dueling) protagonists."[31] Rather than one or even two potential protagonists fighting a mob of minor characters, *The Three Clerks* insists on balancing a triad of protagonists—or, if one counts the Woodward sisters, a sextet. Trollope's novel also explicitly materializes these competitions, which are not only about defining a protagonist against a background of minor characters, but also about which characters will in fact take the "prizes" and rise on the socioeconomic ladder. In the process, Trollope also questions assumptions about how competition works—about how these characters can emerge as distinct individuals through the narrative's and the fictional society's competitions. Trollope sets up a materially limited playing field, populates it with characters who keep getting in one another's way, and invites readers to sympathize while implying through that very sympathy a problem with the playing field's "rules."

Although the novel announces its interest in threes, it has trouble accommodating this many competitors. Instead, the narrative repeatedly tightens its focus on a pair of rivals. The first volume takes up the two older clerks and the two older sisters. As lovers, Alaric is perhaps "a little bolder than his friend [Harry], and a little less romantic." Harry finds Gertrude prettier, while Alaric claims Linda is "by far the prettier of the two" (28). Meanwhile, Linda decides that, although "Harry was the handsomer and the richer, she liked Alaric so much the better of the two" (53). In a decision that will greatly complicate the marriage plots, the two older sisters end up agreeing about Alaric being the better match: Gertrude refuses Harry's proposal of marriage, and accepts Alaric's—who, it seems, has decided she is the prettier sister after all. (Presumably, it doesn't hurt that their uncle has recently decided to settle his savings on Gertrude.) This plot twist is concurrent with Harry and Alaric competing for the same promotion by examination; both the marriage and the career plot resolve in Alaric's favor.

Significantly, it is in the chapter describing Gertrude's marriage that the youngest, Katie, suddenly becomes a full-fledged individual (i.e., she reaches a marriageable age). The narrator draws attention to this, noting, "Her story has yet to be told. To her belongs neither the soft easiness of her sister Linda nor the sterner dignity of Gertrude. But she has a character of her own, which contains, perhaps, higher qualities than those given to either of her sisters"

(176). It is only when Gertrude's marriage plot is resolved that Katie's can begin. And then Linda and *Katie* can bicker over who is the more eligible young man, with Katie claiming she is "quite sure that Charley is much the cleverer," and Linda defending Harry, as she is also "quite sure" Charley is neither "half so clever; nor nearly so well educated" (270). The young people's affections take shape via such comparisons, as if a love interest comes into relief only when set beside someone else.

Given how relentlessly these characters compare one another, it is not surprising that they also imagine how they themselves stack up in competition. For example, Linda realizes that Gertrude is "entitled" to more in her marriage plot, and she assumes that Gertrude therefore deserves Harry Norman's slightly higher status. Yet Linda is not envious; she does not "begrudge Gertrude Norman's superior beauty, nor his greater wealth; she knew that Gertrude was entitled to more, much more, than herself"(53). (In the process, Linda presumably picks up more of a share of the reader's sympathy, as a self-deprecating underdog.) Harry, too, is aware of how he compares to Alaric: at the prospect of their imminent competition against one another for the promotion, Harry confesses that he knows Alaric is better suited—"I know your superiority to myself." Alaric apparently agrees, turning an evaluative eye on himself: "He was made of a more plastic clay than they, and despite the inferiority of his education, he knew himself to be fit for higher work than they could do" (76). When we compare ourselves with another, it involves a different affective negotiation than when we compare two other subjects. In comparing the self with others, one is liable to feel pride or envy. And this gives rise to yet another type of comparison: how these underdog characters handle their losses. Linda comes out on top in this respect when she manages to forgive her sister. The narrator laments, "Oh! what a lesson [Harry] might have learnt from Linda! And yet what were his injuries to hers?" (165).

Although I have concentrated on the three main couples thus far, the minor characters are also differentiated via systems of comparison. These characters are similarly introduced as if they were entering a competition. When Alaric and Gertrude marry and set up house in London, new friends appear, including Clementina, whose fortune Alaric will eventually embezzle. Clementina is introduced with her friends the Neverbends: "And yet the Misses Neverbend were quite as estimable as the divine Clementina, and had once been, perhaps, as attractive as she is now. They had never waltzed, it is true, as Miss Golightly waltzes." After comparing the sisters, in their present and past state, as a unit to Clementina, the narrator then proceeds to disambiguate them, finally using their rather unfortunate first names: "The two sisters were as unlike in their inward lights as in their outward appearance. Lactimel walked ever on the earth, but Ugolina never deserted the clouds. Lactimel talked prose and professed to read it; Ugolina read poetry and professed to write it" (286). Such passages exemplify how Trollope's comparative language develops in this novel, relying not only on easily spotted terms like "more" and "less," but also on subtler syntax.

This sort of parallelism is a marker of Trollope's style. Hugh Sykes Davies has described Trollope's parallelisms as "not unlike that found in the heroic couplet of the Augustans, less compressed, less witty, but with the same power to make words modify one another by being held in a pattern of contrast."[32] I would suggest that this style, so associated with Trollope's writing across his career, is inextricably linked to comparisons, specifically comparisons involving two terms. Davies comes close to the same conclusion in his brief but illuminating analysis. In his argument, what he terms Trollope's "cadence" relies on the words "and" and "but" to explore "the relation between principles and practice": these conjunctions are "used to establish an antithesis between two very closely related phrases, and the repetition of words and phrases is nearly as characteristic an aspect of this special cadence as the conjunction itself."[33] Whereas we might infinitely add "and" to a sentence, the use of "but" implies a pivot that requires and is limited to two clauses. John W. Clark, in his extensive work on Trollope's language, has likewise noticed this use of conjunctions: "In passages of 'internal debate,' balanced sentences, and pairs of sentences balancing each other, the clauses or sentences being joined by adversative conjunctions, are noticeably common." Clark implicitly addresses the importance of two terms ("pairs of sentences"), even if he does not pursue this line of inquiry.[34] By holding up two characters or qualities for comparison, Trollope reveals an interest in these linguistic and mental balancing acts—how to distinguish similarities and differences on a small scale.

Such comparisons structure Charley's marriage plot, which is unique among those of the three clerks for its involvement of choices outside of the Woodward household. Charley has a long-standing flirtation with a barmaid, Norah Geraghty, and he has been encouraged by Alaric to pursue Clementina and her fortune. Of course, as so often happens in Trollope's novels, we do not feel much risk from these minor rivals—reminiscent of Trollope's suspense-killing reassurance in *Barchester Towers* that Elinor Bold will *not* marry Mr. Slope. Instead, these outside options seem to be doing something else.

This makes sense in terms of the novel's formal logic: as the older sisters marry, Katie needs some competition so she can be individuated and emerge as the clear choice. For example, both Katie's qualities and Trollope's "comparative style" emerge across these paragraphs weighing Charley's options: "Norah Geraghty was a fine girl. Putting her in comparison with Miss Golightly, we are inclined to say that she was the finer girl of the two; and that, barring position, money, and fashion, she was qualified to make the better wife." After comparing their educations, the narrator sums up: "Neither of them had ever read anything beyond a few novels. In this respect, as to the amount of labour done, Miss Golightly had certainly far surpassed her rival competitor for Charley's affections." But then, as Charley approaches Norah, he compares her not to Miss Golightly but to Katie with her "young lustrous eyes" (226). This pattern reflects a comparative process that recurs across Trollope's marriage plots: in choosing among three options, the narrator and characters tend first to compare A and B, then B and C, before settling on a decision. Examining this comparative style reveals the extent to which Trollope's classic vacillation plot depends on an underlying structure of comparisons, particularly on comparisons structured by pairs at the level of the sentence as well as of the plot.

Critics have long identified Trollope's novelistic structures with vacillation and decision making. In her work on emotions and the stock market in Trollope, Audrey Jaffe analyzes how characters "waver" in the process of making decisions. She observes that, in *The Prime Minister*, "Wharton's thoughts display not the unwavering certainty of the clear moral line but rather the jittery peaks and valleys of the stock-market graph." In particular, Wharton's reaction to Ferdinand Lopez "takes shape as a mental wavering" as the narrator traces "the fluctuating movements of characters' thoughts as they wend their way from one side of a question to the other," giving "narrative form and identity to those peaks and valleys."[35] I want to point here to both Trollope's language and the language critics use to describe it: these expressions—for example, "waver" and "wend their way from one side of a question to the other"—suggest that characters are choosing between two options.

To sum up the argument so far: Trollope differentiates and stages competitions between his characters beginning at the scale of sentence-level comparisons; by layering comparisons these competitions gradually build, across much wavering, into decisions and into individualized characters with clear preferences. We have seen how Trollope's comparative language works at the level of sentences and the level of paragraphs, and how Trollope and his characters default to comparing two terms at once. These patterns become even clearer if we turn to the larger structures of the novel. Trollope's narrator initiates a structural comparison when he draws parallels across the marriage plots. For example, when Katie initially rejects Charley for being too unsteady, we learn that he "walked up to town, as Norman once had done after a parting interview with her whom he had loved. It might be difficult to say which at the moment suffered the bitterest grief" (502). Such passages insist that we compare characters not only in a particular moment, but also across the plots of the novel.

Such longer- and wider-flung comparisons also emerge across the characters' aspirations and their actions. A key term in *The Three Clerks* is "excelsior," which is repeated thirty-five times by the narrator and characters alike. Although it is most frequently invoked by Alaric's character, Charley also adopts it, and the narrator uses it to contrast the various characters' more or less worthy desires. For example, at the "same moment" that Charley is thinking the word, Alaric is exulting in having written his resignation in order to pursue something better (327). When the eligible young Clementina thinks, "How delightful to have such a dancer for her lover!" the narrator sarcastically notes, "That was her 'Excelsior'" (318). Similarly, as much as Charley aspires to marry Katie, the young barmaid Norah looks up to him: "She also had her high aspirations; she desired to rise in the world, to leave goes of gin and screws of tobacco behind her, and to reach some position more worthy of the tastes of a woman. 'Excelsior,' translated doubtless into excellent Irish, was her motto also" (319). We also learn that "Mrs. Val had her ideas of 'Excelsior,' her ambition to rule, and these ideas and this ambition did not at all suit Gertrude's temper" (400). Trollope juxtaposes the desires that drive these various competitions and power dynamics, while illustrating how these "high" ambitions (i.e., aspirations that look strictly upward) actually involve getting around others (i.e., maneuvering or cutting around side references) in a competitive system.

This insistence that we compare characters' ambitions across the plots is strongest in the final chapters, when the fallen Alaric and Gertrude take their small family to Australia. Trollope's narrator zooms out to compare the fates of the elder two couples: "How different were their lots now! Harry was Mr. Norman of Normansgrove, immediately about to take his place as the squire of his parish . . . Gertrude was the wife of a convicted felon, who was about to come forth from his prison in utter poverty, a man who, in such a catalogue as the world makes of its inhabitants, would be ranked among the very lowest" (508). With these comparisons, Trollope draws attention to the endpoints of the plots, and particularly to how the characters have won or lost the novel's competitions: we are reminded that, while some characters have risen, others have fallen. Mrs. Woodward's earlier analogy of the competitive fishpond has apparently been borne out by the workings of the novel's structure. It also suggests that the plot's competitions have drawn out characters' true colors—who deserves to live comfortably ever after and who deserves to be sent packing to redeem themselves in exile.

There is a tension here between whether characters in fact "deserve" to win or lose or whether the plot, structured as a limited system, has forced characters into these roles. Amplifying the sense that the novel's structure is the problem—in having offered too limited a playing field—the narrative has trouble accommodating more than one or two plotlines at a time. Alaric's plot often threatens to take over entirely. For example, when Alaric's investments fail and he is put on trial for embezzlement, his story puts a hold on those of the other clerks. Harry and Linda postpone their marriage until after the trial, and we don't hear about Charley's progress until afterward. As it turns out, the disgraced Alaric leaves a gap in the Civil Service—well timed for Charley's own rise. Ruth apRoberts wryly notes that Trollope is "naively faithful to chronological order—if he does give us a flashback it seems to be because there is something he forgot to tell."[36] But this example of Charley's suspended plot, which appears in discourse time only after it has taken place in story time, demonstrates that in some cases Trollope might not forget something but rather finds that his plot structure cannot accommodate his characters. From this view, it is not only the trial that makes it impossible for Alaric to stay in England; Trollope needs to exile him in order to give due attention to Harry's and Charley's marriages and promotions. Although the novel is ostensibly about *three* clerks, then, both Trollope's language and narrative can more easily accommodate two subjects than three. Marriage plots boil down to two rivals, and the exam is not really about the entire office but only Alaric and Harry. In Trollope's novels, as much as these competitions are suggestive of a crowd of rivals—like Mrs. Woodward's fishpond—they must be narrated as occurring between two characters.

We can see this tendency across Trollope's work, and particularly across his marriage plots. Even when they announce otherwise, these plots tend to simplify themselves into systems of two rivals. For example, when Violet Effingham has a chapter devoted to her *four* suitors in *Phineas Finn*, we know that only Phineas and Lord Chiltern stand a chance—Violet immediately dismisses the idea of marrying Lord Fawn or Mr. Appledom. And indeed, it is Finn and Chiltern who travel abroad and fight a duel over the lady in question (the duel again exemplifying how certain forms can accommodate only two competitors).

Similarly, Lizzie in *The Eustace Diamonds* is presented as having a group of suitors, but they take turns competing—Lord Fawn and Frank Greystock begin as rivals, Lord Fawn exits the competition, and then Joseph Emilius enters. Most of Trollope's marriage plots, however, do not even pretend to more than two options. The typical form—the basis of his classic vacillation plot— is two options that emerge in stark opposition: Frank Greystock must choose between Lizzie Eustace and Lucy Morris; the eponymous *Lady Anna* must choose between her childhood sweetheart, the tailor's son Daniel Thwaite, and her cousin, the young Earl Lovel; Adolphus Crosbie jilts Lily Dale for Lady Alexandrina de Courcy in *The Small House at Allington*; in *Framley Parsonage*, Lord Lufton decides against Griselda Grantley and marries Lucy Roberts; and, as if amplifying this common device, in *Can You Forgive Her?* Alice Vavasor jilts both the "wild man" George Vavasor and the "worthy man" John Grey, while Glencora Palliser dithers over whether to stay with her steady husband, Plantagenet, or to run away with her former flame, Burgo Fitzgerald.

Isolating Trollope's comparative style, which is so dependent upon comparing two characters or options, resolves an implicit paradox in Trollope's writing. Trollope's style is famously described as mirrorlike or transparent, beginning with Nathaniel Hawthorne's praise of the novels as "just as real as if some giant had hewn a great lump out of the earth and put it under a glass case, with all its inhabitants going about their daily business" (*Autobiography* 133). Kincaid writes that Trollope "achieves his effects very largely through a uniform and plain style . . . The style is so unmetaphoric that the very rare bursts . . . are very startling . . . This deceptively plain language can be used to make the most intricate artistic maneuverings unobtrusive."[37] Many of these "intricate artistic maneuverings" are in service of representing a character's psychological state. Such intricacy serves to test and formulate morality in his novels. As apRoberts has theorized, Trollope's ethical judgments are made not through general principles but through the messiness of unique situations. As she concludes, this is a writer who is "everywhere a complicator."[38]

These two assessments of Trollope—as both "plain" in style and a "complicator" in content—ultimately pull in the same direction. Trollope's style feels particularly plain when we notice how rarely he invokes figurative language that compares unlike things. Critics going back to David Aitken have observed that "the largest number of [Trollope's] similes and metaphors are not expressions of original imaginative perceptions at all, but are drawn straight from the stock of conventional figures of speech preserved in our language in clichés and familiar quotations."[39] In fact, as apRoberts adds, Trollope's images barely register as such because they are so commonplace—"the world is one's oyster, the beautiful woman is the candle to the moth, people row in the same boat, and so on."[40] Instead, he compares more or less similar characters and situations, presenting small differences in simple language and sentence structures. Trollope draws explicit, even plain, parallels to compare his characters' decisions—and to complicate our readerly sympathies. Despite the seemingly paradoxical terms, then, Trollope complicates by simplifying and comparing two rather similar things, teasing out their subtle differences.

Trollope develops a "comparative language" and logic in *The Three Clerks* that structures not only the novel's narrative discourse and plot but also larger formal and ethical patterns across Trollope's writing. Although his plots rely on zero-sum games—which decide between winners and losers, innocent and guilty characters—Trollope reveals the "more or less" thinking that informs the broader sympathies of his characters and narrators, who realize that the subjects being compared are not in fact starkly different but often simply variations on a theme. When Harry drops out of the competitive exam and Alaric wins the promotion, the youthful Katie asks, "Why were there not two prizes?" (138). Her Uncle Cuttwater likewise expresses his sympathies, telling the young men that he is "sorry you couldn't all win" (139). Here, the naïve question and the trite platitude express a fundamental tension between the needs of the plot and the sympathetic desires of the characters. The plot's interest depends on the suspense generated by a limited system, even as Katie and Cuttwater express their sympathy by imagining a material world that could multiply its prizes (or spaces in the fishpond) to accommodate all the competitors. In moving toward a conclusion, I want to draw out this tension by turning to Trollope's most metafictional comparison in *The Three Clerks*— between the dictates of the trial system and the sympathetic, "more or less" thinking of his characters. I suggest we read this as a comparison between the dictates of the plot and the sympathies of the characters and reader.

Throughout Alaric's trial, his lawyer, Chaffanbrass, makes every effort to paint Alaric sympathetically even while admitting his guilt. His strategy is risky: he must admit that Alaric *is* guilty of embezzling Clementina's fortune, but that he is *less* guilty of this crime than his associate Undy Scott. In the following passage, the judge warns the jury that it will be difficult to deliver a judgment of "guilty" or "not guilty" when the trial has concentrated, thus far, on relative guilt:

> An endeavour has been made to affix a deep stigma on one of the witnesses who has been examined before you; and to induce you to feel, rather than to think,

that Mr. Tudor is, at any rate, comparatively innocent—innocent as compared with that gentleman. That is not the issue which you are called on to decide; not whether Mr. Scott, for purposes of his own, led Mr. Tudor on to guilt, and then turned against him; but whether Mr. Tudor himself has, or has not, been guilty under this Act of Parliament that has been explained to you. (487)

The judge emphasizes the discrepancy between judging Alaric Tudor in comparison with Undy Scott and judging Alaric Tudor in comparison with the Act of Parliament. Next to Undy, Alaric is "comparatively innocent—innocent as compared with that gentleman," but according to the law, Alaric is guilty. And the judge further compares these types of judgments (relative or absolute) by opposing them: he associates the first with feeling and the second with thinking. This opposition of course finds echoes in Victorian systems of judgment and morality—particularly in the differences between an intuitive morality and a principle-based system. What I want to concentrate on here is the strange way in which, despite the judge's warning, the jury insists upon ruling by comparative guilt. The jury ultimately finds Alaric "guilty" on one count, but "not guilty" on four others. Further hedging their judgment and again asserting the necessity of understanding Alaric in comparison to Undy, they appeal to the judge: "We beg, however, most strongly to commend the prisoner to your lordship's merciful consideration, believing that he has been led into this crime by one who has been much more guilty than himself" (491).

The strategies of the trial and of the novel's plot are put into tension in this scene. The judge asks that we see only a defendant and prosecutor in competition and hold the defendant to the letter of the law. But the narrator and Chaffanbrass ask that we also understand Alaric's guilt in relation to Undy's. We might analogize the trial to the form of Trollope's novel, and the comparative thinking of the jury to Trollope's mode of characterization. Trollope critiques the plot devices so common to the Victorian novel by showing how they are implicitly or explicitly at odds with his understanding of character. At the same time, these are the very devices he uses to individuate his characters.

## "Competition between Two Such Dear Friends": Trollope versus Dickens

*The Three Clerks* is the first novel that Trollope was able to sell outright. In the *Autobiography* Trollope describes how he first tried to sell it to Longman, who offered only half profits. Undaunted, Trollope then offered his manuscript to Bentley, "and on the same afternoon succeeded in selling it to him for £250"

(100–101). In Trollope's eyes, *The Three Clerks* marked a turning point in his writing career: from signing away half the profits of his novels in exchange for the risk the publisher would run to seeing his novels as a sure investment, worthy of the "lump sum" that Trollope found "more pleasant than a deferred annuity" (*Autobiography* 99).

I recount the publishing background of this novel to emphasize Trollope's position as an "aspirant" making his way in the literary marketplace. It's useful to situate Trollope in that marketplace that he rather avoids thinking about in his *Autobiography*: When *The Three Clerks* was published in 1857, it entered a field crowded by Thackeray, who was between *The Newcomes* and *The Virginians*, and Dickens, whose *Little Dorrit* concluded its serialized run in June of the same year. Given Trollope's position as an emerging name, it is all the more intriguing that he invokes Dickens repeatedly in *The Three Clerks*. In fact, this pattern begins on the first page, as Trollope compares his branch of the Civil Service, the Weights and Measures, to Dickens's Circumlocution Office: "It may be said to stand quite alone as a high model for all other public offices whatever. It is exactly antipodistic of the Circumlocution Office" (1). Trollope not only compares the Weights and Measures (immediately suggestive of calibrations) to Dickens's office; he also compares himself as a writer in relation to Dickens. And as we have seen in the earlier sections of this chapter, such comparisons invite competitions that individuate the players—as competitions tend to demand teasing out differences versus admitting similarities.

Fittingly, Trollope includes the highest concentration of Dickens references when Charley makes his foray into the literary marketplace. Charley's interpolated story includes some familiar characters: the heroine's dresses "were made at the distinguished establishment of Madame Mantalini in Hanover Square" (246), while the nurse attending her lying-in is Mrs. Gamp (266). At the end of *The Three Clerks*, Trollope alludes to Bill Sykes, as he compares "Poor Bill" to his own villain, Undy Scott. And in the final chapter, Trollope drops in a Wellerism, as Charley uses a similar turn of phrase—"it's good fun to you, I dare say, as the fly said to the spider" (549). Trollope sprinkles such cameos throughout his text, and sometimes seems to show off how faithfully he can "do" Dickens. He gives Mrs. Gamp her favorite drink (gin), keeps her water hot, and even reproduces her speech patterns—"It's just half-past heleven, this wery moment as is . . . and the finest boy babby as my heyes, which has seen a many, has ever sat upon" (267). As Trollope pulls characters and references from *Oliver Twist, Nicholas Nickleby, Martin Chuzzlewit*, and Dickens's latest, *Little Dorrit*, he implicitly sets up his competition with the Inimitable.

Not surprisingly, then, critics have drawn parallels between this novel and Dickens, even when they have not explicitly noted how Trollope invokes him. Sadleir writes that the novel is "undoubtedly" "derivative—in ultimate resort from Dickens, nearer at hand from such a Dickens imitator as Frank Smedly."[41] Bareham calls *The Three Clerks* "Dickensian" for its "use of symbolism to ramify message."[42] And Kincaid observes that this novel is unique in being "a really brilliant tale," "as if Trollope had tried his hand at becoming a disciple of Dickens and then withdrew."[43] I find Jerome K. Meckier's analysis most convincing, however, as he reads *The Three Clerks* less as an imitation or homage and more as a challenge: noting many of the Dickensian allusions, Meckier reads both *The Three Clerks* and *Rachel Ray* as challenges to "Dickens as a social realist"—particularly to *Oliver Twist*'s version of villainy, which Meckier suggests Trollope finds "passé."[44] In support of Meckier's claim, Undy is a unique character across Trollope's oeuvre. Critics have long argued that Trollope does not usually give us true villains. As Walter Kendrick observes, Trollope seldom even uses the word "villain"[45]—and even when he does, he tends to sympathize with such characters. As Sadleir notes, "There is hardly a sinner in his books who is not in some way also a claimant on our sympathy."[46] And as Polhemus argues, "We find fewer cheap moral victories over 'wicked' characters than we find in any other Victorian novelist."[47] To illustrate this tendency, one has only to think of Trevelyan in *He Knew He Was Right*: although he terrorizes his wife and family with his jealousy, Trevelyan is supposed to be a sympathetic character. In fact, Trollope considered this character a failure because he could not make him sympathetic *enough*.[48] Unlike Dickens, Trollope is most interested in holding up characters who are more or less similar, more or less sympathetic. The incorrigible Undy thus makes more sense in the context of Trollope's work if we understand him as a challenge to Dickens.

After Alaric's trial, and after comparing Alaric's to Undy's guilt, Trollope's narrator introduces a new sort of competitive trial. He extends his examination of villainy beyond the pages of his novel, comparing Undy to these *other* fictional villains: "I have ventured to introduce to my readers, as my devil, Mr. Undy Scott, M.P. for the Tillietudlem district burghs; and I also feel myself bound to dispose of him, though of him I regret I cannot make so decent an end as was done with Sir Richard Varney and Bill Sykes" (516). Trollope here sets Undy Scott next to Sir Walter Scott's villain from *Kenilworth* and Dickens's villain from *Oliver Twist*. He compares these characters' fictional deserts and finds his own villain's punishment lacking—he cannot "make so decent an end." As this comparison proceeds, Varney quickly drops out because, as the narrator notes, he lived in a different time. Narrowing in on Bill and Undy, the narrator decides that "Bill could not boast the merit of selecting the course which he had run . . . he was born and bred and educated an evil-doer." In contrast, Undy has freely chosen his course and thus deserves "a warmer reward" (516–17). After running these comparisons, the narrator decides he would hang Bill Sykes with "soft regret" but Undy "with what a savage joy, with what exultation of heart." However, neither the hand of the law nor the hand of the author can touch Undy—and so the narrator concludes with the rather anticlimactic "if I could but get at his throat for such a purpose!" (518).

This is rather a startling moment in the grand tradition of Trollope's narrators breaking the fourth wall. Henry James accused Trollope of taking "a suicidal satisfaction in reminding the reader that the story he was telling was only, after all, a make-believe . . . [He] was fond of letting the reader know that this novelist could direct the course of events according to his pleasure."[49] And yet here, instead of reminding his readers that he is in control of the plot, the narrator admits that he would like to hang Undy but cannot. Instead, Undy takes himself off to wander the Continent and gambling tables—"to Hamburg perhaps, or to Ems, or the richer tables of Homburg" (522)—before sinking into obscurity, in an echo of Becky Sharp's fate. Trollope's narrator feels the injustice of this and takes a card from the novel's jury when he pleads in Bill's favor: "And yet poor Bill Sykes, for whom here I would willingly say a word or two, could I, by so saying, mitigate the wrath against him, is always held as the more detestable scoundrel . . . Poor Bill! I have a sort of love for him, as he walks about wretched with that dog of his, though I know that it is necessary to hang him" (517). Trollope repeats with Bill and Undy the comparison we see earlier with Alaric and Undy, which, by exaggerating a greater guilt, allows a character to remain sympathetic.

Undy Scott's character is one of the elements in *The Three Clerks* that shows Trollope's indebtedness not only to his competition with Dickens but also to the fairy tale and to realism, a duality that starts in the title: "three" is suggestive of fairytales, while "clerks" lands us squarely in Victorian London. As Shuman has observed, the novel's "almost ritualistic predictability makes good on its title's promise of a fairytale formula: three city clerks match up with three country sisters in three plots structured by testing and temptation. As is usual in such tales, the youngest and least promising protagonist gains the most sympathy and the most significant success, marrying the youngest, sweetest, and prettiest sister."[50] But this novel, in the process of Trollope individuating his style against that of other established authors like Dickens, does not work primarily in terms of "prettiest" and "sweetest" but rather in terms of "prettier" and "sweeter"—the middling comparisons of realism. The plot is more closely structured around a Goldilocks principle: Alaric has too much ambition, Harry perhaps a tad too little, and Charley just enough.

What I hope to suggest here is that Trollope is interested in comparing the excesses of fairy tales with the "averages" of the realist novel. It's telling that, in his later novels, Trollope doesn't return to extreme villains like Undy—perhaps aligning with his commitment to holding up realistic characters that could more easily serve as examples (whether good or bad) for readers. By leveling the playing field and exploring more or less average characters, Trollope generates a different sort of competitive, comparative logic. As Schoeck argues, it is social proximity that gives rise to envy, which is "usually directed only towards persons with whom it has been possible to compete."[51] Noticing small distinctions among one's peers gives rise to envy, whereas, to take one of Schoeck's favorite examples, a commoner isn't likely to have reason to compare themselves to a king (or, updated to our own moment, the middle class is more likely to compare themselves to the Joneses than to the top 1 percent who live in exclusive, cordoned-off communities). In short, we seem more liable to make comparisons—and to imagine competitions—in exactly those situations where the differences weighed are, in the end, rather insignificant— even as competitions tend to demand significantly different outcomes for winners and losers. It is these differences that preoccupy Trollope. As Henry James early noted, "Trollope's heroines have a strong family likeness, but it is a wonder how finely he discriminates between them."[52] What starts as an insult (all of Trollope's heroines are similar) resolves in commendation—coming from James, to "finely" discriminate sounds like high praise. Trollope is at his most convincing when he directs his attention to what is distinctive about his characters' very similarities, their very ordinariness.

The risk of this similarity, of course, is that characters do not stand out in marked ways and are therefore less memorable. As Polhemus has observed, "Few of Trollope's people can stand out of context like a Don Quixote or a Mrs. Gamp."[53] Even Trollope himself had trouble remembering his characters sometimes. In discussing *Ralph the Heir* in his *Autobiography*, Trollope compares the "life" of his characters: "Ralph the heir has not much life about him; while Ralph who is not the heir, but is intended to be the real hero, has none. The same may be said of the young ladies,—of whom one, she who was meant to be the chief, has passed utterly out of my mind, without leaving a trace of remembrance behind" (313). I quote this not only for its comedy, but also for how Trollope's memories here use the sort of comparative language I have examined in this chapter. One Ralph has "not much life," while the hero "has none"; of the young ladies, the "chief" is completely forgotten. It is worth noting that here the excesses—the closest things these novels get to a fairy tale-like hero—are what Trollope forgets. What remains, however faintly, are the young ladies, who apparently left a trace of remembrance behind, and the heir, with his little bit of life.

Trollope individuates his characters by such comparisons—and in terms that emphasize not the best or worst excesses but rather the small differences, the "more or less" of this or that quality. It is only through comparisons with the less ambitious Norman and Charley that Alaric emerges as excessively ambitious. In short, to be individuated is not to stand out from a crowd but in one. As much as Trollope seems to endorse the assumptions of individualism—with his interest in these ambitious characters "making their way" in a world that lies at their feet full of opportunity, just like, as he so often reminds us, "an oyster to be opened"—he forms his individuals out of comparisons and competitions that suggest individualism's limits and dependencies.

Even in the baggy Victorian novels examined here and in the previous chapter, competitively ambitious characters run up against real limits—of socioeconomic and legal structures as well as the character system. And, tellingly, when those characters like Becky Sharp, Undy Scott, and Alaric Tudor hit one of those hard limits, they are sent off the scene to roam around the Continent or start over in Australia. This is of course a recurring trope in the Victorian novel, from Micawber to Magwitch, as well as in reality—with Dickens and Trollope sending their actual as well as fictional children off to make their fortunes in Australia or New Zealand. And as we saw in chapter 2, these ideas about how to siphon off a surplus population (and its ambitions) via emigration and imperial expansion were long standing, with Malthus inaugurating fears about Britain's scarce resources. But as more authors wrote back to Britain from these colonial spaces, they attested to how these imagined solutions simply staged the conflicts elsewhere. The next chapter takes up these concerns with the case study of Miles Franklin and her autobiographical writing, and in the socioecological system of Australia, where the logic of settler colonialism resulted in violence to peoples, cultures, and environments.

# CHAPTER 6

# Placing and Displacing Ambition

## Miles Franklin's *My Brilliant Career* and *My Career Goes Bung*

> I should like to write. It's the universal Australian ambition, of
> course.
>
> —Miles Franklin, *Prelude to Waking*

Since the publication of Miles Franklin's *My Brilliant Career*, the ambition of its restless protagonist, Sybylla Melvyn, has been associated with that of the emerging Australian nation. The novel was published in 1901, joining a wave of nationalist literature, music, and art on the heels of the Commonwealth of Australia Constitution Act. As Franklin remembered it, the book "burn[ed] with the nationalism rampant at the time."[1] Franklin herself was immediately hailed as an authentic voice of Australia. The writer Henry Lawson, in his preface to Franklin's work, proclaimed the novel "born of the bush" and "true to Australia—the truest I ever read."[2] A. G. Stephens, writing for the *Bulletin* in Sydney, called it "Australian through and through; the author has the Australian mind, she speaks Australian language, utters Australian thoughts, and looks at things from an Australian point of view absolutely."[3] In London, too, reviewers characterized the novel as a tale of bush life, noting its "intense patriotism"—and "not English patriotism, Imperialist reader, but Australian patriotism."[4] Franklin's protagonist struggles to realize her ambitions as a young woman without money in the bush, but, in the process, she gives voice to what came to be imagined as the experience of an entire class of young women—the "lively, dreamy Australian girls whose queer, uncomprehended ambitions are the despair of the household."[5] As the figure of the New Woman developed in these distinct ways in settler literature, it was frequently used to build and claim a national identity while also arguing for greater rights for women—or at least white women. Franklin's outspoken protagonist became the quintessential Australian Girl, the counterpart of the British New Woman.

The reception history of *My Brilliant Career* exemplifies these strands of influence, as well as how they have sometimes come into tension. Franklin's novel has been called "an iconic Australian novel," with all the ingredients required of national fictions in Australia: "a central, individualistic character who is at home in the rural landscape, and detailed depictions of that environment and its challenges."[6] After its early popular reception, *My Brilliant Career* fell off readers' radar (in part because Franklin cut off further editions until after her death). But later in the century, feminist critics recovered Franklin's novel and *My Brilliant Career* was amplified in classrooms and on screen[7]—with the film adaptation becoming a "smash" that marked the rise of Gillian Armstrong's career.[8] Feminist readings of *My Brilliant Career* have proved popular and enduring, from Jennifer Byrne's 2012 preface to the novel to an essay for The Criterion Collection claiming Sybylla's "spirit is tonic—and timeless," "in sync with "independent-minded women of every era, including our own."[9] Of course, such popular, feminist readings of Victorian and "classic" texts are common, particularly via film and television adaptations that help to bridge critical and popular reception, from the way the Brontës and their characters have been claimed as rebellious, feminist icons to the many defenses of Becky Sharp that seek to recast her ambition and selfishness as feminist acts. But such feminist readings are especially complicated in the case of texts like Franklin's, when they can too easily ignore those earlier, nationalist readings. In claiming Sybylla as a timeless, independent-minded woman, there's a tendency to elide the role of that earlier context and the specific setting—those elements that, from the start, readers saw as uniquely bound up with the novel's "patriotism." In this chapter, I want to recenter this Australian context and specifically the environment, which Franklin imagines as both inspiring and limiting Sybylla's ambition—and I want to do so in a way that attempts to resituate that context in light of how settler literature (and its reception and adaptation) has tended to avoid its history of violence and erasure.

Franklin's depiction of a young white woman's ambition unfolding in the Australian environment is complicated. On the one hand, Franklin presents the Australian bush as a metaphorical plane on which to project her ambitions: the setting inspires Sybylla to write, and, in turn, she justifies her ambitions in the follow-up, *My Career Goes Bung*, by linking them to the nation. Much like Sybylla, Franklin invested herself in the formation of a national Australian literature. In fact, her final legacy was to support such writing beyond her death, with her will instructing that the literary award in her name "shall be awarded for the Novel for the year which is of the highest literary merit and which must present Australian Life in any of its phases."[10] On the other hand, both versions of Sybylla portray an Australia hampered by gender and class norms and stricken by drought, which kills off the imported livestock and crops along with the settlers' aspirations. And, like her characters, Franklin herself looked beyond Australia in search of other opportunities, spending much of her career in Britain and the United States. Taken together, Franklin's novels critique the usual narratives that imagined colonial spaces like Australia as playing fields for British settlers' ambitions, instead portraying ambitions that seem displaced[11]—because they are located in a young woman or in Australia's climate.

These questions about ambition and displacement take on further urgency, as this chapter explores, in light of the zero-sum logic of settler colonialism, which pushed so many Indigenous people from their land, across the empire and the globe, and sought to "develop" that land with imported practices. If with naturalism the novel was moving, as Elizabeth Miller argues, "toward ecological realism by locating the human squarely within the environment and by placing environmental limits on human agency,"[12] then such limits are especially important in the context of settler colonialism, and perhaps especially in Australia, which presented particular challenges to the white settlers' modes of farming. With this in mind, this chapter outlines how ideas about women's and settlers' ambitions, both suggestive of excessive and displaced ambition, took form in novels that thematize the relation between ambition and environment. As earlier chapters have explored, the self-help narrative as it emerged in Britain in the nineteenth century provided a cover story for ambitious individualism. By focusing on how one's ambition would lift the nation as well as the individual, texts like Samuel Smiles's *Self-Help* avoided concerns about ambition—specifically the concern that ambitious individuals would have to compete for scarce opportunities. One such opportunity and space for improvement was land itself. In fact, as Andrew H. Miller has argued, the concept of improvement in Britain "has its roots in agriculture and economics, in the practice, most notably, of improving one's estate."[13] The self-help narrative thus easily coincided with the project of empire and the way many European powers imagined they would siphon off and "harness" individual ambition in the name of Christian and national interests.[14] And, even more specifically, the self-help narrative aligned with settler colonialism and the idea of appropriating land and "improving" it into estates.

Much of settler colonial literature seeks to justify the appropriation of land by depicting settlers' hard, physicalized work on it—with that land and local environment often themselves becoming the obstacle settlers must overcome to improve themselves and the empire. Franklin's novels *My Brilliant Career* and *My Career Goes Bung* suggest how such obstacles could in fact present hard limits. But she elides the fuller competitive stakes of settler colonialism, specifically how white settlers did violence to Aboriginal Australian and Torres Strait Islander populations. This silence was and is systemic in white settler colonialism, its literature, and ongoing ideologies.[15] In this chapter, then, I want to read for the silences, using the hints, even if in the margins, of the human and environmental costs of settler colonialism that were already marking Australia in the 1890s.

The first section of this chapter foregrounds how Franklin uses the setting to draw out the conflict between the mythology of Australia as an "open" playing field and the reality of the limitations posed by gender and class structures as well as the environment. In the second section I turn to the feedback loops between the environment and the settlers who attempt to reshape the Australian landscape by transplanting English agriculture. In Franklin's depiction of this dynamic, as she repeatedly reworks the story of ambitious young women's careers, we get a sense—even if obliquely—of how the empire, in circulating and displacing peoples and natures, wreaked havoc that continues to unfold. Franklin's depictions of a changed ecosystem and perpetual drought are eerily prescient of how Australia and the wider world would be shaped by imperial and capitalist forces—with an immediate example being how the lack of Indigenous land practices, combined with climate change, has made droughts, bushfires, and wildfires increasingly deadly.[16]

## "Australia Has No Background": Erasure and Colonial-Settler Ambition

The colonies had long been imagined as a space for the overflow of Britain's ambitions as well as its population. Self-help discourse was, as Melissa Walker puts it, "integral to the success of mid-Victorian British emigration and colonialism"[17]—and, as we've seen, this discourse carried with it ideas about hard work and perseverance that generally assumed a gendered, able-bodied subject acting on an open playing field. Malthus claimed that the happiest condition was that of "new colonies, where the knowledge and industry of an old State operate on the fertile unappropriated land of a new one."[18] The idea of "unappropriated" colonial spaces inspired and justified fantasies of unfettered ambitions. As G. J. Goschen put it, whereas the "old country's" civilization is "more complex, more crowded," "the colonies have more breathing space": "There, individual energy can expand with less encroachments on neighbours' interests. There, movement is freer."[19] Or as Dickens wrote to Forster, "Now, I wonder if I should make a good settler! I wonder, if I went to a new colony with my head, hands, legs, and health, I should force myself to the top of the social milk-pot, and live upon the cream! What do you think? Upon my word I believe I should."[20] When opportunities seemed limited in England, both Dickens and Trollope sent their real and fictional progeny to America, Australia, and New Zealand. Australia, with its history as a penal colony, was imagined as a sort of escape valve for ambitions that bordered on the criminal. Australia is where Dickens's Magwitch can make a fortune and where, as we saw in the previous chapter, Trollope's Alaric Tudor can start over after serving a sentence for embezzlement. And in fact, Franklin was named "Miles" after a relative, Edward Miles, who came to Australia as a convict on the First Fleet in 1788.

Dating back to the Cook expedition and the first convicts-turned-"settlers," the British imaginary fashioned Australia as a land of resources waiting to be turned into property and goods, while often conveniently avoiding mention of Aboriginal people.[21] As many critics have examined, settlers used the myth of terra nullius, or "empty land," as well as concepts about "civilization" versus "savagery," to erase or deny Indigenous people and their rights in order to justify the appropriation of land for pastoral settlement.[22] This subcategory of imperialism uniquely exemplifies a sort of zero-sum thinking. It is distinct, as Patrick Wolfe argues, in that it is "at base a winner-take-all project whose dominant feature is not exploitation but replacement."[23] In its "purest form," Wolfe explains, this logic "strives to replace [I]ndigenous society with that imported by the colonizers." Although other scholars have importantly nuanced this history, illustrating where settler-colonial powers not only acknowledged but also sought out Indigenous populations, they note that these powers were often motivated by a desire to put Indigenous peoples' knowledge and ability to work—to be "harnessed, exploited, and controlled."[24]

In Australia, the colonial settlers' goal was largely pastoral settlement. As Wolfe writes, this "requirement for territory was inherently exclusive": "The introduced cattle and sheep competed with indigenous fauna for subsistence, consuming the tubers, shoots and seeds whereby the indigenous fauna reproduced itself and rapidly reducing waterholes to mud."[25] As Eve Tuck and K. Wayne Yang observe, the most important concern in settler colonialism is "land / water / air / subterranean earth": "Land is what is most valuable, contested, required. This is both because the settlers make Indigenous land their new home and source of capital, and also because the disruption of Indigenous relationships to land represents a profound epistemic, ontological, cosmological violence."[26] In the wider British empire, ideas about Australia and specifically its potential for pastoral settlement evolved across the nineteenth century—as the associations with punishment and exile gave way to imagery of a "working-man's paradise."[27] But this was far from the reality. Most of the land suitable for the sort of agriculture the white settlers brought with them was already appropriated by other settlers.[28] The accumulation of large tracts of land in the hands of the few gave rise to concerns about the power of the "squattocracy" and to debates about potential solutions, including the single tax, which sought to prevent property speculation (and was premised on ideas about ownership of land deriving from work on that land). Such concerns must have been heightened by the increased sense of competition, as the population of Australia was rapidly growing after the Gold Rush in Victoria and New South Wales, tripling just between 1850 and 1860, and then again by 1900, from 1,146,000 to 3,765,000.[29]

Given the importance of land, literally and financially as well as metaphorically and ideologically, to the project of settler colonialism, it is especially important to read novels like Franklin's with attention to the setting and environment. I want to turn specifically to the Goulburn Mulwaree region where Franklin lived, which became a key setting for her novels. As a recent study sums up, the Aboriginal people living in this region included the Gandangara (Gundungurra, Gundungari, Gurra-gunga, and Burragorang) and the Ngun(n)awal (Ngunuwal, Ngoonawal, Wonnawal, Nungawal, Yarr, Yass tribe, Lake George, Five Islands tribe, or Molonglo tribe).[30] White settlers did not always understand or recognize Aboriginal and Torres Strait Islander peoples' land practices—practices that have been documented in recent important work by (for example) Bruce Pascoe, Dale Kerwin, and Bill Gammage.[31] But European colonizers did see the effects, repeatedly remarking on the park-life landscape—including what were effectively paddocks for game, including kangaroo. On one 1798 expedition to Mt. Towrang, east of Goulburn, John Wilson called it "a most beautifull country, being nothing but fine large meadows with ponds of water in them; fine green hills, but very thin of timber."[32] As settlers appropriated land, bringing their imported farming practices to what they perceived as "open forest," they damaged the previously "abundant natural resources."[33] The surveyor William Romaine Govett, familiar with the region in the 1820s and '30s, described these results—both the dwindling population of the Aboriginal people and the changed landscape. Govett particularly lingered on this landscape: "The kangaroos have either been killed, or have fled in search of more retired forests. Sheep and cattle have taken their place, the emu and turkey are seldom seen, the millions of parrots have even become scarce."[34] Govett seems here to acknowledge the violent logic of replacement, with sheep and cattle "taking the place" of the kangaroo.

Settler literature across many contexts romanticizes and projects ideologies onto the natural world while eliding its own violence against these environments. But such tendencies manifest in particular ways in New Woman novels coming from the British empire[35]—sometimes in ways that acknowledge avoidance. At times, New Woman novels' preoccupation with gender and class inequality enables or rationalizes their other silences around the settler project. As Kirstine Moffat has put it, "The predominant silence regarding the [I]ndigenous population in the New Zealand New Woman novels points to the ambivalent position of white settler women in an invader settler nation; preoccupied with their own predicament as an oppressed gender, most of these authors fail to acknowledge their complicity as imperial subjects in the subjugation of Māori people."[36] Such texts require criticism to look for the gaps and elisions. For example, as Ryan Fong has argued, Olive Schreiner's *The Story of an African Farm*—a novel that has offered a point of comparison to Franklin's since the publication of *My Brilliant Career*—leaves out the "expressive worlds of the novel's Khoisan communities" because it is "largely focalized through its white settler characters." One site of entry, as Fong demonstrates, is the San cave art, which the characters project their own ideas onto or even quite literally turn their backs on[37] ("the girls sat with their backs to the paintings").[38] The novel itself turns away from such images and acknowledgment of the Indigenous people and their history.

Other critics have found a similar pattern specific to Australian women's writing that, in taking up the idea of the nation—even if to fight against sexist structures—became complicit in the colonial project. For example, Carole Gerson has studied various examples of the "wild colonial girl," including Sybylla in *My Brilliant Career*, who attempt to resist patriarchal structures but are "ultimately defeated by the complicity of their colonial backgrounds (manifested in their internalized values as well as in their actual home communities) with the norms of the imperial centre."[39] Further, Tanya Dalziell has shown that although the feminism of *My Brilliant Career* represents important progress, it problematically depends upon colonial and racial tropes that are ultimately regressive. Most important to my own argument, Dalziell concludes that the novel employs racial metaphors to represent class conflict, with Franklin "displacing" questions about race and colonialism onto questions about gender and class.[40] Given these readings and the importance of land (literally and metaphorically) in the history of settler colonialism, I want to reconsider the role of the setting, the environment, and ideas about the natural in Franklin's novels. Even as *My Brilliant Career* and *My Career Goes Bung* very explicitly thematize the Australian setting and its particular environment, they elide these stakes of settler colonialism.

It is the Australian setting that both inspires Sybylla's ambitions and that limits them, and it is the representation of Australia that launches both Sybylla's fictional and Franklin's actual writing career. The projection or displacement of ambition was certainly on Franklin's mind: while the protagonists of *My Brilliant Career* and *My Career Goes Bung* are outspoken about their ambitions, Franklin toyed with how much of her own to reveal. This hesitation is of course highly gendered. If ambition had long been a suspect drive, equally liable to manifest in violent self-seeking and competition as in collective or national progress, then this drive was all the more suspect when embodied in a woman. Not surprisingly, Franklin relied, like so many women writers before her, on pen names that hid her gender.[41] She cut the parts of her full name that were feminine—Stella Maria Sarah—and retained Miles Franklin; she also gravitated toward androgynous or masculine pen names, including, for example, Brent of Bin Bin. Such strategies are especially useful for a young woman writing another ambitious young woman into the story of the emerging nation. As Sybylla describes herself in *My Brilliant Career*, she is "cursed with a fevered ambition for the utterly unattainable" (221).

Despite her various distancing strategies, Franklin was closely associated with her protagonist, then and now. The *Saturday Review* went so far as to call *My Brilliant Career* "a semi-autobiographical story" while reviews of the film claimed it was "based on a true story" and adapted from an "autobiographical novel."[42] This all problematically extends historical tendencies to discount women writers by imagining that they merely record what's around them—versus relying on genius to invent material of their own.[43] Even otherwise positive reviews imagined that Franklin had "simply turned her girlish diary into a book," making "literature out of the little things that lay around her."[44] Franklin was very aware of these tendencies to conflate the author with her protagonists. In fact, the preface to *My Career Goes Bung* explains that this follow-up novel was "planned as a corrective" to the "literalness with which *My Brilliant Career* was taken." Franklin might have faced problems in her circle if her family and neighbors were guilty of taking the novel literally—given the less than flattering portraits of so many of the characters (which may have led to Franklin's decision to stop further editions). At the same time, such "literalness" meant that "girls from all over the continent" identified with Sybylla and wrote to Franklin to say that she "had expressed their innermost lives and emotions."[45] The draft form of this follow-up novel, "The End of My Career," includes another attempt to dodge such associations with an "afterlogue":

> I have been dreaming but now I have awakened to find I am not a young girl named Sybylla Melvyn, but an old, grey-headed man bearing as appelation Selim Nilknarf. On my desk I find an MS—a story in the form of a confession.
>     Did I write it?[46]

Although this passage was not ultimately included in *My Career Goes Bung,* Franklin's follow-up novel repeatedly anticipates and overtly engages with the desire of readers and critics to conflate the author with her characters. The novel is narrated by another Sybylla Melvyn, who is the author, we learn, of *My Brilliant Career.* Franklin uses this premise to create some entertaining metafictional confusion. In one of my favorite examples, Henry Beauchamp arrives to court Sybylla after hearing that she has written a book in which a certain *Harold Beecham* marries the (first) fictional Sybylla. Sybylla protests that she "never thought of you—never heard of you." But Henry insists he is indeed the pattern for her marriage plot. He backs up his claim with the facts that he was nearly christened Harold and that Beauchamp is pronounced Beecham (96). The novel delights in these metafictional registers. As the title of chapter 9 puts it, "It was all real, but how much was true?" Franklin's depiction of the (different) ambitious Sybyllas in her two early novels, as well as a series of tales written around 1900 and called Bush Life, effectively displaces Franklin's own authorial ambition into a series of nesting dolls.

Even when this authorial ambition is located in the Sybylla of *My Career Goes Bung,* we learn that this ambition is itself a "diversion" from Sybylla's first goal, to enter politics. To prepare herself for public life, Sybylla begins to read the autobiographies of great people (a plan Samuel Smiles and other practitioners of the self-help genre would surely approve of). But she finds herself annoyed with the "egotism" of the authors (28). This inspires Sybylla to write a "spoof autobiography" (54): "I was diverted from the idea of becoming great myself by the notion of constructing a fictitious autobiography to make hay of the pious affectations of printed autobiographies" (30). All this pokes further metafictional fun at the way *My Brilliant Career* was in fact read as an inspiring novel for young women similarly feeling trapped and limited by gender norms. It also suggestively resituates the way Franklin's earlier novel employed the Australian setting: with her energy "diverted" into this new project, Sybylla begins writing with an English landscape in mind, complete with an "ancient castle on an English moor" (34). As important as Australia and "Australianness" were to Franklin's writing and reception history, *My Career Goes Bung* thus plays with the idea of setting *My Brilliant Career* not in Australia but in England.

Fortunately, Sybylla's teacher Mr. Harris—channeling the advice of creative writing teachers everywhere—counsels her to write what she knows: "Why not try reality? . . . instead of the roses on that castle wall, why not this fragrant bower of wattle? Instead of the wind moaning across the moor, why not the pitiless sun beating down on the cracked dusty earth?" (35). Sybylla seizes on the suggestion: "This was an expanding idea, like opening a window and letting me look into a place I had not known before" (35). Significantly, Sybylla's inspiration and her metaphor for that inspiration revolve around place. This is fitting when we consider how important the setting is to both novels: *My Brilliant Career* and *My Career Goes Bung* are set in the drought years of the 1890s, and both portray spaces recognizable as actual locations Franklin had lived in. The most notable example is the arid Possum Gully, which Franklin's biographer, Jill Roe, reads as a "thinly disguised" version of Franklin's actual home in Stillwater.[47] Roe repeatedly uses the term "thinly disguised" to describe Franklin's habit of using autobiographical material in her works, suggesting that Franklin failed in her attempt to translate the personal into fictional terms. But clearly this was an intentional and repeated decision—a desire to stick closely to the reality of the Australian setting while keeping this sort of poetic, authorial license. Years later, Franklin chose to continue this practice in her memoir, *Childhood at Brindabella*, changing all the place-names and referring to people by their initials.

These place-names suggest without directly locating spaces, thus bridging the literal and metaphorical import of the settings. In *My Brilliant Career*, Sybylla associates her ambition with the broad Australian landscape, proclaiming that "my ambition was as boundless as the mighty bush in which I have always lived" (42). But the immediate environs of Possum Gully limit her "boundless" ambition. In a passage full of gender play, Sybylla recounts how she "manfully endeavoured to squeeze [her] spirit," "crushed, compressed, and bruised" (44), into Possum Gully, which begins to sound rather like a corset with its "narrowing, stagnant monotony" (47). When Sybylla "managed it on one side it burst out on another, and defied me to cram it into the narrow box of Possum Gully" (44). Casting Possum Gully as itself in need of Malthusian outlets for the surplus population, Sybylla claims that "there was not room enough" for the boys growing up, who instead leave town as soon as they can (12). In contrast, the wider landscape promises an Australian dream, with "the dreaming peaks of the mountains beyond the Murrumbidgee" presenting a "banner of spiritual strength raised for me to follow away from 'Possum Gully limitations" (*MCGB* 227). *My Brilliant Career* also contrasts Possum Gully with the lush Caddagat, where Sybylla visits her grandmother. This "Caddagat, draped by nature in a dream of beauty" (40), replicates many aspects of Brindabella, where Franklin grew up among her extended family, and which she also had to leave, in what she remembered as an "exile from Eden."[48]

These different geographies shape Sybylla's ambitions in strikingly different ways across the two novels. In *My Brilliant Career* Sybylla's ambitions shift depending on her environment. The drought inspires Sybylla to voice her poetic epiphany—her "drought idyll." In this scene Sybylla helps her family lift the cows back to their feet to keep them from succumbing to the heat and dehydration—an operation that involves a system of ropes, poles, and sheer force. Such hard labor inspires her fear that this will be the entirety of her experience: "This was life—my life—my career, my brilliant career! I was fifteen—fifteen!" (28). Imagining ways out of this "brilliant career," she in turn proposes becoming an author, an actress, and a singer, as she flirts with marriage. While she is living happily with her grandmother's family at Caddagat, she loses interest in writing: "Yes, life was a pleasant thing to me now. I forgot all my wild, unattainable ambitions in the little pleasures of everyday life. Such a thing as writing never entered my head. I occasionally dreamt out a little yarn which, had it appeared on paper, would have brimmed over with pleasure and love—in fact, have been redolent of life as I found it" (176). Paradoxically, the ambitions that were limited in Possum Gully dissipate when Sybylla finds herself in Caddagat.

In contrast, in *My Career Goes Bung* the arid Possum Gully landscape emerges as the catalyst as well as the means for Sybylla's ambition. This is first a question of material conditions: it is because of the extreme drought in Possum Gully that Sybylla has time to write at all: "The drought made work in the garden superfluous. I had leisure to utilise that ream of paper. The burlesque autobiography grew apace" (34). But here, too, it is also an imaginative catalyst. In response to Mr. Harris's advice to write about the setting she knows, Sybylla immediately describes her surroundings in a passage that encompasses the indigenous plants and animals, as well as those overlaid on them by the colonial settlers:

Our home was of wood and of the usual pattern and situation in a particularly ugly portion of the bush. We were dished in a basin of low scrubby ranges which are familiar to the poorer settlers where the fertile patches are land-locked in a few big holdings by hard-headed fellows who got in early with capital and grants and convicts.

Instead of hedges we had dog-leg and brush fences, and stumps in the cultivation paddocks. There were fowl-houses covered with tin to render them safe against sharp-snouted spotted marsupial cats; the mess-mate roosting trees also had wide rings of tin around the trunks to save the turkeys by night. Cowsheds were roofed with stringy-bark. Fields of briars and rugged ranges were all around; a weedy water hole in the middle; the not-yet-bleached bones of beasts were a common decoration. No roofs but our own were within sight . . . Such reality as mine would look mighty queer in a book, something like a swaggie at a Government House party, but it was as easy to describe as falling off a log. (38–39)

Such passages demonstrate how exactly the landscape is posed as an imaginative catalyst for a white settler woman's ambition. Sybylla describes her surroundings while comparing them with what they are not—those large "fertile patches" associated with those who "got in early." The novelty of imagining in print this particular Australian landscape, overlaid with the settler-class system, is what inspires Sybylla's wide-ranging and vivid descriptions—many of which anticipate a non-Australian reader (such as the note about the tin covers on the fowl houses). It is striking that Sybylla first considers the setting and specifically the landscapes of her potential novel—not the characters or plot. The one potential character in this passage emerges when Sybylla imagines how out of place the Australian setting would seem on the printed page ("something like a swaggie at a Government House party").

The setting again serves as the key avenue for imagining her writerly ambitions when Sybylla travels to Sydney and debates the value of Australian versus English literature. It is here that Mr. Wilting, a literary Englishman, proclaims that Sybylla has "germs of genius" that "if fostered and cultivated . . . may bear fruit in time" (150). To work on her writing, Wilting argues, Sybylla needs to "gain a perspective. You must burst the bonds of your environment" (151). He recommends "immediate transplantation to England" (152). Processing this conversation with another character, Gad, Sybylla reports Wilting's critique that "Australia has no background." Gad counters that "England has so much [history] that she is a museum of what has been, while Australia is an experimental laboratory of what will be. I prefer foreground to background" (154–55).

Taking up this challenge, Sybylla merges her individual ambition with the project of imagining such a national literature with her repeated question, "Shouldn't we do something on our own hook?" (152). In such scenes, we can see the ways in which claiming the nation allowed a young white woman a path for her ambition via the emerging nation—even as this went hand in hand with imagining Australia as a place without a past, thus suggesting the underlying violence of settlers' ambitions that denied and erased the actual long background of Australia's Aboriginal and Torres Strait Islander cultures.

This pattern—of pursuing a path for women's ambition in Australia while being complicit in the project of settler colonialism—aligns with the tendencies outlined by such critics as Gerson and Dalziell. But the way this plays out particularly through the idea of the natural setting is important, not only for how it highlights the metaphorical as well as literal ways in which settlers claimed Australia, but also for how settlers employed ideas about the natural to limit certain people's ambitions. As critics have long argued, nature, coded as feminine, is subject to tropes of possession in service of specifically male ambition.[49] In both novels, Sybylla is told that it is "NATURE" or "God" that has established the social and economic systems that leave her so few avenues for her ambition. And in both, marriage is urged upon her. Even when Gad recognizes Sybylla's artistic potential, his solution is to marry her: "You need a patron, who would let you be yourself, and then you would have a brilliant career" (*MCGB* 194). Franklin's novels thus overtly thematize these clashes between the supposed freedoms of the colonies and the gendered expectations for women—and this frequently happens via the rhetoric of nature and the natural.[50]

Both versions of Sybylla rebel against the idea that gendered systems and norms are natural. When Father O'Toole chastises Sybylla for her career ambitions, arguing, "Ye musn't interfere with Nature" (*MCGB* 67), Sybylla forcefully contradicts him. When her mother tells her that all girls wish they were men but soon settle down to the work of wives and mothers, Sybylla is taken aback: "Never in my life had I a wish to be a man. Such a suggestion fills me with revulsion. What I raged against were the artificial restrictions" (*MCGB* 16). This language crops up in Franklin's memoir as well: "The artificial bonds called feminine were presented to my understanding" (141). In *My Career Goes Bung*, Sybylla carefully itemizes the paths not entirely restricted by such "artificial bonds": she would love to attend the university, except that she can't afford the cost; she could work as a pupil-teacher but would have "to do the same work as a man for less pay"; she could be a nurse "and do twice the work of a doctor for a fraction of his pay or social importance"; and so on. As Sybylla concludes, "This brought me to consider my prospects and to find that I hadn't any" (20–21). Later in the novel she declares that "women were compelled to marry by nearly all other occupations being closed to them, and by the pressure of public opinion" (*MCGB* 190).

Imagining how these artificial limitations become naturalized, in *My Career Goes Bung* Sybylla introduces the language of "grafting" to describe her own gendered behavior. When Sybylla plays at flirting with Goring Hardy, she draws on an embodied, inherited femininity: "My attitude and very tone of voice had been ingrafted by generations of conventionalized, continent mothers who had swallowed the prescriptions laid down for them by men instead of developing themselves in the exercise of natural law, and with nothing to ease their lot but the superstition that the impositions foisted upon them had been God's will" (*MCGB* 188). Sybylla contrasts these "ingrafted," gendered conventions with "the exercise of natural law," which would allow for self-directed development. This sets up a spectrum between natural, individualistic development and the gendered systems that prescribe behavior until it seems natural.

At various points in *My Brilliant Career*, Sybylla invokes similar ideas about the natural to critique the economic structures that create a class of dispossessed men. Sybylla especially sympathizes with the plight of the homeless men who regularly stop by her grandmother's house in Caddagat—"all shapes, sizes, ages, kinds, and conditions of men" who had been "on the tramp" so long "that the ambitions of manhood had been ground out of them, and they wished for nothing more than this" (99). Far from romanticizing the figure of the "swagman," Franklin sees these individuals as a class that has been created through structural and constructed failures. She asks, "In a wide young country of boundless resources, why is this thing?" (*MBC* 100). (Again, the "young" insists on erasing Australia's past.) Looking to the "millions oppressed, downtrodden, God-forsaken," she concludes that "the wheels of social mechanism needed readjusting—things were awry" (*MBC* 45). Sybylla elides the widest-scale dispossession of Indigenous people, while focusing on the hierarchies within the settler system—the immediate drama of men "talk[ing] wildly" about "bust[ing] up the damn banks," "driv[ing] all the present squatters out of the country," and "put[ting] the people on the land" (*MBC* 100).

Sybylla's description of this class oppression recalls the "squeezing" effects of Possum Gully. Addressing her fellow Australians, she writes, "Bravely you jog along with the rope of class distinction drawing closer, closer, tighter, tighter around you: a few more generations and you will be as enslaved as were ever the muzhiks of Russia. I see it and know it, but I cannot help you. My ineffective life will be trod out in the same round of toil—I am only one of yourselves, I am only an unnecessary, little, bush commoner, I am only a— woman!" (*MBC* 253). In combination with the above discussion of squatters and land, Sybylla's allusion to "the muzhiks of Russia," the peasant class of serfs who could not own land, suggests she was thinking about class in terms of land ownership (another "ingrafted" rather than natural system). As Bruce Scates has argued, Sybylla's concern that the few are unfairly monopolizing the soil at the expense of everyone else can be tracked back to contemporary debates in Australia about the single tax. Owning property was imagined as a way to formalize the claim to and sense of belonging to these spaces—versus the transient men "on the tramp" that Sybylla encounters. Franklin herself lived in areas that were monopolized by a few landowners, while those without property crowded for limited resources.[51] These concerns about scarcity were heightened in the 1890s, as Roe has documented. Goulburn experienced both drought and depression in these years, with the real version of Possum Gully suffering from the "over-crowded, under-capitalized and drought-afflicted land."[52] This restages exactly the sort of competition in a limited system that had motivated many settlers and their ancestors to emigrate.

As much as Franklin's novels draw attention to how women as well as working-class and homeless Australians found themselves "squeezed," roped "tighter" and "closer," or blocked from some paths altogether, these settlers are all of course part of the settler-colonial project, with British and American empires depending on the displacement of Indigenous populations—a project that goes largely unmentioned in both Sybyllas' narrations. (What is left only implicit in the above passage, for example, is the fact that those "continent mothers" were themselves grafted onto the Australian landscape.) Compounding the difficulty of teasing out these entangled and displaced strands are the obviously regressive elements in Franklin's thought. Paul Giles has argued that Franklin not only displaced but also repressed attention to racism.[53] And yet there are suggestive moments in Franklin's novels that point to what could have been attention to how race, gender, and empire intersect—and to how these hierarchical forms might, to borrow Caroline Levine's terminology, unsettle or disrupt rather than merely reinforce one another.[54] When Father O'Toole claims that "common" white women in Australia need to marry and have children to thwart the "Yellow Peril," Sybylla immediately reacts against the idea that settlers need to "fill up Australia." Sybylla archly replies that "the unfortunate Yellow Peril women might be relieved to enter into an alliance with us to stem the swarming business" (*MCGB* 67). Although this comment is made sarcastically, it suggestively imagines how women could unite across and, as a result, disrupt racial and national lines—refusing the underlying logic of a competitive race to claim a finite space.[55] Sybylla's rejoinder also points to how amorphous a symbol the Australian landscape is, and how, even in this metaphorical register, a sort of competition emerges, now not of material resources but of meaning. While she looks at the landscape and sees an echo of her own boundless ambition, Father O'Toole sees a mutually exclusively meaning—an imperial and racist imperative to fill Australia up with white settlers.

Both ambitions are displaced by the literal reality of Possum Gully, where the settlers, their livestock, and their crops fail. In these descriptions, Franklin tellingly contrasts these "transplants" with the indigenous plants suited to the Australian climate. As the next section argues, Franklin's representations of the environment across these early novels and her childhood memoir raise questions about what it means to be "native" versus "transplanted." In these depictions Franklin hints, if obliquely, at how the ambitions of settlers and imperial powers displaced Indigenous populations. Reading for the setting thus suggests the larger context of Sybylla's ambitions: the wider debate about how place and people, the manmade and natural, shape one another.

## "Without an Indigenous Literature, People Can Remain Alien in Their Own Soil": Natives and Transplants in Franklin's Writing

The rhetoric of "transplanting" was frequently invoked in discussions about colonialism around the British empire.[56] Addressing a new colony in South Australia in the 1830s, for example, George Grote draws on this common metaphor, asking, "But how can England so effectually secure an extended foreign market for her commodities as by planting, in all the inviting and attractive spots of this fair earth, colonies of industrious Englishmen, carrying with them the tastes and habits of their countrymen, . . . and thus creating a great and continuous demand for the surplus labour and capital of this country?" Grote claims that such emigration will divert the "competition which now overflows and chokes up all the channels of employment" "to another soil, where the reward of labour is rich and sure, and where the exertions of the transplanted artisan, instead of impeding those left behind, will, by their mutual intercourse materially aid and assist each other." Where competition initially seems to work like a fluid, "overflowing" the "channels" of employment, Grote switches, mid-sentence, to the metaphorical register of planting—with "transplanted" workers finding rich rewards in other soil.[57]

In striking contrast, Franklin's *My Brilliant Career* and *My Career Goes Bung* imagine not a "rich and sure" soil that rewards transplanted workers but an environment that actively rejects the colonial settlers. The "hot, dry, pitiless" drought of the 1890s makes for an almost biblically cursed landscape in Sybylla's description: "The scorching furnace-breath winds shrivelled every blade of grass; dust and the moan of starving stock filled the air; vegetables became a thing of the past." The settlers, calling on their specifically British dispositions, battle against this hostile climate, "[fighting] our way against all odds with the stubborn independence of our British ancestors. But when 1894 went out without rain, and '95—hot, dry, pitiless '95—succeeded it, there came a time when it was impossible to make a living" (*MBC* 24). These harsh conditions pervade both of Franklin's novels: the drought is mentioned thirty-two times in *My Brilliant Career* and nineteen in *My Career Goes Bung*. In *My Brilliant Career*, letters carry news about the weather, neighbors "yarn" about prices and "the continuance of the drought" (237), and, in a pivotal scene with her would-be lover, Sybylla pauses to note "a blue sea breeze, redolent of the bush fires which were raging at Tocumwal and Bombala" (239). In *My Career Goes Bung*, it is a sign of Sybylla's success when she learns that "people are magging more about your book than the drought or the price of wool" (61). As we have seen, the drought often serves as an active agent in the plot, as when it spurs Sybylla's drought idyll in *My Brilliant Career* or when it gives her time to start writing in *My Career Goes Bung*.

Much as the drought dramatizes the limits and catalysts around Sybylla's youthful ambitions, so too does it point, more broadly, to the limits of the colonial settlers' ambitions, specifically the practice of transplanting and cultivating foreign livestock and crops in the Australian climate. The cows and horses register the severity of the drought in their failing health and eventual deaths. After spending most of *My Career Goes Bung* in Sydney, Sybylla returns to find that "only the hardiest plants in the garden survived" (214), while many animals have died. She laments their "emaciated carcasses" and cries over the fate of the horses—"panting, trembling, staggering through their purgatory under lash and objurgation." Sybylla points to the settlers' mistakes when she imagines these dying animals reproaching their "incompetent" Australian masters (213). This is most explicit when she observes how "the starving stock lacked strength to bring their young to birth, and the moan of dying creatures throughout that country side was a reproach to whatever power had placed them there" (33). Such descriptions admonish the British settlers' attempts to reshape the land, even as it obscures the agency behind these attempts ("whatever power had placed them there").

Sybylla contrasts these failed efforts with the thriving "native" flora: "Isolated shrubs and plants, that had been the pride of settlers' drudging wives and daughters, died in spite of efforts to keep them alive with the slop water collected after household use. The wattle trees, however, because they were natives, were putting forth an unstinted meed of bloom with an optimism rivalling 'God's in His Heaven, all's right with the world' . . . This loveliness lacked competition in the grim landscape" (33). There is a sense that, in an ongoing "competition," the "native" wattle trees will reclaim the land. In such descriptions, suggestive of actual competitions over space, we might read the submerged conflict inherent to the settler-colonial project in Australia. It was exactly the practice of pastoral settlement, as Wolfe argues, that set up a zero-sum game between the indigenous and the transplanted landscape.

There are other hints of this ecological conflict in Franklin's writing, particularly in her *Childhood at Brindabella*. Franklin was intimately familiar with the gardening habits of the colonial settlers and how they had been imported—along with stock and plants—from England. In her memoir Franklin spends many pages recounting the gardens of her childhood. Given that gardens were such loaded spaces for signaling socioeconomic class as well as national or imperial affinities, it's telling that Franklin describes her family as a "tribe of inveterate gardeners" thanks to a servant who "trained on one of the ducal estates in England" and assisted Franklin's great-grandfather, teaching "three generations of both sexes to sow and prune and set both gardens and orchards" (50). In these descriptions she pays pointed attention to native and transplanted species, using the language of "emigrants" and "wild Australians": "Many of the English garden flowers that could endure frost flourished in the virgin soil. Mother's garden was a preserve for emigrants stoutly fenced in from wild Australians. A native violet persistently resisted extirpation . . . Like other native plants they resisted alike extermination and transplantation" (52). The "wild Australians" are hardy and inclined to take over garden plots and yet resistant to intentional cultivation—a stark contrast to the docile English species, preserved in their safe enclosures. Across such descriptions, Franklin suggests material and ecological limitations, from the borders of the gardens to the modest power settlers wield in the face of the Australian ecosystem and climate. She also taps into rhetoric often used in discussions of colonization, comparing people and plants.

As much as colonial spaces were imagined as open playing fields—or gardens—for imperial and individual ambitions to act upon, they were also, in turn, understood to be acting upon their inhabitants. In fact, European writers repeatedly pointed to environment and climate to explain variations across human populations, with these ideas feeding into nineteenth-century ideas about race. Before turning to this context, I want to preface it with Marlon B. Ross's important research into how, exactly, the nineteenth century thought about race: "The tenets of race (and thus of racism) were . . . disjointedly sloppy during the time (as they still are in our time)," making race "fungible, pliable, seductive in a way that shields it from both the niceties and the outrages of moral, polemical, and artistic discourses even as such discourses are mounted as heavy weapons of partisan attack stemming from the harms of racism."[58] In Britain, some of this "disjointedly sloppy" thinking came from Hippocratic theories about environmental determinism, which imagined that "climate exerted a powerful effect upon human health, and even upon physical characteristics."[59] Although he did not see climate as a primary cause for such variations, Darwin addresses these inherited ideas in *The Descent of Man*. He observes that "it was formerly thought that the color of the skin and the character of the hair were determined by light or heat." Climate was also thought to affect disposition and psychology; as Darwin notes, "It has often been remarked, that a cool climate from leading to industry and the various arts has been highly favorable, or even indispensable for [progress]."[60] These ideas are perhaps most memorably expressed (at least in the context of Victorian studies) in John Ruskin's theories about architecture. In explaining the impulses behind Gothic architecture, Ruskin puts his first emphasis on climate: "There is, first, the habit of hard and rapid working; the industry of the tribes of the North, quickened by the coldness of the climate, and giving an expression of sharp energy to all they do as opposed to the languor of the Southern tribes."[61]

This tangle of ideas about race, climate, and acclimatization came to the fore in Victorian discussions about the emigration of populations or, in the case of slavery, the forced movement of people. Different theories were proposed for how much and how quickly populations could adapt. As Darwin observed, "Through the combined influences of climate and changed habits of life, European settlers in the United States undergo, as is generally admitted, a slight but extraordinarily rapid change of appearance. There is, also, a considerable body of evidence showing that in the Southern States the house-slaves of the third generation present a markedly different appearance from the field-slaves."[62] Or as a writer in the *Anthropological Review* put it in 1866,

"As an instance of the effect of climate and change of life on the human species, we need only compare the Yankees of the present day with the people of the mother countries."[63] As a result, even as tropes about environmentally driven racial difference were used to justify British imperial projects, these spaces were seen as acting on settlers in the same way they had supposedly shaped Indigenous populations.

Given the widespread racist attitudes against these populations, such ideas about the environment raised concerns about how white British settlers might "deteriorate" over generations. For example, the *Pall Mall Gazette* criticized the plan to annex and colonize New Guinea, observing, "Surely we have learned by this time that our race cannot go on long in the tropics without great deterioration." This writer proceeds to raise concerns specifically about those born in Australia: "Grave doubts have been raised by the colonists themselves whether native-born Australians who remain all their lives in New South Wales, Victoria, or South Australia, can be physically equal to those who have been brought up in the more favourable climates of Tasmania, New Zealand, or England. The children of the second, and still more of the third generation, present that weedy appearance which may be noticed in English children born and brought up in India."[64] Once settled in the colonies, British subjects were supposedly shaped, over generations, by the climate. But, as Mark Harrison notes, these theories about acclimatization were also giving way as "the perceived boundaries between races began to harden," with the result that "Europeans came to regard themselves as exotica in foreign soil: feelings of superiority and vulnerability were two sides of the same imperial coin."[65] The larger context helps make sense of how, even in Franklin's depictions of the colonial settlers struggling against the Australian climate, she gestures to these racialized ideas.

With this context as a lens, we can better see the hints or elisions in Franklin's writing that gesture, even if vaguely, to the real violence behind these settlers' ambitions. Even if Franklin largely avoids any mention of Aboriginal people, she painstakingly describes how white settlers, including her family, sought to replace the Australian landscape with imported crops and livestock. Given this context, I want to return to those passages where she insists on her British—and specifically white—identity. Allusions to race often intersect with other hierarchies that get at ideas about agency explored in earlier chapters, as for example, the introduction to *My Brilliant Career*, where the narrator claims her authorship via ideas about race, slavery, and ability: "Better be born a slave than a poet, better be born a black, better be born a cripple!" (4). I'm also thinking of the sprinkle of passages across these novels that insist, in turn, on a purity of white, English, and British identity. For example, Sybylla claims her mother's lineage back to "one of the depraved old pirates who pillaged England with William the Conqueror" in *My Brilliant Career* (6), while, in *My Career Goes Bung*, Henry Beauchamp insists that the "breed" is there in Sybylla because her father is the "whitest man in Australia" (84). Sybylla also describes the settlers fighting the drought with the "stubborn independence of our British ancestors" (*MBC* 24). Such passages insist on the settlers' difference from and opposition to the Australian environment—as if to protest that they have retained their racial identity rather than acclimatizing—even as this setting is held up, in the abstract, as a sort of blank slate for settlers' ambitions to act upon.

By reading for the setting in these ways, we get a sense of how colonial settlers, "transplanted" in an environment that starkly demonstrated the limits to their systems of knowledge and agriculture, made sense of a project that did such violence to the people and ecosystems of Australia. As much as Franklin's novels dramatize the encounter between Sybylla's (and the settlers') "boundless" ambitions and a resistant environment, she elsewhere acknowledged how Australia was ultimately reshaped by families like her own. Remembering a favorite swimming hole in her memoir, Franklin laments that "the unique shrubbery of the streams" is now gone, "so that men can swirl expensive lines and artificial flies in some sort of fishing ritual analogous to foxhunting." She reminisces about sporting with platypuses and fishing "for the small speckled indigenous trout called slipperies," the "sweetest fish ever tasted"—a native species that "disappeared" when the "drier, larger, greedier, imported rainbow trout" were introduced. These changes are not always by design but sometimes redound from small actions. It was Franklin's own family who effected some of these changes: "It was my youngest uncle, with me looking on, who first let loose in those streams the invaders that came tiny as tadpoles in milk-cans from government hatcheries" (126). Such a scene lends weight to readings of Franklin's complicity in the colonialist project—"looking on" as the English "invaders" take over. It also speaks to how settlers obscured or avoided the responsibility for such violent reworkings of the Australian ecosystems—how Franklin's own sense of loss (much like her own oppressions of class and gender) distracts us from seeing the larger losses to the Aboriginal and Torres Strait Islander people and cultures as well as the ecosystems of Australia.

Franklin imagines this movement of flora and fauna across the empire as a key way of thinking about what links British subjects—even as such movement is often violently destructive. For example, after recalling a favorite kind of plum from her childhood, Franklin recounts how, while going down Tottenham Court Road years later, she was "dumbfounded" to find the exact fruit at a local market: "I sallied out dazed, never more integrally of the British Empire" (*Childhood at Brindabella* 133). Franklin poses this as a positive recognition of belonging, even as it overlays an uncanny experience of reconceptualizing origin stories—the plum that was associated with her Australian childhood emerges as, in fact, English. Other recognition scenes are more disturbing. For example, Franklin sees a woman in Chicago wearing a fur coat bought in a shop in Vienna made from Australian cat—a species that was exterminated, with the result that the "imported foxes have increased to take their places" (98). This movement confuses the actual origin points of various species, which, like other goods, circulate in a wider globalizing marketplace.[66] It also points out the violence and loss that comes with such circulation, with introduced species displacing the slipperies and Australian cat into extinction.

Both versions of Sybylla raise similar questions about how subjects and objects circulate or are displaced around the empire specifically in reference to authors and literature. For example, Sybylla imagines her identity as a writer in terms of Australia, the larger empire, and the globalizing marketplace. But whereas Sybylla ends *My Brilliant Career* by claiming her Australianness— "I am proud that I am an Australian, a daughter of the Southern Cross, a child of the mighty bush" (252)—at the end of *My Career Goes Bung*, this version of Sybylla turns instead to England. This conclusion seems to contradict everything that this version of Sybylla has spent most of the novel propounding to the other characters. After all the discussions about a specifically Australian literature, Sybylla fantasizes about "England with her ancient historic beauty— tradition—the racial rooftree," claiming that "through song and story it has permeated every fibre of my mind since I could first scan a pictured page, while I have spent scarcely a month in but one corner of Sydney. London— THE BIG SMOKE—London, where our dreams come true" (232). Downplaying the importance of directly experiencing a setting, the actual wattle trees pale in comparison to the metaphorical "racial rooftree" of England—a manmade structure imitating the natural form. In the end, fantasies about white, British, and perhaps even more specifically "English" identity become more powerful than the lived experience of generations of colonial settlers in Australia. In the process, Sybylla retreats from imagining the British empire, to England, to its very center, London.

By the time Franklin established the literary prize in her name, she had many more years, most of them abroad, to consider how authors and national literatures circulate in a global system—and how the competitive prize in her name might hold up representations of Australia both to Australians and to a wider world. Exactly what representations are awarded has been a topic of perennial debate, with this prize effectively setting up a competition for a literary vision of Australia. As Patrick Allington muses, "One historically mysterious element of the Miles is how a judging panel weighs 'Australian life' against the stipulation that the winner should also be 'of the highest literary merit.'" The trustees of the prize revisited this question in 2012, when the Trust Company's CEO, John Atkin, authorized the judges to "use their discretions to modernise the interpretation of 'Australianess' [sic] beyond geographical boundaries to include mindset, language, history and values, as is in keeping with the current Australian literary landscape."[67] Atkin's instructions confront what constitutes Australianness, inviting judges (and, implicitly, authors) to venture beyond mere "geographical boundaries" to imagine a wider metaphorical "literary landscape."

There are good reasons to continually reevaluate which visions of "Australian life" are held up by the Miles. The economy of literary and artistic production is largely shaped by such prizes that bestow cultural capital, directing readers' attention to "winners."[68] As Miles judge Richard Neville has noted, it's not uncommon for a novel that's been shortlisted for the Miles to go from selling nine hundred copies to, with the prize name, twelve thousand.[69] On the website that explains the prize and accepts submissions, the trustees stress these material conditions of literary production and how Franklin "had firsthand experience of struggling to make a living as a writer." In today's similarly competitive field, the Miles acts to "support" and "foster" writers, serving as the patron that Franklin (and both versions of Sybylla) lacked.[70] Given this context, it is important to question which writers as well as which visions are awarded recognition and support, not only from the Miles but also from the larger literary prize culture and the publishing industry. The *New York Times* has recently revealed the results of a sweeping study of fiction books published in English from 1950 to 2018. Shocking even the researchers, 95 percent were by white people.[71] Earlier studies have found similarly disheartening results. The *Bookseller* reports that of the top five hundred titles published in Britain in 2016 (up to the time of the study's publication), just six were by British writers of an ethnic minority background; in the United States, that figure was thirty.[72]

These alarming representational disparities intersect with similarly worrying statistics tracking gender. As numerous studies have shown—although to corroborate these findings one need only take a cursory glance at the lists of winners of prestigious literary prizes not intentionally set aside for writers of certain backgrounds or identities—books by white men are far more often recognized than books by women and people of color. There is a terrible irony in the fact that the Miles, established and named for a writer who was outspoken about women's rights and ambitions, has historically been disproportionately awarded to men. The disparity was so marked that a competing prize named for Miles Franklin, the Stella Prize, was established with the intent to recognize specifically women writers in Australia. This is of course part of a wider pattern. To sum up this gender disparity in broad strokes, men tend to win prestigious awards about two-thirds of the time. Nicola Griffith's examination of six prestigious prizes, awarded across 2000–15, revealed that the more prestigious the prize, the more likely it was to be awarded to men. Even when women took the prize, they often wrote about a male character.[73] As Natalie Kon-yu has observed, this pattern holds for the Miles: "By and large, the women writers awarded the Miles Franklin in the last twenty years write novels either about male protagonists, or about historical events such as war." Such disparities are all the worse when we consider how disproportionately women are in fact writing and reading these novels that aren't as likely to be recognized. One study of Australia's writers found that 65 percent of literary fiction authors, 76 percent of genre fiction writers, and 87 percent of children's authors are women.[74] As the Royal Society of Literature found in the British context, even as "literature's readers are more likely to be female than male, its recognized writers are more likely to be male than female," at 69 percent.[75]

Such questions about the literary representation of experiences other than those of white men are not merely academic. Books—and, by virtue of our "prestige culture," literary prizes—amplify certain experiences that come to represent groups and nations. The amplification of experiences that speak more directly to readers' own lives was, of course, a major goal of establishing robust local literary traditions in the first place. As the trustees of the Miles put it, this prize cultivates Australian *readers* as well as writers. While authors are of course financially supported—both by the prize money itself and by the proceeds from an increased readership—readers are imagined as metaphorically nurtured. As the trustees claim, citing Franklin, "Without an indigenous literature, people can remain alien in their own soil."[76] Such a passage returns to the connection between the novel and the nation that we started with. It is also suggestive of how claiming Australia, the literal land and the metaphorical space, has long relied on the rhetoric of planting and belonging—including how Franklin justified her own ambitions as a young white woman writer by grafting them onto the nation.

Again, these ways of thinking have real consequences, as exemplified by a recent exchange between Aboriginal activist Noel Pearson and conservative commentator Andrew Bolt. In defining the "essence of [I]ndigeneity" as a people's "connection with their ancestors whose bones are in the soil," Pearson comes to the "somewhat uncomfortable conclusion" that even Bolt is "becoming Indigenous because the bones of his ancestors are now becoming part of the territory." Insisting on a competitive logic, Bolt goes on to argue that, having been born in Australia six years before Pearson, he is "more [I]ndigenous than Pearson."[77] This logic—of contesting Indigenous peoples' claims to the land via such equivocating definitions of race and identity—has a long history. Zoë Laidlaw and Alan Lester have observed that "from the very beginnings of colonization . . . there was a critical relationship between the assumed identity of Indigenous peoples—their degree of 'pristine purity,' and their tenure on the land." Descendants had less claim to the land, even as, paradoxically, colonial settlers had more. Settler colonial states have thus used understandings of race, as Laidlaw and Lester put it, "to collude in dispossessing Indigenous peoples."[78]

With this longer history in mind, we can better see how Franklin's use of such rhetoric is loaded across her writing, raising questions about what it means for a person or literature to be "Indigenous"—and how this term relates to the history and zero-sum logic of settler colonialism that has done violence to Indigenous peoples and ecosystems around the world. These questions have changed since Franklin's writing, from Australia's establishment as the Commonwealth of Australia in 1901, through contemporary debates about Australia Day or Invasion Day, and how to face the ongoing history of settler colonialism while also, as Shino Konishi puts it, recognizing "local histories of Indigenous experience that do not revolve around settler colonial domination, expropriation, exploitation or elimination."[79] At the time of writing, Australia's national anthem has only just replaced "young and free" with "one and free"—a few years after studies dated arrival back to sixty-five thousand years ago. The judges of the Miles have good reason to further the debate over what it means for today's novels to represent Australia as well as its many inhabitants, past and present—as Franklin's own writing becomes the distant literary background and the Miles continues to shape the material conditions of literary production in Australia.

It is encouraging that the Miles has recognized a number of women and Indigenous writers in recent years, with the 2019 prize going to Melissa Lucashenko's *Too Much Lip*—a novel that speaks directly to the history of colonial and racial violence, identity, and environmental destruction. *Too Much Lip* follows the protagonist, Kerry, as she returns to her hometown of Durrango, where her grandfather is dying and her family is struggling, financially and emotionally, with historical and ongoing traumas. The novel foregrounds the land, both its history and its continuing appropriation by the Australian government via greedy realtors. Kerry finds that her Aboriginal family's ancestral ground, where previous generations have been buried, is slated as the site for a new prison. Kerry also confronts the difficulties of conceptualizing her identity as she learns more about her family's history. While Kerry's sister has been rising in the real estate business, "passing" and disavowing her ancestry, Kerry and the rest of her family have tried to resist the local real estate industry behind the prison project. In the process, the family learns that they are all related to the same white colonial settlers who have perpetrated violence on their family and taken (or threatened to take) their ancestral land. The novel thus overtly thematizes the relation among the land, history, and belonging. In an interview, Lucashenko revisited questions about the literary landscape of Australia and the work both literature and prizes can do now: as she observes, the recognition of her work, as well as "that of other Aboriginal authors like Alexis Wright and Claire G. Coleman," "shows that Australian literature is changing to recognize Aboriginal voices as critical to the field and the nation."[80]

In this chapter, my hope has been to reimagine how to read Franklin's *My Brilliant Career* and *My Career Goes Bung* in light of this longer history—and the ways this longer history of setter colonial practices and narratives has resulted in the destruction and inequities that are impossible to elide, from the recent devastating bushfires to COVID-19 policies. Franklin's novels mostly adhere to the larger patterns of Australian New Woman fiction, focusing on white women settlers whose ambitions are limited by gender and class oppression—putting these narratives to use in forming a national identity. But Franklin also suggests the way that this ambitious subject is continually displaced, across the nesting doll versions of Sybylla (with their echoes of Franklin's own ambitions to write), in Sybylla's restless movements and shifting goals, and in setting the novels during a drought that uniquely highlights the failures of the settlers to understand and adapt to the Australian climate. It can be tempting to read such displacements as a faint gesture to the stakes of the settler project and what and whom it displaced.

If the self-help narrative previously justified and moralized ambition by dressing it up as a driver of national and imperial progress, there is additional reason to look for such hints around the margins, a lurking awareness of the actual stakes of white settlers' ambitions. As Victorian studies, the larger field of literary studies, and, one hopes, Western cultures with long histories of colonial and racial violence try to make sense of how this violence has been ignored and elided in the name of patriotism and national pride, it feels like a fitting moment to grapple with the difficulties of reading Franklin's work now. Even as Sybylla was held up as a distinctively Australian character and the sort of "independent-minded" woman who could inspire later generations on screen and in syllabi, she points us to the legacy of how white women in settler societies have used ideas about the nation and race to justify their ambitions. Even as Franklin portrays Sybylla identifying with and metaphorically claiming the Australian landscape, today we can read this with more awareness of the stakes of appropriating and reshaping these ecosystems. If Sybylla is indeed a "timeless" character, teachers and readers need multiple critical lenses to consider Franklin's representation of race, gender, and place.

# Coda

If texts like Samuel Smiles's *Self-Help* initially provided a cover story for ambition by linking the good of the individual to that of the collective, by the end of the Victorian era, the mask had slipped. Taking the occasion of Smiles's 1905 *Autobiography* to critique *Self-Help* and the age that had produced it, the *Saturday Review* remembered the mid-century as an age that lived by the mantra "help yourself and never mind the others." This mantra had led to the lionization of "the self-made man . . . who by pinching and screwing and overreaching his competitors . . . succeeded in making a large fortune."[1] The reviewer laments how such texts—and particularly William Arthur's biography of Samuel Budgett, *The Successful Merchant*—"formed the ideals and created the ambitions of more people than can ever be reckoned." And the danger of these ambitions is, specifically, how they turn into competition:

> It was the era of the Mechanics' Institution and the Mutual Improvement Society when everybody was making frantic efforts to become what they called educated in order to be better equipped for beating their rivals in trade . . . They were the days of Libraries of Useful Knowledge; and the readers of them were the Gradgrinds whose dearest principle was that if the hardest headed only had full liberty to wage war with each other, and use the cheapest labour in the human slave market, this would result in the greatest happiness of the greatest number. (551)

This passage draws a direct line between self-help narratives, the ambition to improve oneself, and ensuing competition. And the danger of this competition is that, far from allowing for individuals to develop in unique ways, it compels a factorylike uniformity in these "frantic efforts" to beat out rivals and "wage war" in trade.

Such critiques of Smiles's *Self-Help* and the wider genre fit into narratives familiar to us today—about how this genre has functioned, as Beth Blum puts it, as "an instrument of neoliberal governance, a tool of systemic oppression, or an agent of colonial subjection."[2] Of course, as chapter 1 argued, *Self-Help* was more complicated, aligning with what some historians have seen as a radical call for education and upward mobility, even inspiring socialists like Robert Blatchford. But this critique of Smiles and the self-help ethos draws out an even more specific line of reasoning about what, exactly, worried this earlier era's readers: that self-help texts would encourage ambitions that would inevitably lead to competition and conflict. As much as authors like Smiles and George Lillie Craik tried to direct readers' ambitions toward a sort of "wealth" that would have "the property of multiplying itself to meet the wants of all"[3]— like knowledge or character—self-help still seemed merely to prepare readers to compete for limited economic opportunities.

Across this book, I've explored how Victorian-era writers and readers returned over and over to narratives about the hardworking and successful individual, even while pointing to concerns that ambition was dangerous in a limited system. The most immediate example of such a limited system is the individual who has finite energies, abilities, and time. As much as Smiles and others preaching the self-help ethos celebrated ambitious work for how it could make individuals and nations, its limits were always suggested in its very power. Ambition could backfire on the subject who wielded it, whether through overwork, injuries, or illness (including, in nineteenth-century terms, monomania). It is what makes and differentiates but also what "takes possession" of the individual. Using this drive to catalyze narratives, particularly the baggy monster of the multiplot Victorian novel, authors rendered the logic of the zero-sum game into various competitions—tracking marriage choices, career trajectories, legal contests, and the outcomes of primogeniture or inheritance. Even narratives that appear unreservedly to tout such self-helping individualism, like *John Halifax, Gentleman*, end up implying that one's rise entails another's losses. Victorian fiction dramatized ambition by showing where it runs up against the limits of an individual's energy and ability, where it turns into competition, or where it risks upsetting a socioecological system of finite resources. In doing so, such narratives explore how zero-sum thinking works as well as how it feels. Reading across such fiction and writers' autobiographies reveals the extent to which these authors were in fact grappling at close quarters with how to frame narratives about ambition and competition, often, as in the case of Trollope, with explicit concerns about how to offer up one's life as well as one's characters as examples for how to work hard and deserve one's success.

The "problem" of ambition continues to haunt sociopolitical systems that rely on mythologies about individualism, meritocracy, and economic competition. Presumably, the writer at the *Saturday Review* would be disappointed to learn that—as much as he imagined that Smiles's *Self-Help* "would not be popular if written now"[4]—politicians would invoke this text to neoliberal ends in the 1980s and '90s, and that the nineteenth century's "frantic efforts" and "full liberty to wage war" would come to rhyme with the twentieth and twenty-first centuries' "hustling" and "deregulation." Our understanding of ambition is still plagued by uncertainties about how the individual relates to the collective, particularly through competition. At their basis, competitions are always suggestive of a limited system with unequal outcomes. As William Davies puts it, "To argue in favour of competition and competitiveness is necessarily to argue in favour of inequality, given that competitive activity is defined partly by the fact that it pursues an unequal outcome." As much as competition is supposed to "[guarantee] that markets are a 'positive sum game,'" then, it is also always suggestive of scarcity and zero-sum games.[5] Today's neoliberal policies and ecological realities accentuate this paradox and this sense of scarcity, with economic inequality reaching crisis levels at the same time that natural resources are ever more limited, while entire regions experience or anticipate increasingly extreme droughts, fires, and weather, as well as rising sea levels. And competition for space can become quite literal, as many cities with better job opportunities don't have sufficient housing. Such looming or ongoing economic and environmental disasters demonstrate and exacerbate the deeply unequal distribution of opportunities and resources.

In recent years, study after study has shown that narratives about the hardworking, successful individual rising in a meritocracy are false as well as dangerous. Those at the top claim that they worked hard for their success and shouldn't owe anything to the common good, while everyone else who didn't "win" in a rigged system misses the chance to contribute their talents (while also shouldering the blame for that failure). Robert H. Frank has shown why our tendency to ascribe success to self-efficacy is especially false in today's "winner-take-all markets," where luck and chance play outsized roles.[6] And Jo Littler has recently explored how the myth of a meritocracy has sold "a ladder system of social mobility, promoting a socially corrosive ethic of competitive self-interest which both legitimises inequality and damages community 'by requiring people to be in a permanent state of competition with each other.'" Such beliefs are that much more corrosive when they're so clearly false, with the data showing that the potential for social mobility among most working- and lower-middle-class people in the UK and the United States has declined over the past few decades.[7] These trends are only exacerbated when the data is examined at different intersections of gender, race, and generation.[8]

Heightening this sense that one must compete for ever-more-limited op-portunities, we seem to be programmed for zero-sum thinking. Researchers have studied how the average person (i.e., for the purposes of this study, not a trained economist) observes the act of trading, including barter and cash transactions. Two people agreeing to a trade should technically be seen as a positive-sum game (that is, each person agrees because they are trading for something they value more). And yet, observers tended to see even these mu-tually beneficial transactions as zero-sum—one's gain requires another's loss.[9] If zero-sum thinking is so ready to hand, it is all the easier for politicians to invoke ugly feelings by prompting us to imagine that we're in competition with others, or that our ambitions can't be realized in a limited and unequal socio-ecological system. In turn, this surely affects the ways voters weigh everything from economic policies to trade negotiations. The result of such thinking was on display in Brexit and Trumpism, with Trump epitomizing these patterns every time he framed a trade deal as a zero-sum game or claimed the United States was too "full" to accept refugees or immigrants.[10]

The global rise of populists like Trump who blame those at the periphery or bottom of the system—immigrants, women, and people of color—for per-ceived disadvantages is a profound reminder of the real stakes of thinking about ambition and competition. After all, the actually dangerous ambitions aren't those of the people seeking to escape climate disasters, war, or poverty—they're the ambitions of the 1 percent, who never feel they have enough. As Tim Harford puts it, "The focus on zero-sum rhetoric has drawn attention away from more plausible solutions, many of which are purely domestic: higher quality education, publicly funded infrastructure investment, antitrust action to keep markets functioning competitively, and a more constructive welfare state which supports and encourages work rather than stigmatises and punishes idleness."[11] Uncertainties about ambition and competition affect the material conditions that will, in turn, shape which and whose ambitions are realized in the next generation.

Even before the COVID-19 pandemic threw so many into further and deeper economic hardships, the supposedly booming US economy was de-fined by a strange paradox—growth and low unemployment wasn't substan-tially benefiting workers and their salaries. Pankaj Mishra has investigated how preaching individualism in such a limited system tends to result in vio-lent backlashes: "Can the triumphant axioms of individual autonomy and interest-seeking, formulated, sanctified and promoted by a privileged minor-ity, work for the majority in a crowded and inter-dependent world? Or, are today's young doomed to hurtle, like many Europeans and Russians in the past, between a sense of inadequacy and fantasies of revenge?"[12] When a culture preaches the power of ambition and individualism, these drives can seem, like Marx's theory of capital, to be characterized by a "limitless drive to go beyond its limiting barrier. Every boundary [*Grenze*] is and has to be a barrier [*Schranke*] for it."[13] But even a "limitless drive" must encounter real boundaries in a material and crowded world—especially when that world has been rigged for those who already have money and power, and when one person's upward mobility appears increasingly to depend on another's downward mobility.[14]

Victorian narratives still have much to say about this tension. Even as they employ the inherent interest and narrativity contained in the ambitious individual, and even as they keep us reading for who will "win," they remind us of what's at stake: how ambition might backfire on individuals, societies, and the natural world when the unquestioned goal is always doing or having more. As much as it must remain far beyond the scope of a monograph on Victorian literature to solve our many intersecting crises, these nineteenth-century narratives offer a space to reconsider how we approach and respond to the mythology of the hardworking individual and their well-deserved success. Then and now, such narratives capitalize on readerly desires not only "to see what happens next" but also, more specifically, "to see who wins" in a structure that necessitates that someone else lose.

## Introduction

1. For more on such readings, see Meckier's "*Great Expectations* and *Self-Help*"; and R. Gilmour's chapter "Dickens and *Great Expectations*" in *The Idea of the Gentleman in the Victorian Novel.*

2. Dickens, *The Pickwick Papers*, 432.

3. Kathryn Hughes describes the sensation Eliot's first novel made, with critics loudly praising *Adam Bede* and pushing sales up to sixteen thousand in the first year. Hughes, *George Eliot*, 204.

4. Meckier, "*Great Expectations* and *Self-Help*," 541.

5. Leckie, "Reader-Help," 14.

6. Smiles, *Self-Help*, 94. Hereafter cited parenthetically in the text.

7. For more on the longer history of this transition in the Anglo-American tradition, see King, *Ambition, a History.*

8. For an extended and earlier version of this argument in relation to *Our Mutual Friend*, see my essay "Bradley Headstone's Bad Example." For another reading of self-help in Dickens, see Meckier, "*Great Expectations* and *Self-Help*." For further context on Dickens's portrayal of upward mobility, see R. Gilmour, *Idea of the Gentleman*; Moynahan, "The Hero's Guilt"; Carey, *The Violent Effigy*; and Jordan, "The Social Sub-text."

9. Orwell, "Charles Dickens," 417.

10. As Orwell observed, "It is the thought of the 'pure' Agnes in bed with a man who drops his aitches that really revolts Dickens" ("Charles Dickens," 439).

11. Jordan has argued that Dickens provides David with a scapegoat: David "tends to disavow his social ambition and aggression" while condemning these qualities in Uriah Heep. This strategy allows David to pursue "his own parallel course under the cover of moral superiority" (78). Moynahan suggests that ambition has been repressed and redirected into a villain: "Ambition as the instinct of aggression, as the pitiless drive for power . . . is both coalesced and disguised in the figure of Orlick." Far from exercising Smilesian hard work and perseverance himself, Pip is bestowed money and status. Meanwhile, any overtly aggressive ambition is "disguised" in Orlick, his "double, alter ego, and dark mirror-image" (69).

12. Bodenheimer, *Knowing Dickens*, 2.

13. Welsh, *From Copyright to Copperfield*, 2.

14. Forster, *Life of Charles Dickens*, 1.68.

15. Forster, *Life of Charles Dickens*, 1.66.

16. *Speeches of Charles Dickens*, 281.

17. *Speeches of Charles Dickens*, 48.

18. *Speeches of Charles Dickens*, 405–6. Dickens addressed the Birmingham and Midland Institute on September 27, 1869.

19. Dickens, *David Copperfield*, 613.

20. Cochrane, *Risen by Perseverance*, 175. This biography includes the oft-repeated anecdote about Gadshill Place (so much repeated in fact that it appears twice in this text). As a child, Dickens noticed Gadshill Place on a walk with his father, who told him that "if he worked hard enough he might himself live in such a house" (173).

21. Gissing, *Collected Works*, 80 and 51.

22. Chesterton, *Charles Dickens*, 57–58.

23. Forster, *Life of Charles Dickens*, 1.72.

24. Forster, *Life of Charles Dickens*, 2.455.

25. Cochrane, *Risen by Perseverance*, 219.

26. An excellent counterexample is Goodlad's *Victorian Literature and the Victorian State*, which frequently quotes Smiles in outlining the movement from prescriptive to descriptive character. Although Goodlad's work does not center ambition or expand on the role of inspirational biography or the wider genre of self-help, it does contribute a much-needed consideration about how ideas of character were developing in the era.

27. Stout, *Corporate Romanticism*, 18.

28. Steinlight, *Populating the Novel*, 19.

29. See Mitchell and Snyder, *Narrative Prosthesis*, 51.

30. For more recent work in the area of Victorian studies, narrative, and the novel, see also Hingston's *Articulating Bodies*; and Gore's *Plotting Disability*.

31. Wolfe, *Settler Colonialism*, 163.

32. In *Upward Mobility and the Common Good*, Robbins identifies the patron or benefactor as a recurring trope in fictional narratives about upward mobility—a trope that nonfictional texts like *Self-Help* depart from, in their unabashed interest in the powerful individual.

33. Trollope, *The Three Clerks*, 121.

34. Ferguson, "*Emma* and the Impact of Form," 177.

35. King, *Ambition: A History*, 117.

36. Hirschman, *Passions and the Interests*, 100.

37. Pettigrove, "Ambitions," 67.

38. "Influence of Ambition," 116.

39. Google Books.

40. Carlyle, *On Heroes*, 265–66.

41. The *Oxford English Dictionary* breaks down the Latin *ambit-us*, "a going round, a compass," into *amb-* (about) and *-itus* (going).

42. Alger, *Solitudes of Nature*, 120–21.

43. Thackeray, "Small-Beer Chronicles," 122.

44. Travers, *Samuel Smiles*, 166.

45. Carlyle, *Sartor Resartus*, 79.

46. Trendafilov, "Origins of *Self-Help*," 8.

47. Travers, "Samuel Smiles and the Origins of 'Self-Help,'" 177. For more on Smiles's influences, see also Tyrrell's articles, "Class Consciousness in Early Victorian Britain" and "Samuel Smiles and the Woman Question."

48. Emerson, "Self-Reliance," 196.

49. Trendafilov, "Origins of *Self-Help*," 10.

50. Trendafilov, "Origins of *Self-Help*," 11.

51. Briggs, *Victorian People*, 116.

52. See R. Gilmour, *Idea of the Gentleman*.

53. Sinnema, introduction to *Self-Help*, vii.

54. Huber, *American Idea of Success*, 147 and 149.

55. Marden, *Pushing to the Front*, 96.

56. Wyllie, *The Self-Made Man*, 128.

57. "Literature and Art," 413.

58. Smiles, *Autobiography*, 228–30.

59. Smiles, *Autobiography*, 229.

60. "Spirit of Smiles," 551.

61. Lubbock, *Choice of Books*.

62. Tobias, *Ella's Englishman*, 3. It should be noted, however, that in this scene *Self-Help* is found among a group of books with "very handsome bindings, but looking unread."

63. Blum, *Self-Help Compulsion*, chapter 1.

64. Brewer, *Pleasures of the Imagination*, 509.

65. Robinson, *Self-Education*, v.

66. Sinnema uses the term "secular hagiography" to explain the book to new readers on the back cover of the Oxford edition.

67. Booth, *How to Make It*, 51.

68. Atkinson, *Victorian Biography Reconsidered*, 25.

69. Booth, *How to Make It*, 50.

70. Smiles, *Autobiography*, 222. Smiles was also influenced by Louis Aimé-Martin's *Éducation des mères de famille: Ou de la civilisation du genre humain par les femmes (The Education of Mothers of Families; or, The Civilization of the Human Race)* and Baron de Gérando's *Du perfectionnement moral, ou De l'éducation de soi-même (Self-Education; or, The Means and Art of Moral Progress)*. See Tyrrell, "Samuel Smiles and the Woman Question," 195 and Blum, *Self-Help Compulsion*, 46. Although less reliant on inspirational biography, De Gérando similarly stresses the importance of imitation and holding up good examples (for example, the 1830 English translation has a chapter titled "Imitation and Example").

71. G. L. Craik, *Pursuit of Knowledge*, 1.1. Further citations are quoted parenthetically in the text.

72. *Fortunes Made in Business*, iii.

73. *Fortunes Made in Business*, iii–iv.

74. *Success in Life*, iv.

75. Boucherett, *Hints on Self-Help*, 126.

76. W. Anderson, *Self-Made Men*, 18.

77. W. Anderson, *Self-Made Men*, 122 and 139.

78. Arthur, *Successful Merchant*, 67.

79. H. Mayhew, "Men Who Have Helped," 92.

80. Watt, *Myths of Modern Individualism*, 238 and 241.

81. Lukes, *Individualism*, 3 and 22.

82. Smiles, *Thrift*, 183. Hereafter cited parenthetically in the text.

83. Watt, *The Rise of the Novel*, 13.

84. B. Anderson, *Imagined Communities*, 25–26. Jonathan Culler has noted that Anderson seems to be saying here that *any* novel creates this sense of homogenous empty time—which is "a formal condition of imagining the nation—a structural condition of possibility." In distinction, many of Anderson's examples, as well as later critics, suggest a more specific claim: that novelistic representations of a nation "help to encourage, shape, justify, or legitimate" it. See Culler, "Anderson and the Novel," 23 and 37.

85. Armstrong, *How Novels Think*, 3 and 59.

86. Blum, *Self-Help Compulsion*, 7.

87. Blum, *Self-Help Compulsion*, 41.

88. Pettigrove, "Ambitions," 55.

89. *Millionaires and How They Became So*, 101. Tellingly, the author switches between "everybody" and "every man" in these passages—making it unclear who all is accounted for in this calculation.

90. Hirschman, *Passions and the Interests*, 100.

91. Hirschman, *Passions and the Interests*, 51–52.

92. Mill, *Principles of Political Economy*, 453. Engels, *Condition of the Working-Class*, 75–76.

93. Davies, *Limits of Neoliberalism*, 61.

94. Mill, *On Liberty*, 91–92.

95. Perkin, *Origins*, 2.

96. Rubinstein, *Men of Property*, 127, 38, and 46.

97. For more on the ubiquity of war during the Victorian era, see Hensley, *Forms of Empire*.

98. Daly, *Demographic Imagination*, 1–2.

99. Mill, *Principles of Political Economy*, 453.

100. See, for example, Kornbluh's *Realizing Capital*; Poovey's *Genres of the Credit Economy*; Lynch's *The Economy of Character*; and Gallagher's *The Body Economic*.

101. See, for example, Armstrong's *How Novels Think*; Plotz's *The Crowd*; Daly's *Demographic Imagination*; and Emily Steinlight's *Populating the Novel*.

102. Woloch, *The One vs. the Many*, 13.

103. Robbins, *Upward Mobility*, 84 and 243.

104. Levine, *Forms*, 108–9.

105. Hornborg, "Cornucopia or Zero-Gum Game?," 214.

106. Hornborg, "Zero-Sum World," 246.

107. Trollope, *Autobiography*, 248.

108. Ritchie, introduction to *The Biographical Edition*, xiii–xxxvi, xxxiv–xxxv.

109. Bourrier, *Victorian Bestseller*, 93–94.

110. Martineau, *Autobiography*, 197.

111. Gissing, *New Grub Street*, 123.

112. Smiles, *Autobiography*, 296–98. Such concerns about work and overwork were surely informed by contemporary labor debates that sought to define who could do what type of work for how many hours per day and week (from the Ten-Hour Movement to the series of Factory Acts that regulated the work of women and children). In the context of such debates, writing was uniquely difficult to account for. Many authors attempted to measure their work by time spent or words written, with Trollope tracking both in his diaries to give a day-by-day account of his writing activity. And the product of all this literary labor also raised questions about value: a text might be valued based on its popularity, its aesthetic value, the time it took to produce, or the number of pages it occupied. In short, literary labor puzzled attempts to rationalize and measure work in the Victorian era, while it also crystallized concerns about the physical effects of overwork and how it could manifest across classes and occupations.

113. R. Gilmour describes Craik's novel as "the classic novel of self-help, in the sense that it presents the ideology in its purest, least critical form" (*Idea of the Gentleman*, 86). Brantlinger calls the novel "a moral exemplum of the creed of Samuel Smiles" (*Spirit of Reform*, 119).

114. M. Franklin, *My Brilliant Career*, 24 and 42.

115. Littler, *Against Meritocracy*, 8–9 and 212.

116. "Caretaking Your Own Well-Being."

117. "Contemplation by Design 2018."

118. Blum, "The Self-Helpification of Academe."

119. R. G. Smith, *Affect and American Literature*, 2.

120. Melvin Lerner conducted early foundational research into just world beliefs. For recent critiques of meritocracy and the tendency to attribute one's success to hard work, see Frank, *Success and Luck*; and Littler, *Against Meritocracy*.

121. Foucault, *Birth of Biopolitics*, 119–21; and Mirowski, "The Thirteen Commandments of Neoliberalism."

122. "The Thirteen Commandments of Neoliberalism."

123. Ngai, *Our Aesthetic Categories*, 202.

## Chapter 1 · Forming the Ambitious Individual in Samuel Smiles's *Self-Help*

1. Smiles, *Self-Help*, 7. Hereafter cited parenthetically in the text.

2. Goodlad, *Victorian Literature and the Victorian State*, 146.

3. This last quality was added to the title in the 1866 edition, to become *Self-Help: With Illustrations of Character, Conduct, and Perseverance*.

4. For a thorough examination of Smiles's early radical politics, see Tyrrell's work, especially "Class Consciousness in Early Victorian Britain"; and "Samuel Smiles and the Woman Question." See also Clausen, "How to Join the Middle Classes"; and Travers, *Samuel Smiles*.

5. I. Gilmour, *Dancing with Dogma*, 336–37. As Alex Tyrrell notes, there is an "endless supply" of such "attempts to force Smiles into a late twentieth-century ideological strait-jacket" ("Samuel Smiles and the Woman Question, 185n2).

6. "The Hand in Your Pocket."

7. Meacher quoted in Dannreuther and Perren, *Political Economy of the Small Firm*, 50.

8. Harris, foreword to Smiles, *Self-Help*, vi–vii.

9. Joseph, introduction to Smiles, *Self-Help*, 12.

10. Blum, *Self-Help Compulsion*, 41.

11. Briggs, *Victorian People*, 125 and 121.

12. For more on this, see the introduction and Trendafilov, "Origins of *Self-Help*."

13. For more on such organizations and their politics, see especially Rose, *The Intellectual Life of the British Working Classes*; Altick, *The English Common Reader*; and E. P. Thompson, *The Making of the English Working Class*.

14. R. J. Morris, "Samuel Smiles and the Genesis of Self-Help," 108.

15. Fielden, "Samuel Smiles and Self-Help," 164.

16. Tyrrell, "Samuel Smiles and the Woman Question," 185–216, 200–201. Smiles's thinking here, as in so many places, is messy. Smiles did address cooperative or collective action in his later work *Thrift* (1876), although he sometimes praises it (as when speaking of the Rochdale Pioneers) and sometimes criticizes it (as when he suggests that workers' unions are not always "healthy" and result in strikes that are usually "unfortunate") (116). For more on Smiles's discussion of unions, see Melissa, "On the Move," 612n61.

17. Tyrrell, "Samuel Smiles and the Woman Question," 214.

18. Tyrrell, "Class Consciousness in Early Victorian Britain," 116.

19. Blatchford, *A Book about Books*, 233, 234, and 245.

20. Goodlad's *Victorian Literature and the Victorian State* is a noteworthy exception, situating ideas about character across a range of texts, including Smiles's *Self-Help*.

21. In addition to Blum, see Leckie, "Reader-Help," which questions how readers, especially in Britain and America, actually encountered Smiles's text.

22. Clausen, "How to Join the Middle Classes," 408.

23. Interestingly, Marden's full title (*Pushing to the Front, or Success under Difficulties: A Book of Inspiration and Encouragement to All Who Are Struggling for Self-Elevation along the Paths of Knowledge and of Duty*) mixes different ways of thinking about ambition and aspiration—both "pushing" against others to reach the front and overcoming "difficulties" via a sort of upward "self-elevation" without side references.

24. Matthews, *Getting On in the World*, v–vi.

25. Adams, *The Secret of Success*, xv.

26. Wyllie, *The Self-Made Man*, 127.

27. This sets up an interesting tension between the hard work of Smiles's examples and the ease with which the reader can flip through the text. For a reading of this disconnect, see Leckie, "Reader-Help."

28. Smiles, *Autobiography*, 222.

29. Smiles, *Autobiography*, 52.

30. Kant describes genius as "the innate mental predisposition (*ingenium*) *through which* nature gives the rule to art" (*Critique of Judgment*, 174). Even the genius cannot trace his steps, as "he himself does not know how he came by the ideas for it; nor is it in his power [*Gewalt*] to devise such products at his pleasure, or by following a plan, and to communicate [his procedure] to others in precepts that would enable them to bring about like products" (175, brackets in original). Kant differentiates between artistic genius and mechanical thought, noting that we can follow Newton's steps to his "great and profound discoveries," but not those of the artistic genius (176–77).

31. Hood, *Peerage of Poverty*, 139.

32. Hood, *Peerage of Poverty*, 136.

33. For examples of these terms in usage, see S. Smiles, *Autobiography*, 138; and Paxton, *Peerage of Poverty*, 168.

34. "Self-Help," *Fraser's*, 784. Sadly, between editions Smiles removed some of these "apt and happy" sayings.

35. Robinson, *Self-Education*, 84.

36. "Inspiration," *Oxford English Dictionary*.

37. Huber, *American Idea of Success*, 147 and 149.

38. Marden's publishers claimed to receive "thousands of letters from people in nearly all parts of the world, telling how the book has aroused their ambition, changed their ideals and aims, increased their confidence, and how it has spurred them to the successful undertaking of what they before had thought impossible" (*Pushing to the Front*, v). Smiles writes about the letters he received in his *Autobiography*; see especially 224–28. For another reading of readers' responses to Smiles, see Lecki, "Reader-Help." Another example, perhaps more strictly of confirming rather than inspiring ambition, comes from Louis Pasteur's biography: Pasteur "had a profound faith in hard work as the means of rising in the world, and when he had a cerebral haemorrhage at the age of fifty-six, from too much of it, he read Samuel Smiles's *Self-Help* during his convalescence." Zeldin, *A History of French Passions*, 582.

39. Smiles, *Character*, 215–16.

40. Hood, *Peerage of Poverty*, 136.

41. Schalk, "Reevaluating the Supercrip," 73.

42. Schalk, "Reevaluating the Supercrip," 77. For more on this important subject, see also Kafer, *Feminist, Queer, Crip*; and Scott, "Time Out of Joint." In the fuller passage I quote from in the body, Schalk synthesizes how this critical discussion has theorized the supercrip narrative: "Catherine Scott, in her work on Christopher Reeve's memoir, identifies two additional mechanisms of supercrip narratives: suppression or masking of negative emotions such as stress or depression, and emphasis on personal, individualized attributes such as willpower and determination . . . Alison Kafer writes that a focus on individuality depoliticizes disability by strategically deploying 'rhetorics of disability acceptance and inclusion' in the name of 'decidedly un-crip ends.'" Schalk, "Reevaluating the Supercrip," 77. Chrisman also suggestively points to how "self-help" rhetoric has circulated in descriptions of disability: "In Disability Studies, the inspirational narrative has become intrinsically bound to the narrative of overcoming: that is, the idea that one can take sole responsibility for conquering one's disability and its attendant challenges. The belief that a person with a disability can and should pull oneself up by the bootstraps despite overwhelming odds is an impediment to understanding the sociocultural barriers that people with any given disability may face." ("A Reflection on Inspiration," 173).

43. Adams, *The Secret of Success*, 40.

44. W. Anderson, *Self-Made Men*, 18.

45. Goldstein, *Console and Classify*, 153.

46. Davis, *Obsessions: A History*, 68.

47. T. C. Morgan, "Monomania and Monomaniacs," 44.

48. Goldstein, *Console and Classify*, 157.

49. L. Parker, "Effects of Certain Mental and Bodily States," 55–56.

50. Goldstein, *Console and Classify*, 160.

51. Goldstein, *Console and Classify*, 161.

52. Spitzka, *Insanity*, 295–96.

53. Parker, "Effects of Certain Mental and Bodily States," 70 and 72.

54. Parker, "Effects of Certain Mental and Bodily States," 72. Interestingly, Parker imagines that passions are more liable to result in insanity than "literary or scientific pursuits"—even as he cites the example of the man obsessed with perpetual motion—certainly a scientific pursuit.

55. Van Zuylen, *Monomania*, 44.

56. Smiles's message—and his example of going home to write late into the night—has interesting through lines with academia today. Blum, for example, examines these tropes in "The Self-Helpification of Academe."

57. Morgan, "Monomania and Monomaniacs," 45.

58. Spitzka, *Insanity*, 296. Spitzka's choice of the word "caricature" seems particularly apt in light of how frequently representations of monomania and obsessive-compulsive disorder have relied on comedy. See Cefalu, "What's So Funny about Obsessive-Compulsive Disorder?"

59. Parker, "Effects of Certain Mental and Bodily States," 56.

60. "Success," 700.

## Chapter 2 · Expanding the Story of Ambition, Work, and Health in a Limited World

1. Martineau, *Autobiography*, 202. Hereafter cited parenthetically in the text.

2. Adams, *Woman's Work and Worth*, 201–2.

3. Goodlad, *Victorian Literature and the Victorian State*, 146. While Smiles's *Self-Help* of course appeared later in Martineau's career, Craik's *The Pursuit of Knowledge under Difficulties* was published in the 1830s, including his follow-ups that focused particularly on women (and especially women writers). The 1830s also saw "self-help" emerge as a new term, as outlined in the introduction.

4. As Klaver writes, "By 1834, Martineau's publisher, Charles Fox, was selling 10,000 copies of each monthly volume, with the whole series reaching an estimated 144,000 readers." Klaver, *A/Moral Economics*, 58.

5. Freedgood, "Banishing Panic," 213.

6. Logan, introduction to *Illustrations of Political Economy*, 34.

7. Martineau, preface to *Illustrations of Political Economy*, 1.viii–ix.

8. Peterson, *Becoming a Woman of Letters*, 10.

9. For example, in speaking of women and the vote, Martineau writes, "I have no vote at elections, though I am a tax-paying housekeeper and responsible citizen; and I regard the disability as an absurdity, seeing that I have for a long course of years influenced public affairs to an extent not professed or attempted by many men" (*Autobiography*, 305).

10. Freedgood, "Banishing Panic," 38.

11. Hobart, "Harriet Martineau's Political Economy."

12. Appropriately, this anecdote appears in Hamilton's biography of Martineau in *Women Writers* (72).

13. Martineau, *Life in the Sick-Room*, 41–42.

14. G. L. Craik, *Pursuit of Knowledge under Difficulties*, 1.286.

15. Crawford, "Harriet Martineau," 465.

16. Ablow, "Harriet Martineau and the Impersonality of Pain," 685 and 677.

17. E. Wright, *Reading for Health*, 119.

18. Martineau, *Illustrations of Political Economy*, 1.xv–xvi.

19. *Life in the Wilds*, 3–4. Martineau's depiction of these Indigenous people is sketchy at best and taps into racist ideas (they are described as a "race of men, more fierce than wild beasts"). They seem to be included only to motivate the plot revolving around the settlers and their resourcefulness.

20. For more on this subject, see especially Logan, *Harriet Martineau, Victorian Imperialism, and the Civilizing Mission*; and Brantlinger, *Dark Vanishings*.

21. See especially Martineau's *Ireland* and *Homes Abroad*.

22. As Elizabeth Miller writes, with the rise of naturalism the novel moves "toward ecological realism by locating the human squarely within the environment and by placing environmental limits on human agency" ("Dendrography and Ecological Realism," 701).

23. Klaver in particular focuses on this topic, tracing where Martineau's fictionalization of economic principles comes into tension with the source texts. See Klaver, *A/Moral Economics*.

24. MacDuffie, "Environment," 682. MacDuffie draws on Pearce, "From 'Circumstances' to 'Environment,'" 247–48.

25. See especially Dzelzainis, "Malthus, Women and Fiction."

26. "ART. VII.—*Illustrations of Political Economy*," 136.

27. Watt, *Rise of the Novel*, 86–87.

28. Martineau, *Ella of Garveloch*, 143. Hereafter cited parenthetically in the text.

29. Freedgood, "Banishing Panic," 33.

30. Hirschman, *Passions and the Interests*, 51–52.

31. Kropotkin, *Mutual Aid*, 227.

32. For more on this aspect, see my article "Imagining Environmental and Economic Systems."

33. Macpherson, *Political Theory of Possessive Individualism*, 3.

34. Russell, *Reading Embodied Citizenship*, 4–5.

35. Other recent work in ecocriticism and eighteenth- and nineteenth-century studies—including Ashton Nichols's *Beyond Romantic Ecocriticism* and Kate Rigby's *Dancing with Disaster*—also points out that such rethinking of agency is not entirely new, even in the British and imperial context, but developed alongside those traditional binaries.

36. Malthus, *Principle of Population*, 65. This passage appears in Malthus's 1798 edition of the *Essay*.

37. Malthus, *Principle of Population*, 128.

38. Malthus, *Principle of Population*, 61.

39. Malthus, *Principle of Population*, 531–32.

40. Martineau, *Weal and Woe*, 68. Hereafter cited parenthetically in the text.

41. See, for example, Plotz, *The Crowd*; Daly, *Demographic Imagination*; and Steinlight, *Populating the Novel*.

42. See R. J. Mayhew's *Malthus*, especially chapter 5.

43. Chapman, *Memorials of Harriet Martineau*, 208.

44. See Klaver, "Imperial Economics," especially 26–27.

45. As the reviewer for the *Dublin University Magazine* put it, "Miss Martineau was determined to outmalthus Malthus" ("Miss Martineau's Tracts," 561). Another reviewer pondered, "By what criterion is each labourer to know how many men and women in his parish ought to marry, and when his turn should take place?" ("ART IV. *Illustrations of Political Economy*," 336). As this reviewer goes on to point out, such a rule would mean sacrificing one's own desires for the greater good not only of an unappreciative public but also of a *future*

unappreciative public: "And what is the preventive check to accomplish? The possible rise of wages, from a diminution of labour, some twenty years hence! How can the prospect of so happy a consummation fail to reconcile the labourer to all the privations of celibacy, especially when supported under them by the approbation of Society!" (341). And, as the particularly scathing *Quarterly Review* pointed out, all of this assumed that people could even determine the right number of workers needed: "When it is notorious that in these districts the relative supply and demand for labour often oscillates from one extreme to the other within a year or two—we are to be informed by Miss Martineau, in delicate phrase, that the labourers have the power, and they alone, by more or less of continence, to adjust the supply of labour exactly at all times to the demand!" ("ART. VII. *Illustrations of Political Economy*," 144).

46. Dalley, "On Martineau's *Illustrations of Political Economy*."

47. Holmes, *Fictions of Affliction*, 3–4.

48. Garland-Thomson, *Extraordinary Bodies*, 43.

49. See Samalin, "Exploitation."

50. See Peterson, "From French Revolution to English Reform," 444 and 434. Aware of what ideologically troubled waters she was treading, Martineau attempted to remain an independent voice. To Martineau's credit, Peterson finds only one misstep—when she "succumb[ed] to Lord Brougham's plea that she write tales illustrating the new poor law for the Society for the Diffusion of Useful Knowledge," which was associated with the Whig party (449n70). Suggestive of the extent to which Martineau did remain independent is the fact that she drew criticism for her *Illustrations* from so many quarters, from publications like the Tory *Quarterly Review* as well as from working-class newspapers—especially after the publication of *Weal and Woe* (Peterson, "From French Revolution to English Reform," 447n64). Peterson draws on N. W. Thompson, *The People's Science*.

51. Russell, *Reading Embodied Citizenship*, 21.

## Chapter 3 · Enabling the Self-Help Narrative in Dinah Craik's *John Halifax, Gentleman*

1. R. Gilmour, *Idea of the Gentleman*, 101; Brantlinger, *The Spirit of Reform*, 119; and Bourrier, *Victorian Bestseller*, 92.

2. See, for example, Holmes, *Fictions of Affliction*; Bourrier, *The Measure of Manliness*; Hingston, *Articulating Bodies*; and Gore, *Plotting Disability*.

3. James, "Dinah Maria Mulock Craik," 846.

4. Holmes argues that Victorian melodramas primed readers to respond with emotion to portrayals of characters with disabilities in *Fictions of Affliction*. Bourrier demonstrates how Victorian novels repeatedly paired strong men with ill or disabled men in order to develop masculine characters through their opposites, who serve as affective focalizers or narrators. See Bourrier, *The Measure of Manliness*. For other recent disability studies work concentrating on the nineteenth-century novel and addressing Craik, see Gore, *Plotting Disability* (on Phineas's character versus the hetero-ablist assumptions of the marriage plot); and Hingston, *Articulating Bodies* (on *The Little Lame Prince*).

5. D. M. Craik, *John Halifax, Gentleman*, 79. Hereafter cited parenthetically in the text.

6. R. Gilmour, *Idea of the Gentleman*, 86.

7. See Showalter, "Dinah Mulock Craik," 6.

8. Mitchell, *Dinah Mulock Craik*, 105. As Mitchell notes, both novels explore the fate of a woman who gives birth out of wedlock.

9. Bourrier, *Victorian Bestseller*, ix.

10. Mitchell, *Dinah Mulock Craik*, i.

11. Bourrier, *Victorian Bestseller*, 107.

12. Bourrier, *Victorian Bestseller*, 84–85 and 119–20.

13. Oliphant, "Mrs. Craik," 83.

14. Shaylor, introduction to D. M. Craik, *John Halifax, Gentleman*, vii.

15. "Obituary," 269.

16. Showalter, "Dinah Mulock Craik," 10.

17. Bourrier, *Victorian Bestseller*, 108.

18. Showalter, "Dinah Mulock Craik," 18.

19. Matheson, "Introduction," xii.

20. Bourrier, *Victorian Bestseller*, 93–94.

21. Bourrier, *Victorian Bestseller*, 93.

22. Oliphant, "Mrs. Craik," 82.

23. Oliphant, "Mrs. Craik," 82.

24. Showalter, "Dinah Mulock Craik," 9.

25. Matheson, introduction to D. M. Craik, *John Halifax, Gentleman*, xxv.

26. Matheson, introduction to D. M. Craik, *John Halifax, Gentleman*, xi–xii.

27. Peterson, *Becoming a Woman of Letters*, 132.

28. Oliphant, "Mrs. Craik," 84. Such stories were recounted well after Craik's death. Annie Matheson's introduction to the novel similarly notes that Craik "held that the world at large had no right to cross the threshold of a woman's home for any other reason than that of personal friendship, and that gratitude for her writing, if she happen to be a writer, is best shown by respecting the modesty of her reserve" (xxiv–xxv).

29. D. M. Craik, *Olive*, 2.32.

30. D. M. Craik, *Olive*, 1.55. Craik alludes to a heroine who had long generated debates about the proper outlets for women's ambitions. Germaine de Staël's 1807 *Corinne; ou, L'Italie* focuses on a woman artist and performer. In this passage, Craik echoes Felicia Hemans's questions about Corinne's happiness versus that of an everyday married woman:

> Radiant daughter of the sun!
> Now thy living wreath is won.
> Crown'd of Rome!—Oh! art thou not
> Happy in that glorious lot?—
> Happier, happier far than thou,
> With the laurel on thy brow,
> She that makes the humblest hearth
> Lovely but to one on earth!

See Hemans, "Corinne at the Capitol," in *Poetical Works*, 478.

31. Bourrier, *Victorian Bestseller*, 118.

32. D. M. Craik, *A Woman's Thoughts about Women*, 41.

33. D. M. Craik, *A Woman's Thoughts about Women*, 13.

34. King, *Ambition, a History*, 121.

35. "John Halifax, Gentleman," *Literary Gazette*, 178.

36. Quoted in Showalter, "Dinah Mulock Craik," 18.

37. "John Halifax, Gentleman," *Saturday Review*, 85.

38. "John Halifax, Gentleman," *Athenaeum*, 520.

39. James, "Dinah Maria Mulock Craik," 845.

40. "John Halifax, Gentleman," *Examiner*, 293 and 292.

41. Bourrier, *Victorian Bestseller*, 98–99.

42. Hutton, "Novels," 472.

43. D. M. Craik, *John Halifax, Gentleman*, 68. Hereafter cited parenthetically in the text.

44. Bayard is in fact an example included in Smiles's *Self-Help*. Beyond John himself, many of the characters in *John Halifax, Gentleman* look for models: the childish Edwin's "great object of hero-worship [is] his eldest brother," Guy (360); Ursula is twice compared to Cornelia, a

model of feminine virtues; and as for Ravenel, the young aristocrat of the neighborhood, his "hero-worship had fixed itself, with an almost unreasoning trust" on John Halifax (452).

45. "John Halifax, Gentleman," *Athenaeum*, 520.
46. Malm, *Fossil Capital*, 57.
47. Mitchell, *Dinah Mulock Craik*, 49.
48. "The Country of John Halifax," 316.
49. Matheson, Introduction to *John Halifax, Gentleman*, xxi.
50. "Memorial to the Author of 'John Halifax, Gentleman,'" 72.
51. Dames, *Amnesiac Selves*, 4.
52. Dames, *Amnesiac Selves*, 12.
53. Lacom, "'The Time Is Sick,'" 547.
54. Mitchell and Snyder, *Narrative Prosthesis*, 29.
55. See Bourrier, *Measure of Manliness*.
56. Garland-Thomson, *Extraordinary Bodies*, 48.
57. Garland-Thomson, *Extraordinary Bodies*, 48.
58. Garland-Thomson, *Extraordinary Bodies*, 9.
59. E. Wright, *Reading for Health*, 119.
60. Sparks, "Dinah Mulock Craik's *Olive*," 360. For another reading of Craik, the marriage plot, and disability, see Gore, *Plotting Disability*.
61. Hutton, "Novels by the Authoress of 'John Halifax,'" 475.
62. See Garland-Thomson, *Extraordinary Bodies*, 27 and 20.
63. Dames, *Amnesiac Selves*, 236.
64. Martineau, *Life in the Sick-Room*, 148.

## Chapter 4 · "At What Point This Ambition Transgresses the Boundary of Virtue"

1. Thackeray, "Small-Beer Chronicle," 122.
2. Thackeray, *The Snobs of England*, 2. Hereafter cited parenthetically in the text.
3. Puckett, *Bad Form*, 41.
4. Garcha, *From Sketch to Novel*, 7.
5. Byerly, "Effortless Art," 349.
6. Trollope, *Thackeray*, 79.
7. Trollope locates a tension here between aesthetic and financial considerations: they were simply "too good to be brought to an end, and therefore there were forty-five of them. A dozen would have been better" (*Thackeray*, 83).
8. Trollope, *Thackeray*, 90.
9. Shillingsburg, "The 'Trade' of Literature," 741.
10. Sundell, introduction to *Twentieth Century Interpretations of Vanity Fair*, 1. For more on Thackeray's periodical work, see Gary Simon's "'Show Me the Money!,'" especially 64 and 91.
11. Puckett, *Bad Form*, 36.
12. Puckett, *Bad Form*, 37.
13. See, for example, Fisher's "The Aesthetic of the Mediocre"; and Byerly's "Effortless Art."
14. Thackeray, "A Brother of the Press," 336.
15. Thackeray "A Brother of the Press," 336–37.
16. Thackeray, "May Gambols," 706.
17. Thackeray, "On Men and Pictures," 99.
18. Thackeray, "A Brother of the Press," 336–37.
19. Thackeray, *The Paris Sketch Book*, 64.
20. Gigante, *Taste: A Literary History*, 2.
21. Thackeray, "On Men and Pictures," 101.

22. Thackeray, "On Men and Pictures," 101.

23. Thackeray, "On Men and Pictures," 101.

24. See A. H. Miller, *Novels behind Glass*, 27.

25. Thackeray, *Letters and Private Papers*, 198 and 216.

26. Thackeray, "A Pictorial Rhapsody," 119.

27. This way of thinking about artistic ambition through the comparison of sketches and oil paintings was current in Victorian culture. It also came up in chapter 3 in relation to Dinah Craik—with Annie Matheson claiming that the "charm" of *John Halifax, Gentleman* "is that of a noble and single-minded sincerity, and of that untutored poetry which, never seeking to pass its boundaries or to strain after effect, has its own distinction of fine and simple phrasing, and achieves what more complicated and ambitious effort could not have touched. It is a pastel sketch in which the colours are translucent and delicate, rather than an elaborate oil-painting on a crowded canvas" (introduction to *John Halifax, Gentleman*, xii).

28. Thackeray, *The Newcomes*, 213–214.

29. Felski, *The Limits of Critique*, 135.

30. Felski, *The Limits of Critique*, 134.

31. A. Anderson, *The Powers of Distance*, 7.

32. A. Anderson, *The Powers of Distance*, 32.

33. Carey, *Thackeray: Prodigal Genius*, 111–12, 115.

34. K. M. Rogers, "The Pressure of Convention," 259.

35. K. M. Rogers, "Pressure of Convention," 62n1.

36. It's worth noting that this phenomenon has been studied by researchers in psychology and political science, where the appeal and "motivating power" of the underdog has been more quantitatively measured. The power of the underdog is wrapped up with ideas about merit: observers perceive underdogs as working harder, which makes them more likable—and, perhaps, more deserving of success. See especially Vandello, Goldschmied, and Richards, "The Appeal of the Underdog." See also Rogers and Moore, "The Motivating Power of Under-confidence"; and Goldschmied and Vandello, "The Advantage of Disadvantage."

37. Thackeray, *The Luck of Barry Lyndon*, 142. Hereafter cited parenthetically in the text.

38. Harden, "Historical Introduction," 233–34.

39. Trollope, *Thackeray*, 75–76.

40. Ritchie, introduction to Thackeray, *Biographical Edition*, xxxiv–xxxv.

41. As I've argued elsewhere, this leaves much room for ambiguity, in the novel and in later adaptations—and particularly around the question of sexuality and sexual violence. See my article "Becky Sharp, Gender, and Likability."

42. Gilbert, *Better Left Unsaid*, 42.

43. See Courtemanche, *The "Invisible Hand" and British Fiction*.

44. Courtemanche, *The "Invisible Hand" and British Fiction*, 166.

45. Jadwin, "Clytemnestra Rewarded."

46. A. H. Miller, *Novels behind Glass*, 47.

47. A. H. Miller, *Novels behind Glass*, 47.

48. Richardson, "Becky Sharp, Gender, and Likability."

49. Marks, "'Mon Pauvre Prisonnier,'" 78.

50. Tillotson, *Thackeray the Novelist*, 92. I am indebted to Kurnick's allusion to Tillotson in *Empty Houses*, 61.

51. See Ngai, *Our Aesthetic Categories*.

52. See Cohn, *Transparent Minds*, 26–33.

53. Kurnick, *Empty Houses*, 50.

54. A. Armstrong, *How Novels Think*, 80–81.

55. Thackeray, *A Collection of Letters*, 447.

56. Lionel Stevenson notes many parallels between Lady Morgan and Becky Sharp, as well as interesting echoes in names across Morgan's novels and *Vanity Fair*—echoes that suggest Thackeray had her in mind. See Stevenson, "*Vanity Fair* and Lady Morgan."

57. Clarke, *Thackeray and Women*, 9.

58. Boucherett, *Hints on Self-Help*.

59. For a recent example of this research, see Cha and Weeden, "Overwork and the Slow Convergence in the Gender Gap in Wages."

60. See, for example, Brescoll, Smith, and Thomas, "Constrained by Emotion"; Hack, "Forming Impressions"; and Pierce, *Gender Trials*, especially 114–15.

61. Much recent research has explored how gender biases result in double standards for certain behaviors or traits. For example, male professors might be praised for acting empathetically toward students, whereas the same behavior is expected as a baseline for women's behavior—going unremarked and unrewarded in students' evaluations. For a few recent examples of this literature, see Heilman and Chen, "Same Behavior, Different Consequences"; Driscoll, Hunt, and MacNell, "What's in a Name"; and Boring, Ottoboni, and Stark, "Student Evaluations of Teaching."

62. See Williams and Tiedens, "The Subtle Suspension of Backlash"; and Okimoto and Brescoll, "The Price of Power."

63. From Susan Hampshire's framing of her portrayal of Becky Sharp in the 1967 BBC production, to debates about Reese Witherspoon being too likable, to, most recently, Olivia Cooke's performance and reviews framing the character's selfishness as "a feminist act," this figure still raises fraught debates about gender, ambition, and "likability." I discuss these adaptations at length in "Becky Sharp, Gender, and Likability." For examples of debates about Becky Sharp and feminism, see Colby, "'Scenes of All Sorts . . .'"; Gottlieb, "Becky in the Movies"; and Cohen and Reid, "*Vanity Fair*: Becky's Selfishness Is a Feminist Act."

## Chapter 5 · Individuating Ambitions in a Competitive System

An earlier and shorter form of this chapter appeared in the *Fortnightly Review* as "A Competitive World: Ambition and Self-Help in Trollope's *An Autobiography* and *The Three Clerks*" as the winner of the 2012 Trollope Prize. My thanks to the committee for their thoughtful feedback, and to Denis Boyles and the *Fortnightly Review* for permission to reprint this material in its current form.

1. Trollope, *The Three Clerks*, 121. Hereafter cited parenthetically in the text.

2. See A. Anderson, *Bleak Liberalism*; and D. Wright, *Bad Logic*.

3. Cathy Shuman also points to this fairy-tale logic in *Pedagogical Economies*; see especially 89–90.

4. As Cathy Shuman observes, Trollope's work "is structured by vacillation or unresolvable opposition." *Pedagogical Economies*, 84.

5. Skilton, introduction to Trollope, *An Autobiography*, xiii, quoted in Goodlad, *Victorian Literature and the Victorian State*, 141.

6. Trollope, *An Autobiography*, 40 and 43. Hereafter cited parenthetically in the text.

7. Bareham, "Patterns of Excellence," 67.

8. Smiles, *Self-Help*, 94.

9. Kincaid, "Trollope's Fictional Autobiography," 343.

10. For an alternate reading of these tropes, see Allen, "Trollope to His Readers," 10.

11. As if managing his own ambition, Smiles is careful to note at the start of his *Autobiography* that he did not think his life merited such attention—but that friends urged him on, citing the examples of Benjamin Franklin and Anthony Trollope in particular. See S. Smiles, *Autobiography*, 2.

12. Smiles, *Self-Help*, 119.

13. As James puts it, "The imagination that Trollope possessed he had at least thoroughly at his command." *Partial Portraits*, 98–99.

14. Super, "Truth and Fiction in Trollope's *Autobiography*," 79–80.

15. B. Franklin, *Benjamin Franklin*, 646.

16. Aguirre, "Cold Print: Professing Authorship," 573.

17. See Knelman, "Trollope's Experiments with Anonymity," 21–24.

18. Knelman, "Trollope's Experiments with Anonymity," 23.

19. Sadleir, *Trollope: A Commentary*, 374; and Kincaid, *The Novels of Anthony Trollope*, 73.

20. Sadleir, *Trollope: A Commentary*, 196.

21. See, for example, Ruth, *Novel Professions*; Shuman, *Pedagogical Economies*; and Dames, "Trollope and the Career."

22. Trollope, *Autobiography*, 211–12.

23. "The Civil Service," *Dublin University Magazine*, 412.

24. See Littler, *Against Meritocracy*, 54–55, where Littler uses the example of the British Civil Service specifically to illustrate "covert discrimination."

25. "The Civil Service as a Profession," 227.

26. "The Civil Service," *Dublin University Magazine*, 420. For more on Trollope and his attitudes toward the Civil Service, see Shuman, *Pedagogical Economies* (especially chapter 3); and Goodlad, *Victorian Literature and the Victorian State* (especially pages 139–40).

27. I'm thinking here about how ambition has been read in this novel as a sort of indictment of the Smilesian version of "energy and ambition," which can "disrupt the Novel as Usual." Goodlad, *Victorian Literature and the Victorian State*, 141. But Trollope seems to be at pains to distinguish among different sorts of ambitions and their potential uses.

28. "The Civil Service as a Profession," 225.

29. Shuman, *Pedagogical Economies*, 86.

30. See Dames, "Trollope and the Career."

31. Woloch, *The One vs. the Many*, 13 and 245.

32. Davies, "Trollope and His Style," 77.

33. Davies, "Trollope and His Style," 76 and 82.

34. Clark, *Language and Style of Anthony Trollope*, 19.

35. Jaffe, "Trollope in the Stock Market," 58.

36. apRoberts, *The Moral Trollope*, 34.

37. Kincaid, *The Novels of Anthony Trollope*, 48.

38. apRoberts, *The Moral Trollope*, 41.

39. Aitken, "'A Kind of Felicity,'" 350–51.

40. apRoberts, *The Moral Trollope*, 21.

41. Sadleir, *Trollope: A Commentary*, 375.

42. Bareham, introduction to *Anthony Trollope*, 9.

43. Kincaid, *The Novels of Anthony Trollope*, 71.

44. Meckier, "*The Three Clerks* and *Rachel Ray*," 166.

45. Kendrick, *The Novel-Machine*, 78.

46. Sadleir, *Trollope: A Commentary*, 343.

47. Polhemus, *The Changing World of Anthony Trollope*, 17.

48. Trollope, *Autobiography*, 293.

49. James, *Partial Portraits*, 116.

50. Shuman, *Pedagogical Economies*, 89–90.

51. Schoeck, *Envy*, 22–23.

52. James, *Partial Portraits*, 127.

53. Polhemus, *The Changing World of Anthony Trollope*, 20.

## Chapter 6 · Placing and Displacing Ambition

1. Quoted in Martin, introduction to Franklin, *My Brilliant Career*, 31.

2. Franklin, *My Brilliant Career*, 1. Hereafter cited parenthetically in the text (and, when necessary for clarity, abbreviated as *MBC*).

3. Stephens, "A Bookful of Sunlight."

4. L, R. F. O., "A Bashkirtseff of the Bush," 566.

5. Stephens, "A Bookful of Sunlight."

6. Davies and Martin, "Toward Worlding Settler Texts," 5.

7. Davies and Martin, "Toward Worlding Settler Texts," 3.

8. Donald, "Her Brilliant Career," 108. As Donald notes, Armstrong was "the first female filmmaker from outside the US to be approached by MGM to make a big-budget feature," giving "Oscar winners Geoffrey Rush and Cate Blanchett some of their first roles" (108).

9. Byrne, "The Despair of the Household." Byrne reads the novel as "one of the early works of feminism." Rickey, "*My Brilliant Career*: Unapologetic Women." Rickey also imagines this "timeless" spirit characterizing "the novelist who created her, the filmmaker who put her on-screen, and the star who brought her to life there."

10. Cusack, James, and Franklin, *Yarn Spinners: A Story in Letters*, 377.

11. My use of the word "displace" here is informed by Tanya Dalziell's attention to how Franklin's novel uses the logic of displacement (specifically, in Dalziell's argument, the way the novel draws on racialized tropes when representing socioeconomic hierarchies). I want to build on this work here to suggest the importance of adding ecocritical readings to this complex of issues. See Dalziell, "Colonial Displacements."

12. E. Miller, "Dendrography and Ecological Realism," 701.

13. A. H. Miller, *Burdens of Perfection*, 2.

14. King, *Ambition, a History*, 121.

15. As Sarah Maddison writes of the Australian context: "The deep resistance to acknowledging the foundational illegitimacy of the Australian settler state fuels a limited approach to the administration of memory." "The Limits of the Administration of Memory," 182. Much important work has been done on the long and ongoing violence of settler colonialism and its ideology. For more on how this ideology has erased Indigenous people and their history, and how this has been perpetuated by educational as well as political systems, see, for example Patel, *Decolonizing Educational Research*; and Masta, "Settler Colonial Legacies." Other important work also points to how, in responding to or studying settler-colonial ideology, its history, and ongoingness, we face other risks of turning "decolonization" into a metaphor (Tuck and Yang, "Decolonization Is Not a Metaphor") and "absorbing the knowledge, but once again displacing the bodies out to the margins" (Gaztambide-Fernández and Tuck, "Curriculum, Replacement, and Settler Futurity," 73).

16. For research on Aboriginal practices around agriculture, land management, and fire, see Gammage, *The Biggest Estate on Earth*; Pascoe, *Dark Emu*; and Kerwin, *Aboriginal Dreaming Paths and Trading Routes*. Kerwin also provides much-needed counternarratives about where European colonizers learned practices from Aboriginal Australians. For the importance of Indigenous Ecological Knowledge in the North American context, see, for example, Eisenberg et al., "Out of the Ashes."

17. Walker, "Self-Made Maids," 281. Walker points to studies like Robert Grant's "'The Fit and Unfit'" and Robert Hogg's *Men and Manliness* that name Samuel Smiles as a key source of such self-help discourse in colonial spaces. The degree to which self-help and emigration were linked in Britain and the empire can also be glimpsed in the names of societies that aimed to assist would-be settlers, such as the Self-Help Emigration Society of Liverpool, the Crystal Palace Self-Help Emigration Society, and the Self-Help Emigration Society in London. Writing in 1888, Walter B. Paton tracked the work of emigration societies and advised others on how to get involved; he counted seventy such societies and comments, "I have no doubt there are many more" ("Work and Workers," 129).

18. Malthus, *Principle of Population*, 54.

19. Goschen, *Address*, 16.

20. Forster, *Life of Charles Dickens*, 1.278.

21. For more on early accounts of Australia's environment and the Cook expedition, see, for example, Bewell, *Natures in Translation*; and Hudson, "'Botany Bay' in British Magazines."

22. See Buchan, *Empire of Political Thought*, for an argument that complicates the concept of terra nullius in this context (see especially chapter 3).

23. Wolfe, *Settler Colonialism*, 163. Other work has linked such discussions about settler colonialism, the Australian context, and genocide studies; see A. Dirk Moses, *Genocide and Settler History*.

24. Konishi, "First Nations Scholars," 301. Konishi contributes to and synthesizes the work being done in this area, while also showing the importance of Indigenous-authored extra-colonial histories that go beyond the rhetoric of replacement and exploitation. For more on Indigenous land management and agriculture, and how colonizers benefited from this knowledge, see Kerwin, *Aboriginal Dreaming Paths and Trading Routes*.

25. Wolfe, *Settler Colonialism*, 27.

26. Tuck and Yang, "Decolonization Is Not a Metaphor," 5.

27. Martin, introduction to Franklin, *My Brilliant Career*, 21.

28. Martin, introduction to Franklin, *My Brilliant Career*, 21.

29. Martin, introduction to Franklin, *My Brilliant Career*, 21.

30. Richards, *Goulburn Mulwaree LGA Aboriginal Heritage Study*, 12. Much of the early anthropological work still cited today is of course difficult to rely on, especially without more voices from the Aboriginal groups of the region. The anthropologist Norman Tindale brought dangerous ideologies (from his views on Nazism to eugenics) and assumptions to his work. Some have questioned, for example, the way he grouped people by languages.

31. Gammage, *The Biggest Estate on Earth*; Pascoe, *Dark Emu*; and Kerwin, *Aboriginal Dreaming Paths and Trading Routes*.

32. Gammage, *The Biggest Estate on Earth*, 197.

33. Richards, *Goulburn Mulwaree LGA Aboriginal Heritage Study*, 15.

34. Quoted in Richards, *Goulburn Mulwaree LGA Aboriginal Heritage Study*, 15.

35. For more on these critical discussions, see Jusová, *The New Woman and the Empire*; Crozier-De Rosa, "Identifying with the Frontier"; Hassan, "Jane Eyre's Doubles?"; and Beetham and Heilmann, *New Woman Hybridities*.

36. Moffat, "'Devoted to the Cause of Woman's Rights,'" 307.

37. Fong, "The Stories outside the African Farm," especially 429–430.

38. Schreiner, *The Story of an African Farm*, 10.

39. Gerson, "Wild Colonial Girls," 62.

40. Dalziell, "Colonial Displacements," 53. For another reading of race in Franklin's work, see Garton, "Contesting Enslavement."

41. This is one of many suggestive parallels with the Brontës—from the interest in governessing (Sybylla has a brief and disastrous stint as a governess in *My Brilliant Career*) to the portrayal of ambitious women to the association with "wild" spaces, whether the Yorkshire moors or the Australian bush. A number of early reviews pointed out parallels.

42. "My Brilliant Career," *Saturday Review*, 373; and Martin, introduction to Franklin, *My Brilliant Career*, 33. This tendency to merge Franklin and her narrators has also, often in combination with gendered and Freudian readings, problematically influenced later critical understandings of Franklin's work. Early reviewers seemed to discount Franklin's talent or "genius" when they imagined her as merely reporting her own life. These critical narratives have intersected with Freudian readings that understand Franklin's depiction of a woman's sexuality as evidence of repression and working through something (vs. intentional, even artistic, creation). In fact, one of Franklin's acquaintances explained away the novel's radicalism as the

result of Franklin's "repressed sexuality." According to this reading, "morbid introspection, with sexual frustration, slides below the story like a tidal undertow." See Roderick, *Miles Franklin: Her Brilliant Career*, 71–72, 75, and 126; also quoted in Scates, "*My Brilliant Career* and Radicalism," 370. Even as recently as 2002, Franklin has been described as a "young woman grappling with some very difficult problems," ultimately producing a novel "full of half thought through feelings and experiences." See Garton, "Contesting Enslavement," 344 and 346.

43. Martin, introduction to Franklin, *My Brilliant Career*, 31.

44. Stephens, "A Bookful of Sunlight." This passage comes in an otherwise glowing review, suggesting the extent to which, perhaps in the context of Australia in 1901 as well as in the pages of *Vanity Fair*, a woman's ambitions are more likely to be entertained when they are imagined as ultimately limited, "little."

45. Franklin, *My Career Goes Bung*, 6. Hereafter cited parenthetically in the text (and, when necessary for clarity, abbreviated as *MCGB*). As Martin explains, Franklin withdrew her first novel from publication in 1910—stipulating that further editions had to wait till a decade after her death. "The motivation traditionally assigned to this decision—which Franklin's later comments seem to confirm—was disappointment at her family's angry response to the novel." However, Martin also speculates that Franklin could have had other motivations, given that this "ambitious and increasingly astute writer" had had time to reflect on the novel and on the reviews. Martin, introduction to Franklin, *My Brilliant Career*, 15.

46. "The End of My Career," Mitchell Library MS 445/2. I am indebted to Richard Lansdown's unpublished work on these archival materials.

47. See Roe, *Her Brilliant Career*, 29.

48. Franklin, *Childhood at Brindabella*, 158. Hereafter cited parenthetically in the text.

49. Susan Gardner writes that "many metaphors in colonial writing personify a vanquished, violated, victimized land and people as female." "*My Brilliant Career*: Portrait of the Artist," 42. For a more capacious reading of this phenomenon and its emergence as a literary trope, see R. Greene, *Unrequited Conquests*.

50. As a number of critics have argued, marriage in the colonies comes to represent "a point of irreconcilability of the two roles the bush girl incorporates—'masculine' freedom and independence and 'feminine' domesticity and delicacy." See M. J. Smith and her summary of Martin's "Relative Correspondence" in "The 'Australian Girl' and the Domestic Ideal," 78.

51. See Scates, "*My Brilliant Career* and Radicalism," 372–73.

52. See Roe, "*My Brilliant Career* and 1890s Goulburn," 364.

53. Giles, *Antipodean America*, 332.

54. See Levine, *Forms*, 109.

55. This concern is echoed years later in *Prelude to Waking*, when Merlin reflects that, "since the war," she's not so attracted by the idea of having sons: "There's no safeguard that they wouldn't be cannon fodder, or poison-gas fodder, and it's time for thinking women to consider what careless fecundity means" (Parenthesis 8).

56. See especially Bewell, *Natures in Translation*; Gragg, *Englishmen Transplanted*; and J. P. Greene, *Creating the British Atlantic*.

57. "New Colony of South Australia."

58. Ross, "The Race of/in Romanticism," 27.

59. M. Harrison, "'The Tender Frame of Man,'" 74.

60. Darwin, *The Descent of Man*, 111 and 160.

61. Ruskin, *The Stones of Venice*, 174. For more on such thinking and how it fed into ideas about emigration in the British empire, see Grant, *Representations of British Emigration*, 85.

62. Darwin, *The Descent of Man*, 237.

63. Charnock, "On the Origin of the Gypsies," 90.

64. "Manifest Destiny at the Antipodes." Such rhetoric is in keeping with Patrick Brantlinger's argument in *Dark Vanishings* that white British subjects and settlers imagined other races as "doomed" to extinction.

65. M. Harrison, "'The Tender Frame of Man,'" 70. See also Brantlinger, *Dark Vanishings*, and especially chapter 8 on how Darwin and others applied ideas about evolution and race.

66. For more on this globalizing economy and ecology, see McClintock, *Imperial Leather*, particularly chapter 5 on advertising. See also Bewell, *Natures in Translation*.

67. See Allington, "All Bets Are Off," 18.

68. See English, *The Economy of Prestige*, particularly the fourth section of the book dedicated to "the global economy of cultural prestige."

69. Quoted in Delaney, "'A Dream Come True.'"

70. "Miles Franklin Literary Award."

71. So and Wezerek, "Why Is Publishing So White?"

72. Shaffi, "Publishing Seeks to Address Industry's Lack of Diversity."

73. Griffith, "Books about Women Don't Win Big Awards."

74. See Kon-yu, "On Sexism in Literary Prize Culture."

75. Royal Society of Literature, *Literature in Britain*, 7.

76. "Miles Franklin Literary Award."

77. Bolt, "Racism at the University."

78. Laidlaw and Lester, "Indigenous Sites and Mobilities," 12.

79. Konishi, "First Nations Scholars," 302.

80. Lucashenko, "The Stella Interview."

## Coda

1. "Spirit of Smiles," 551.

2. Blum, *Self-Help Compulsion*, 41.

3. G. L. Craik, *Pursuit of Knowledge under Difficulties*, 1.286.

4. "Spirit of Smiles," 552.

5. Davies, *Limits of Neoliberalism*, 41 and 43.

6. As Frank explains, "Chance events have always mattered, of course, but in some respects they've grown more important in recent decades. One reason for that has been the spread and intensification of what the economist Philip Cook and I have called winter-take-all markets." And this, in turn, "has amplified the importance of chance in a second way. In almost all cases, the prodigious rewards that accrue to a handful of winners in these markets attract enormous numbers of contestants. And the more contestants there are, the more luck matters." See Frank, *Success and Luck*, 9–10.

7. Littler, *Against Meritocracy*, 3 and 8–9.

8. See, for example, Petersen, *Can't Even*; and Chetty et al., "Race and Economic Opportunity."

9. Johnson, Zhang, and Keil, "Psychological Underpinnings of Zero-Sum Thinking."

10. There are also interesting trends for how zero-sum thinking lines up with people's politics. See Davidai and Ongis, "The Politics of Zero-Sum Thinking."

11. Harford, "Trump, Bannon and the Lure of Zero-Sum Thinking."

12. Mishra, *Age of Anger*, 28.

13. Marx, *Grundrisse*, 334.

14. Littler sums up recent research in this area examining both downward as well as upward mobility since the 1980s: "As Vikki Boliver and David Byrne have argued, not only has there been 'little if any sign of [people] becoming any more equal over time' but now with a crumbling middle class, 'upward mobility increasingly necessitates downward mobility' . . . In other words, the 'room at the top' generated by an expanding public sector has shrunk." See Littler, *Against Meritocracy*, 53.

Ablow, Rachel. "Harriet Martineau and the Impersonality of Pain." *Victorian Studies* 56, no. 4 (Summer 2014): 675–97.

Adams, William Henry Davenport. *Celebrated Englishwomen of the Victorian Era.* 2 vols. London: F. V. White, 1884.

———. *Exemplary Women: A Record of Feminine Virtues and Achievements.* London: John Hogg, 1882.

———. *The Secret of Success; or, How to Get On in the World; With Some Remarks upon True and False Success, and the Art of Making the Best Use of Life.* 2nd ed. London: John Hogg, 1880.

———. *Woman's Work and Worth in Girlhood, Maidenhood, and Wifehood: Illustrations of Woman's Character, Duties, Rights, Position, Influence, Responsibilities, and Opportunities; With Hints on Self-Culture and Chapters on the Higher Education and Employment of Women.* London: John Hogg, 1880.

Aguirre, Robert D. "Cold Print: Professing Authorship in Anthony Trollope's *An Autobiography.*" *Biography* 25, no. 4 (Fall 2002): 569–92.

Aitken, David. "'A Kind of Felicity': Some Notes about Trollope's Style." *Nineteenth-Century Fiction* 20, no. 4 (March 1966): 337–53.

Alaimo, Stacy. *Bodily Natures: Science, Environment, and the Material Self.* Bloomington: Indiana University Press, 2010.

———. Foreword to *Disability Studies and the Environmental Humanities: Toward an Eco-crip Theory,* edited by Sarah Jaquette Ray and Jay Sibara, ix–xvi. Lincoln: University of Nebraska Press, 2017.

Alger, William Rounseville. *The Solitudes of Nature and of Man; or, The Loneliness of Human Life.* Boston: Roberts Brothers, 1867.

Allen, Peter. "Trollope to His Readers: The Unreliable Narrator of *An Autobiography.*" *Biography* 19, no. 1 (Winter 1996): 1–18.

Allington, Patrick. "All Bets Are Off [The 2012 Miles Franklin Literary Award and the 'Australianness' Eligibility Criterion]." *Australian Book Review* 342 (2012).

———. "'What Is Australia, Anyway?' The Glorious Limitations of the Miles Franklin Literary Award." *Australian Book Review* 332 (2011): 23–34.

Altick, Richard D. *The English Common Reader: A Social History of the Mass Reading Public, 1800–1900.* Chicago: University of Chicago Press, 1957.

Anderson, Amanda. *Bleak Liberalism.* Chicago: Chicago University Press, 2016.

———. *The Powers of Distance: Cosmopolitanism and the Cultivation of Detachment.* Princeton, NJ: Princeton University Press, 2001.

Anderson, Benedict. *Imagined Communities: Reflections on the Origin and Spread of Nationalism*. London: Verso, 2006. First published in 1983.

Anderson, William. *Self-Made Men*. London: John Snow, 1861.

apRoberts, Ruth. *The Moral Trollope*. Athens: Ohio University Press, 1971.

Archibald, Diana C. *Domesticity, Imperialism and Emigration in the Victorian Novel*. Columbia: University of Missouri Press, 2002.

Ardis, Ann. *New Women, New Novels: Feminism and Early Modernism*. New Brunswick, NJ: Rutgers University Press, 1990.

Armstrong, Nancy. *Desire and Domestic Fiction: A Political History of the Novel*. New York: Oxford University Press, 1987.

———. *How Novels Think: The Limits of British Individualism 1719–1900*. New York: Columbia University Press, 2006.

"ART IV. *Illustrations of Political Economy*." *Eclectic Review* 8 (October 1832): 328–49.

"ART. VII.—*Illustrations of Political Economy*." *Quarterly Review* 49, no. 97 (April 1833): 136–52.

Arthur, William. *The Successful Merchant: Sketches of the Life of Mr. Samuel Budgett, Late of Kingswood Hill*. 11th ed. London: Hamilton, Adams, 1854. First published in 1852.

Atkinson, Juliette. *Victorian Biography Reconsidered: A Study of Nineteenth-Century "Hidden" Lives*. Oxford: Oxford University Press, 2010.

Bareham, Tony. Introduction to and "Patterns of Excellence: Theme and Structure in *The Three Clerks*." In *Anthony Trollope*, edited by Tony Bareham, 7–11 and 54–80. London: Vision Press, 1980.

Bate, Jonathan. *Romantic Ecology: Wordsworth and the Environmental Tradition*. London: Routledge, 1991.

———. *The Song of the Earth*. London: Picador, 2000.

Beetham, Margaret, and Ann Heilmann. *New Woman Hybridities: Femininity, Feminism and International Consumer Culture, 1880–1930*. London: Routledge, 2004.

Bennett, Jane. *Vibrant Matter: A Political Ecology of Things*. Durham, NC: Duke University Press, 2010.

Bewell, Alan. *Natures in Translation: Romanticism and Colonial Natural History*. Baltimore: Johns Hopkins University Press, 2017.

Blatchford, Robert. *A Book about Books*. London: Clarion Press, 1903.

Blum, Beth. *The Self-Help Compulsion: Searching for Advice in Modern Literature*. New York: Columbia University Press, 2020.

———. "The Self-Helpification of Academe." *Chronicle of Higher Education* (July 8, 2018). www.chronicle.com/article/The-Self-Helpification-of/243861#comments-anchor.

Bodenheimer, Rosemarie. *Knowing Dickens*. Ithaca, NY: Cornell University Press, 2007.

Boliver, Vikki, and David Byrne. "Social Mobility: The Politics, the Reality, the Alternative." *Soundings* 55 (December 2013): 50–59.

Bolt, Andrew. "Racism at the University: White Australians Aren't 'Indigenous,' Too." *Herald Sun* (March 30, 2016). www.heraldsun.com.au/blogs/andrew-bolt/racism-at-the-university-white-australians-arent-indigenous-too/news-story/cd9bf55c7b65127b4f39bb93a6ea4201.

Booth, Alison. *How to Make It as a Woman: Collective Biographical History from Victoria to the Present*. Chicago: University of Chicago Press, 2004.

Boring, Anne, Kellie Ottoboni, and Philip B. Stark. "Student Evaluations of Teaching (Mostly) Do Not Measure Teaching Effectiveness." *ScienceOpen Research* (January 7, 2016): 1–11.

Boucherett, Jessie. *Hints on Self-Help; A Book for Young Women*. London: Jarrold and Sons, 1866.

Bourrier, Karen. *The Measure of Manliness: Disability in the Mid-Victorian Novel*. Ann Arbor: University of Michigan Press, 2015.

———. *Victorian Bestseller: The Life of Dinah Craik*. Ann Arbor: University of Michigan Press, 2019.

Bowler, Peter J. *Evolution: The History of an Idea*. Berkeley: University of California Press, 2003.

———. "Malthus, Darwin, and the Concept of Struggle." *Journal of the History of Ideas* 37, no. 4 (December 1976): 631–50.

Brantlinger, Patrick. *Dark Vanishings: Discourse on the Extinction of Primitive Races 1800–1900*. Ithaca, NY: Cornell University Press, 2003.

———. *The Spirit of Reform: British Literature and Politics, 1832–1867*. Cambridge, MA: Harvard University Press, 1977.

Brescoll, Victoria L., Jacqueline S. Smith, and Erin L. Thomas. "Constrained by Emotion: Women, Leadership, and Expressing Emotion in the Workplace." In *Handbook on Well-Being of Working Women*, edited by Mary L. Connerley and Jiyun Wu, 209–24. New York: Springer, 2015.

Brescoll, Victoria L. and Tyler G. Okimoto. "The Price of Power: Power Seeking and Backlash against Female Politicians." *Personality and Social Psychology Bulletin* 36.7 (2010): 923–36.

Brewer, John. *The Pleasures of the Imagination: English Culture in the Eighteenth Century*. New York: Farrar, Straus and Giroux, 1997.

Briggs, Asa. *Victorian People: A Reassessment of Persons and Themes 1851–1867*. Rev. ed. Chicago: University of Chicago Press, 1975. First published in 1954.

Brooks, Peter. *Reading for the Plot*. Cambridge, MA: Harvard University Press, 1984.

Buchan, Bruce. *Empire of Political Thought: Indigenous Australians and the Language of Colonial Government*. New York: Routledge, 2016. First published 2008.

Byerly, Alison. "Effortless Art: The Sketch in Nineteenth-Century Painting and Literature." *Criticism* 41, no. 3 (Summer 1999): 349–64.

Byrne, Jennifer. "The Despair of the Household." In *My Brilliant Career*, by Miles Franklin. Melbourne: Text, 2012. Ebook.

"Caretaking Your Own Well-Being." TeachingWriting, Stanford (Stanford login required). https://teachingcommons.stanford.edu/teachingwriting/pwr-guide/caretaking-your-own-well-being.

Carey, John. *Thackeray: Prodigal Genius*. London: Faber & Faber, 1977.

———. *The Violent Effigy: A Study of Dickens' Imagination*. London: Faber, 1973.

Carlyle, Thomas. *On Heroes, Hero-Worship, and the Heroic in History*. London: Chapman and Hall, 1840.

———. *Past and Present*. New York: Scribner's, 1918.

———. *Sartor Resartus*. London: Chapman and Hall, 1831.

Casid, Jill H. *Sowing Empire: Landscape and Colonization*. Minneapolis: University of Minnesota Press, 2005.

Cefalu, Paul. "What's So Funny about Obsessive-Compulsive Disorder?" *PMLA* 124, no. 1 (January 2009): 44–58.

Cha, Youngjoo, and Kim A. Weeden. "Overwork and the Slow Convergence in the Gender Gap in Wages." *American Sociological Review* 79, no. 3 (June 2014): 457–84.

Chapman, Maria Weston. *Memorials of Harriet Martineau*. Boston: James R. Osgood, 1877.

Chapone, Hester. *Letters on the Improvement of the Mind, Addressed to a Young Lady*. London: J. Walter, 1790.

Charnock, Richard S. "On the Origin of the Gypsies." *Anthropological Review* 4 (1866): 89–96.

Chen, Julie J., and Madeline E. Heilman. "Same Behavior, Different Consequences: Reactions to Men's and Women's Altruistic Citizenship Behavior." *Journal of Applied Psychology* 90, no. 3 (2005): 431–41.

Chesterton, G. K. *Charles Dickens: A Critical Study*. New York: Dodd, Mead, 1907.

Chetty, Raj, Nathaniel Hendren, Maggie R. Jones, and Sonya R. Porter. "Race and Economic Opportunity in the United States: An Intergenerational Perspective." The Equality of

Opportunity Project (March 2018). www.equality-of-opportunity.org/assets/documents /race_paper.pdf

Chilton, Lisa. *Agents of Empire: British Female Migration to Canada and Australia, 1860s–1930.* Toronto: University of Toronto Press, 2007.

Chrisman, Wendy L. "A Reflection on Inspiration: A Recuperative Call for Emotion in Disability Studies." *Journal of Literary & Cultural Disability Studies* 5, no. 2 (2011): 173–84.

Clark, John W. *The Language and Style of Anthony Trollope.* Chatham: W. & J. Mackay, 1975.

Clarke, Micael M. *Thackeray and Women.* DeKalb: Northern Illinois University Press, 1995.

Clausen, Christopher. "How to Join the Middle Classes: With the Help of Dr. Smiles and Mrs. Beeton." *American Scholar* 62 (1993): 403–18.

Cochrane, Robert. *Risen by Perseverance; or, Lives of Self-Made Men.* Edinburgh: William P. Nimmo, 1879.

Cohen, Claire, and Rebecca Reid. "Vanity Fair: Becky's Selfishness Is a Feminist Act." *Telegraph,* August 28, 2018. www.telegraph.co.uk/tv/vanity-fair/importance-of-becky-sharp-for-women/.

Cohn, Dorrit. *Transparent Minds.* Princeton, NJ: Princeton University Press, 1978.

Colby, Robert A. "'Scenes of All Sorts . . .' *Vanity Fair* on Stage and Screen." *Dickens Studies Annual* 9 (1981): 163–94.

Colella, Silvana. "Sweet Money: Cultural and Economic Value in Trollope's *Autobiography.*" *Nineteenth-Century Contexts* 28, no. 1 (March 2006): 5–20.

"Contemplation by Design 2018." BeWell, Stanford. https://bewell.stanford.edu/contemplation -by-design-2018/.

"The Country of John Halifax." *Leisure Hour* 40 (1891): 315–20.

Courtemanche, Eleanor. *The "Invisible Hand" and British Fiction 1818–1860.* Houndsmill: Palgrave Macmillan, 2011.

Craik, Dinah Mulock. ["The Author of 'John Halifax, Gentleman'"]. *A Woman's Thoughts about Women.* Leipzig: Bernhard Tauchnitz, 1860.

———. *John Halifax, Gentleman.* Toronto: Broadview, 2005. First published in 1856.

———. *Olive.* London: Chapman and Hall, 1850.

Craik, George Lillie. *The Pursuit of Knowledge under Difficulties.* 2 vols. London: Charles Knight, 1830–31.

———. *The Pursuit of Knowledge under Difficulties: Illustrated by Female Examples.* London: C. Cox, 1847.

Crawford, Iain. "Harriet Martineau, Charles Dickens, and the Rise of the Victorian Woman of Letters." *Nineteenth-Century Literature* 68, no. 4 (March 2014): 449–83.

Crozier–De Rosa, Sharon. "Identifying with the Frontier: Federation New Woman, Nation and Empire." In *Changing the Victorian Subject,* edited by Crozier-De Rosa et al., 37–58. Adelaide: University of Adelaide Press.

Culler, Jonathan. "Anderson and the Novel." *Diacritics* 29, no. 4 (Winter 1999): 19–39.

Cusack, Dymphna, Florence James, and Miles Franklin. *Yarn Spinners: A Story in Letters,* edited by Marilla North. St. Lucia: University of Queensland Press, 2001.

Daleski, H. M. "Strategies in Vanity Fair." In *Modern Critical Interpretations: William Makepeace Thackeray's "Vanity Fair,"* edited by Harold Bloom, 121–48. New York: Chelsea House, 1987.

Dalley, Lana L. "On Martineau's *Illustrations of Political Economy, 1832–34.*" *BRANCH: Britain, Representation and Nineteenth-Century History,* edited by Dino Franco Felluga. Extension of *Romanticism and Victorianism on the Net.* September 2012. www.branchcollective.org /?ps_articles=lana-l-dalley-on-martineaus-illustrations-of-political-economy-1832-34.

Daly, Nicholas. *The Demographic Imagination and the Nineteenth-Century City: Paris, London, New York.* Cambridge: Cambridge University Press, 2015.

Dalziell, Tanya. "Colonial Displacements: Another Look at Miles Franklin's *My Brilliant Career.*" *Ariel: A Review of International English Literature* 35, nos. 3/4 (2004): 39–56.

Dames, Nicholas. *Amnesiac Selves: Nostalgia, Forgetting, and British Fiction, 1810–1870.* New York: Oxford University Press, 2001.

———. "Trollope and the Career: Vocational Trajectories and the Management of Ambition." *Victorian Studies* 45, no. 2 (Winter 2003): 247–78.

Dannreuther, Charles, and Lew Perren. *The Political Economy of the Small Firm.* New York: Taylor & Francis, 2013.

Darwin, Charles. *The Descent of Man and Selection in Relation to Sex.* New York: D. Appleton, 1871.

Davidai, Shai, and Martino Ongis. "The Politics of Zero-Sum Thinking: The Relationship between Political Ideology and the Belief That Life Is a Zero-Sum Game." *Science Advances* 5, no. 12 (December 2019): 1–10.

Davies, Hugh Sykes. "Trollope and His Style." *Review of English Literature* 1 (1960): 73–84.

Davies, Larissa McLean, and Susan K. Martin. "Toward Worlding Settler Texts: Tracking the Uses of Miles Franklin's *My Brilliant Career* through the Curriculum." *Australian Literary Studies* 32, no. 2 (September 2017): 1–24.

Davies, William. *The Limits of Neoliberalism: Authority, Sovereignty, and the Logic of Competition.* Rev. ed. London: Sage, 2017. First published in 2014.

Davis, Lennard J. *Obsessions: A History.* Chicago: University of Chicago Press, 2008.

Delaney, Brigid. "'A Dream Come True': What the Miles Franklin Award Means to Writers." *Guardian,* August 19, 2017. www.theguardian.com/books/australia-books-blog/2017/aug /20/a-dream-come-true-what-the-miles-franklin-award-means-to-writers.

Dickens, Charles. *Our Mutual Friend.* New York: Penguin, 1997.

———. *David Copperfield.* Rev. ed. New York: Penguin, 2004.

———. *The Pickwick Papers.* New York: Penguin, 2003.

———. *The Speeches of Charles Dickens: A Complete Edition.* Edited by K. J. Fidelity. Oxford: Clarendon, 1960.

Donald, Ella. "Her Brilliant Career: Gillian Armstrong on the Australian Screen Then and Now." *Metro Magazine* 194 (Fall 2017): 108–13.

Dorling, Danny. *Injustice: Why Social Inequality Still Persists.* Bristol: Policy Press, 2011.

Driscoll, Adam, Andrea N. Hunt, and Lillian MacNell. "What's in a Name: Exposing Gender Bias in Student Ratings of Teaching." *Innovative Higher Education* 40, no. 4 (2015): 291–303.

Dzelzainis, Ella. "Malthus, Women and Fiction." In *New Perspectives on Malthus,* edited by Robert J. Mayhew, 155–81. Cambridge: Cambridge University Press, 2016.

Eisenberg, Cristina, Christopher L. Anderson, Adam Collingwood, Robert Sissons, Christopher J. Dunn, Garrett W. Meigs, Dave E. Hibbs, Scott Murphy, Sierra Dakin Kuiper, Julian SpearChief-Morris, Leroy Little Bear, Barb Johnston, and Curtis B. Edson. "Out of the Ashes: Ecological Resilience to Extreme Wildfire, Prescribed Burns, and Indigenous Burning in Ecosystems." *Frontiers in Ecology and Evolution* 7 (November 2019): 1–12.

Eliot, George. *Adam Bede.* New York: Oxford University Press, 2008.

———. *Middlemarch.* New York: Norton, 2000.

Emerson, Ralph Waldo. "Self-Reliance." *Nature and Selected Essays.* New York: Penguin, 2003. 175–203.

Engels, Frederick. *The Condition of the Working-Class in England in 1844.* Reprint of David Price 1892 ed. London: George Allen and Unwin, 1943.

English, James. *The Economy of Prestige: Prizes, Awards, and the Circulation of Cultural Value.* Cambridge, MA: Harvard University Press, 2008.

Esterhammer, Angela. "Spontaneity, Immediacy, and Improvisation in Romantic Poetry." In *A Companion to Romantic Poetry,* edited by Charles Mahoney, 321–36. Malden, MA: Wiley-Blackwell, 2011.

Felski, Rita. *The Limits of Critique.* Chicago: University of Chicago, 2015.

Ferguson, Frances. "Jane Austen, *Emma*, and the Impact of Form." *MLQ: Modern Language Quarterly* 61, no. 1 (March 2000): 157–80.

Fielden, Kenneth. "Samuel Smiles and Self-Help." *Victorian Studies* 12, no. 2 (December 1968): 155–76.

Fisher, Judith L. "The Aesthetic of the Mediocre: Thackeray and the Visual Arts." *Victorian Studies* 26, no. 1 (September 1982): 65–82.

Fong, Ryan. "The Stories outside the African Farm: Indigeneity, Orality, and Unsettling the Victorian." *Victorian Studies* 62, no. 3 (Spring 2020): 421–32.

Forster, John. *The Life of Charles Dickens.* 2 vols. Boston: James R. Osgood, 1875.

*Fortunes Made in Business: A Series of Original Sketches Biographical and Anecdotic from the Recent History of Industry and Commerce; By Various Writers.* Vol. 3. London: Sampson Low, Marston, Searle and Rivington, 1887.

Foucault, Michel. *The Birth of Biopolitics: Lectures at the Collège de France, 1978–79.* Edited by Michel Senellart. Translated by Graham Burchell. New York: Palgrave Macmillan, 2004.

Frank, Robert H. *Success and Luck: Good Fortune and the Myth of Meritocracy.* Princeton, NJ: Princeton University Press, 2016.

Franklin, Benjamin. *Benjamin Franklin: Autobiography, Poor Richard, and Later Writings.* New York: Library of America, 1997.

Franklin, Miles. *Childhood at Brindabella: My First Ten Years.* Sydney: Angus & Robertson, 1963.

———. "The End of My Career." Mitchell Library MS 445/2.

———. *My Brilliant Career.* New York: Penguin, 2007.

———. *My Career Goes Bung.* Essex: Virago Press, 1981.

———. *Prelude to Waking.* Sydney: Angus and Robertson, 1950.

Frawley, Maria. "'A Prisoner to the Couch': Harriet Martineau, Invalidism, and Self-Representation." In *The Body and Physical Difference: Discourses of Disability*, edited by David T. Mitchell and Sharon L. Snyder, 174–88. Ann Arbor: University of Michigan Press, 1997.

Frazee, John P. "The Creation of Becky Sharp in Vanity Fair." *Dickens Studies Annual: Essays on Victorian Fiction* 27 (1998): 227–44.

Freedgood, Elaine. "Banishing Panic: Harriet Martineau and the Popularization of Political Economy." *Victorian Studies* 39, no. 1 (Autumn 1995): 33–53.

Gagnier, Regenia. *The Insatiability of Human Wants: Economics and Aesthetics in Market Society.* Chicago: University of Chicago Press, 2000.

Gallagher, Catherine. *The Body Economic: Life, Death, and Sensation in Political Economy and the Victorian Novel.* Princeton, NJ: Princeton University Press, 2006.

Gammage, Bill. *The Biggest Estate on Earth: How Aborigines Made Australia.* Sydney: George Allen and Unwin, 2011.

Garcha, Amanpal. *From Sketch to Novel: The Development of Victorian Fiction.* Cambridge: Cambridge University Press, 2009.

Gardner, Susan. "*My Brilliant Career*: Portrait of the Artist as a Wild Colonial Girl." In *Gender, Politics, and Fiction: Twentieth Century Australian Women's Novels*, edited by Carole Ferrier, 22–43. Brisbane: University of Queensland Press, 1986.

Garland-Thomson, Rosemarie. *Extraordinary Bodies: Figuring Physical Disability in American Culture and Literature.* New York: Columbia University Press, 1996.

Garton, Stephen. "Contesting Enslavement: Marriage, Manhood and *My Brilliant Career*." *Australian Literary Studies* 20, no. 4 (October 2002): 336–49.

Gaztambide-Fernández, Rubén A., and Eve Tuck. "Curriculum, Replacement, and Settler Futurity." *Journal of Curriculum Theorizing* 29, no. 1 (2013): 72–89.

Gérando, Joseph-Marie (Baron of Gérando). *Self-education; or, The Means and Art of Moral Progress.* Translated by Elizabeth Palmer Peabody. Boston: Carter and Hendee, 1830.

Gerson, Carole. "Wild Colonial Girls: New Women of the Empire." *Journal of Commonwealth and Postcolonial Studies* 3, no. 1 (Autumn 1995): 61–77.

Gigante, Denise. *Taste: A Literary History*. New Haven, CT: Yale University Press, 2005.

Gilbert, Nora. *Better Left Unsaid: Victorian Novels, Hays Code Films, and the Benefits of Censorship*. Stanford, CA: Stanford Law Books, 2013.

Giles, Paul. *Antipodean America: Australasia and the Constitution of U.S. Literature*. Oxford: Oxford University Press, 2013.

Gilmour, Ian. *Dancing with Dogma: Britain under Thatcherism*. London: Simon & Schuster, 1992.

Gilmour, Robin. *The Idea of the Gentleman in the Victorian Novel*. London: George Allen and Unwin, 1981.

Gissing, George. *Collected Works of George Gissing on Charles Dickens*. Vol. 1, *Essays, Introductions and Reviews*. Edited by Pierre Coustillas. Surrey: Grayswood Press, 2004.

———. *New Grub Street*. New York: Penguin, 1985.

Goldschmied, Nadav P., and Vandello, Joseph A. "The Advantage of Disadvantage: Underdogs in the Political Arena." *Basic and Applied Social Psychology* 31, no. 1 (February 19, 2009): 24–31.

Goldstein, Jan Ellen. *Console and Classify: The French Psychiatric Profession in the Nineteenth Century*. Chicago: University of Chicago Press, 2001.

Goodlad, Lauren M. E. *Victorian Literature and the Victorian State: Character and Governance in a Liberal Society*. Baltimore: Johns Hopkins University Press, 2003.

Google Books: British English. "Ambition." https://googlebooks.byu.edu/x.asp.

Goschen, G. J. *Address by the Right Hon. G. J. Goschen to the Members of the Philosophical Institution at Edinburgh on Laissez-Faire and Government Interference*. London: Spottiswoode, 1883.

Gottlieb, Robert. "Becky in the Movies." *New York Review of Books* 51, no. 18 (November 18, 2004). www.nybooks.com/articles/2004/11/18/becky-in-the-movies/.

Gragg, Larry. *Englishmen Transplanted: The English Colonization of Barbados 1627–1660*. Oxford: Oxford University Press, 2003.

Grant, Robert. "'The Fit and Unfit': Suitable Settlers for Britain's Mid-nineteenth-Century Colonial Possessions." *Victorian Literature and Culture* 33, no. 1 (2005): 169–86.

———. *Representations of British Emigration, Colonisation and Settlement: Imagining Empire, 1800–1860*. Basingstoke: Palgrave Macmillan, 2005.

Greene, Jack P. *Creating the British Atlantic: Essays on Transplantation, Adaptation, and Continuity*. Charlottesville: University of Virginia Press, 2013.

Greene, Roland. *Unrequited Conquests: Love and Empire in the Colonial Americas*. Chicago: University of Chicago, 2000.

Griffith, Nicola. "Books about Women Don't Win Big Awards: Some Data." May 26, 2015. https://nicolagriffith.com/2015/05/26/books-about-women-tend-not-to-win-awards/.

Hack, Tay. "Forming Impressions: Effects of Facial Expression and Gender Stereotypes." *Psychological Reports: Mental & Physical Health* 114, no. 2 (April 1, 2014): 557–71.

Hamilton, Catherine J. *Women Writers: Their Works and Ways*. 2nd ser. London: Ward, Lock, & Bowen, 1893.

"The Hand in Your Pocket." *Sun*, September 13, 1976.

Handley, Graham. Appendix A in *The Three Clerks*. New York: Oxford University Press, 1989.

Harden, Edgar F. Historical introduction to *The Luck of Barry Lyndon: A Romance of the Last Century*, 229–36. Ann Arbor: University of Michigan Press, 1999.

Harford, Tim. "Trump, Bannon and the Lure of Zero-Sum Thinking." *Financial Times*, August 25, 2017.

Harris, Ralph. Foreword to *Self-Help*, iv–ix. London: Civitas, Institute for the Study of Civil Society, 1996.

Harrison, J. F. C. "The Victorian Gospel of Success." *Victorian Studies* 1, no. 2 (December 1957): 155–64.

Harrison, Mark. "'The Tender Frame of Man': Disease, Climate and Racial Difference in India and the West Indies, 1760–1860." *Bulletin of the History of Medicine* 70 (1996): 68–93.

Hassan, Narin. "Jane Eyre's Doubles? Colonial Progress and the Tradition of New Woman Writing in India." In *Gilbert and Gubar's The Madwoman in the Attic after Thirty Years*, edited by Annette R. Federico, 111–26. Columbia: University of Missouri Press, 2009.

Hemans, Felicia. *The Poetical Works of Felicia Dorothea Hemans*. London: Oxford University Press, 1914.

Henderson, Ian. "Gender, Genre, and Sybylla's Performative Identity in Miles Franklin's *My Brilliant Career*." *Australian Literary Studies* 18, no. 2 (1997): 165–73.

Hensley, Nathan K. *Forms of Empire: The Poetics of Victorian Sovereignty*. Oxford: Oxford University Press, 2016.

Hess, Scott. *William Wordsworth and the Ecology of Authorship: The Roots of Environmentalism in Nineteenth-Century Culture*. Charlottesville: University of Virginia Press, 2012.

Hingston, Kylee-Anne. *Articulating Bodies: The Narrative Form of Disability and Illness in Victorian Fiction*. Liverpool: Liverpool University Press, 2019.

Hirschman, Albert O. *The Passions and the Interests: Political Arguments for Capitalism before Its Triumph*. Princeton, NJ: Princeton University Press, 2013.

Hobart, Ann. "Harriet Martineau's Political Economy of Everyday Life." *Victorian Studies* 37, no. 2 (1994): 223–51.

Hogg, Robert. *Men and Manliness on the Frontier: Queensland and British Columbia in the Mid-nineteenth Century*. New York: Palgrave Macmillan, 2012.

Holmes, Martha Stoddard. *Fictions of Affliction: Physical Disability in Victorian Culture*. Ann Arbor: University of Michigan Press, 2009.

Holyoake, George Jacob. *Self Help by the People: History of Cooperation in Rochdale*. London: Holyoake, 1857 [1858?].

Hood, Edwin Paxton. *Peerage of Poverty; or, Learners and Workers in Fields, Farms, and Factories*. London: Partridge, 1870.

Hornborg, Alf. "Cornucopia or Zero-Gum Game? The Epistemology of Sustainability." *Journal of World-Systems Research* 9, no. 2 (2003): 205–16.

———. "Zero-Sum World: Challenges in Conceptualizing Environmental Load Displacement and Ecologically Unequal Exchange in the World-System." *International Journal of Comparative Sociology* 50, nos. 3/4 (2009): 237–62.

Huber, Richard M. *The American Idea of Success*. New York: McGraw-Hill, 1971.

Hudson, Hannah. "'Botany Bay' in British Magazines, 1786–1791." *Eighteenth-Century Studies* 54, no. 2 (2021): 261–84.

Hughes, Kathryn. *George Eliot: The Last Victorian*. New York: Cooper Square Press, 2001.

Hutton, R. H. "Novels by the Authoress of 'John Halifax.'" *North British Review* 29 (November 1858): 466–81.

"The Influence of Ambition on Happiness." *Mirror Monthly Magazine* 3, no. 1390 (February 1848): 116–20.

Jadwin, Lisa. "Clytemnestra Rewarded: The Double Conclusion of Vanity Fair." In *Famous Last Words: Changes in Gender and Narrative Closure*, edited by Alison Booth, 35–61. Charlottesville: University of Virginia Press, 1993.

Jaffe, Audrey. "Trollope in the Stock Market: Irrational Exuberance and *The Prime Minister*." *Victorian Studies* 45, no. 1 (Autumn 2002): 43–64.

———. *Vanishing Points: Dickens, Narrative, and the Subject of Omniscience*. Berkeley: University of California Press, 1991.

James, Henry. "Dinah Maria Mulock Craik" [Review: *A Noble Life*. By the Author of *John Halifax, Gentleman*. New York: Harper and Brothers, 1866.] In *Literary Criticism*. Vol. 1, *Essays on Literature, American Writers, English Writers*, edited by Leon Edel and Mark Wilson, 845–48. New York: Literary Classics of the United States, 1984.

———. *Partial Portraits*. New York: MacMillan, 1888.

"John Halifax, Gentleman." *Athenaeum* 1487 (April 26, 1856): 520.

"John Halifax, Gentleman." *Literary Gazette: A Weekly Journal of Literature, Science, and the Fine Arts* (April 19, 1856): 178.

"John Halifax, Gentleman." *Saturday Review of Politics, Literature, Science and Art* 2, no. 30 (May 24, 1856): 84–85.

"John Halifax, Gentleman. By the Author of 'The Head of the Family,' 'Olive,' &c. &c." Edited by Leigh Hunt, Albany William Fonblanque, and John Forster." *Examiner* 2519 (May 10, 1856): 292–93.

Johnson, Samuel, Jiewen Zhang, and Frank Keil. "Psychological Underpinnings of Zero-Sum Thinking." *Social Science Research Network* (January 28, 2018). http://dx.doi.org/10.2139/ssrn.3117627.

Jones, Ashley Bell, Ryne A. Sherman, and Robert T. Hogan. "Where Is Ambition in Factor Models of Personality?" *Personality and Individual Difference* 106 (2017): 26–31.

Jordan, John. "The Social Sub-text of *David Copperfield*." *Dickens Studies Annual* 14 (1985): 61–92.

Joseph, Keith. Introduction to Smiles, *Self-Help*, 7–16. Harmondsworth: Penguin, 1986.

Jusová, Iveta. *The New Woman and the Empire*. Columbus: Ohio State University Press, 2005.

Kafer, Alison. *Feminist, Queer, Crip*. Bloomington: Indiana University Press, 2013.

Kant, Immanuel. *Critique of Judgment*. Translated by Werner S. Pluhar. Indianapolis: Hackett, 1987.

Kaye, Richard A. "A Good Woman on Five Thousand Pounds: *Jane Eyre*, *Vanity Fair*, and Literary Rivalry." *SEL* 35 (1995): 723–39.

Kendrick, Walter M. *The Novel-Machine: The Theory and Fiction of Anthony Trollope*. Baltimore: Johns Hopkins University Press, 1980.

Kerwin, Dale. *Aboriginal Dreaming Paths and Trading Routes: The Colonisation of the Australian Economic Landscape*. Brighton: Sussex Academic Press, 2010.

Kincaid, James R. *The Novels of Anthony Trollope*. Oxford: Clarendon Press, 1977.

———. "Trollope's Fictional Autobiography." *Nineteenth-Century Fiction* 37, no. 3 (December 1982): 340–49.

King, William Casey. *Ambition, a History: From Vice to Virtue*. New Haven, CT: Yale, 2013.

Klaver, Claudia K. *A/Moral Economics: Classic Political Economy and Cultural Authority in Nineteenth-Century England*. Columbus: Ohio State University Press, 2003.

———. "Imperial Economics: Harriet Martineau's *Illustrations of Political Economy* and the Narration of Empire." *Victorian Literature and Culture* 35 (2007): 21–40.

Knelman, Judith. "Trollope's Experiments with Anonymity." *Victorian Periodicals Review* 14, no. 1 (Spring 1981): 21–24.

Konishi, Shino. "First Nations Scholars, Settler Colonial Studies, and Indigenous History." *Australian Historical Studies* 50, no. 3 (2019): 285–304.

Kon-yu, Natalie. "On Sexism in Literary Prize Culture." *LitHub*, July 15, 2016. http://lithub.com/on-sexism-in-literary-prize-culture/.

Kornbluh, Anna. *Realizing Capital: Financial and Psychic Economies in Victorian Form*. New York: Fordham University Press, 2014.

Kropotkin, Pyotr. *Mutual Aid: A Factor of Evolution*. New York: McClure Phillips, 1902.

Kucich, John. *Excess and Restraint in the Novels of Charles Dickens*. Athens: University of Georgia Press, 1981.

———. "Transgression in Trollope: Dishonesty and the Antibourgeois Elite." *ELH* 56, no. 3 (Autumn 1989): 593–618.

Kurnick, David. *Empty Houses: Theatrical Failure and the Novel*. Princeton, NJ: Princeton University Press, 2012.

L., R. F. O. "A Bashkirtseff of the Bush." *Speaker: The Liberal Review* (August 17, 1901): 565–66.

La Berge, Leigh Claire, and Quinn Slobodian. "Reading for Neoliberalism, Reading like Neoliberals." *American Literary History* 29, no. 3 (2017): 602–12.

Lacom, Cindy. "'The Time Is Sick and Out of Joint': Physical Disability in Victorian England." *PMLA* 120, no. 2 (March 2005): 547–52.

Laidlaw, Zoë, and Alan Lester. "Indigenous Sites and Mobilities: Connected Struggled in the Long Nineteenth Century." In *Indigenous Communities and Settler Colonialism: Land Holding, Loss and Survival in an Interconnected World*, edited by Laidlaw and Lester, 1–23. London: Palgrave Macmillan, 2015.

Leckie, Barbara. "Reader-Help: How to Read Samuel Smiles's Self-Help." In *Media and Print Culture Consumption in Nineteenth-Century Britain: The Victorian Reading Experience*, edited by Paul Raphael Rooney and Anna Gasperini, 15–32. London: Palgrave Macmillan, 2016.

Levine, Caroline. *Forms: Whole, Rhythm, Hierarchy, Network*. Princeton, NJ: Princeton University Press, 2015.

"Literature and Art." *Capital and Labour* 227 (June 26, 1878): 413.

Littler, Jo. *Against Meritocracy: Culture, Power and Myths of Mobility*. London: Routledge, 2017.

Litvak, Joseph. *Strange Gourmets: Sophistication, Theory, and the Novel*. Durham, NC: Duke University Press, 1997.

Logan, Deborah A. *Harriet Martineau, Victorian Imperialism, and the Civilizing Mission*. Burlington: Ashgate, 2010.

———. Introduction to *Illustrations of Political Economy: Selected Tales*, edited by Deborah Logan, 9–50. Peterborough, ON: Broadview, 2004.

Lubbock, John. *The Choice of Books*. Philadelphia: Henry Altemus, 1896.

Lucashenko, Melissa. "The Stella Interview: Melissa Lucashenko on *Too Much Lip*." *Stella*, March 12, 2019. https://thestellaprize.com.au/2019/03/stella-interview-melissa -lucashenko-much-lip/

Lukes, Steven. *Individualism*. Worcester: Basil Blackwell, 1973.

Lynch, Deidre. *The Economy of Character*. Chicago: University of Chicago Press, 1998.

MacDuffie, Allen. "Environment." *Victorian Literature and Culture* 46 nos. 3/4 (Fall/Winter 2018): 681–84.

Macpherson, C. B. *The Political Theory of Possessive Individualism: Hobbes to Locke*. Oxford: Oxford University Press, 2011.

Maddison, Sarah. "The Limits of the Administration of Memory in Settler Colonial Societies: The Australian Case." *International Journal of Politics, Culture, and Society* 32 (November 2018): 181–94.

Malm, Andreas. *Fossil Capital: The Rise of Steam Power and the Roots of Global Warming*. London: Verso, 2016.

Malthus, Thomas Robert. *An Essay on the Principle of Population*. Edited by Philip Appleman. 2nd ed. New York: Norton, 2004.

———. *An Essay on the Principle of Population*. London: Printed for J. Johnson by T. Bensley, 1803.

"Manifest Destiny at the Antipodes." *Pall Mall Gazette* 3246 (July 14, 1875): 10.

Marden, Orison. *Pushing to the Front*. New York: Thomas Y. Crowell, 1894.

Marks, Patricia. "'Mon Pauvre Prisonnier': Becky Sharp and the Triumph of Napoleon." *Studies in the Novel* 28, no. 1 (Spring 1996): 76–92.

Martin, Bruce K. Introduction to *My Brilliant Career*, by Miles Franklin, 11–36. Peterborough: Broadview, 2008.

Martin, Susan. "Relative Correspondence: Franklin's *My Brilliant Career* and the Influence of Nineteenth-Century Australian Women's Writing." In *The Time to Write*, edited by Kay Ferres, 54–70. New York: Penguin, 1993.

Martineau, Harriet. *Autobiography*. Edited by Linda H. Peterson. Peterborough: Broadview, 2007.

——. *Ella of Garveloch: Illustrations of Political Economy*. Vol. 2 of 9. London: Charles Fox, 1834.

——. *Homes Abroad: Illustrations of Political Economy*. Vol. 4 of 9. London: Charles Fox, 1834.

——. *Ireland: Illustrations of Political Economy*. Vol. 3 of 9. London: Charles Fox, 1834.

——. *Life in the Sick-Room*. Edited by Maria H. Frawley. Peterborough: Broadview, 2003.

——. *Life in the Wilds: Illustrations of Political Economy*. Vol. 1 of 9. London: Charles Fox, 1832.

——. Preface to *Illustrations of Political Economy*, iii–xviii. Vol. 1 of 9. London: Charles Fox, 1832.

——. *Weal and Woe in Garveloch: Illustrations of Political Economy; Selected Tales*. Edited by Deborah Anna Logan. Peterborough: Broadview, 2004.

Marx, Karl. *Grundrisse: Foundations of the Critique of Political Economy*. Translated by Martin Nicolaus. New York: Penguin, 1993.

Masta, Stephanie. "Settler Colonial Legacies: Indigenous Student Reflections on K–12 Social Studies Curriculum." *Intersections: Critical Issues in Education* 2, no. 2 (2018): 76–88.

Matheson, Annie. Introduction to *John Halifax, Gentleman*, by Dinah Mulock Craik, v–xl. London: Methuen, 1900.

Matthews, William. *Getting On in the World; or, Hints on Success in Life*. Chicago: S. C. Griggs, 1873.

Mayhew, Horace. "Men Who Have Helped Themselves." *Punch* 39 (September 8, 1860): 92.

Mayhew, Robert J. *Malthus: The Life and Legacies of an Untimely Prophet*. Cambridge, MA: Belknap Press of Harvard University Press, 2014.

McClintock, Anne. *Imperial Leather: Race, Gender, and Sexuality in the Colonial Contest*. New York: Routledge, 1995.

Meckier, Jerome. "*Great Expectations* and *Self-Help*: Dickens Frowns on Smiles." *Journal of English and Germanic Philology* 100, no. 4 (October 2001): 537–54.

——. "*The Three Clerks* and *Rachel Ray*: Trollope's Revaluation of Dickens Continued." *Dickens Quarterly* 25, no. 3 (September 2008): 162–71.

"Memorial to the Author of 'John Halifax, Gentleman.'" *Academy and Literature* 951 (July 26, 1890): 72.

Mikhail, Alan. "Enlightenment Anthropocene." *Eighteenth-Century Studies* 49, no. 2 (2016): 211–31.

"Miles Franklin Literary Award." Perpetual Limited. www.perpetual.com.au/MilesFranklin.

Mill, John Stuart. *On Liberty, Utilitarianism, and Other Essays*. Edited by Mark Philp and Frederick Rosen. Oxford: Oxford University Press, 2015.

——. *Principles of Political Economy with Some of Their Applications to Social Philosophy*. Boston: Lee and Shepard, 1872.

Miller, Andrew H. *The Burdens of Perfection: On Ethics and Reading in Nineteenth-Century British Literature*. Ithaca, NY: Cornell University Press, 2008.

——. *Novels behind Glass: Commodity Culture and Victorian Narrative*. Cambridge: Cambridge University Press, 1995.

Miller, Elizabeth. "Dendrography and Ecological Realism." *Victorian Studies* 58, no. 4 (Summer 2016): 696–718.

*Millionaires and How They Became So: Showing How Twenty-Seven of the Wealthiest Men in the World Made Their Money; Reprinted from Tit-Bits.* London: Tit-Bits offices, 1884.

Minoru, Toyoda. *Shakespeare in Japan: An Historical Survey.* Tokyo: Shakespeare Association of Japan by the Iwanami Shoten, 1940.

Mirowski, Philip. "The Thirteen Commandments of Neoliberalism." *Utopian* 11 (June 19, 2013). \www.the-utopian.org/post/53360513384/the-thirteen-commandments -of-neoliberalism.

Mishra, Pankaj. *Age of Anger: A History of the Present.* New York: Farrar, Straus and Giroux, 2017.

"Miss Martineau's Tracts." *Dublin University Magazine* 6, no. 35 (November 1835): 557–66.

Mitchell, David. T., and Sharon L. Snyder. *Narrative Prosthesis: Disability and the Dependencies of Discourse.* Ann Arbor: University of Michigan Press, 2000.

———. "Introduction: Disability Studies and the Double Bind of Representation." In *The Body and Physical Difference: Discourses of Disability,* edited by Mitchell and Snyder, 1–31. Ann Arbor: University of Michigan Press, 1997.

Mitchell, Sally. *Dinah Mulock Craik.* Boston: Twayne, 1983.

Moffat, Kirstine. "'Devoted to the Cause of Woman's Rights': The New Zealand New Woman Novel." *Women's Writing* 26, no. 3 (2019): 304–27.

Moler, Kenneth L. "Evelina in Vanity Fair: Becky Sharp and Her Patrician Heroes." *Nineteenth-Century Fiction* 27, no. 2 (September 1972): 171–81.

Moretti, Franco. *The Bourgeois: Between History and Literature.* New York: Verso, 2013.

———. *The Way of the World.* New ed. New York: Verso, 2000.

Morgan, Sydney. *Lady Morgan's Memoirs: Autobiography, Diaries, and Correspondence.* 3 vols. Leipzig: Bernhard Tauchnitz, 1863.

Morgan, T. C. "Monomania and Monomaniacs." In *The New Monthly Magazine and Humorist,* part 2, edited by Thomas Hood, 43–51. London: Henry Colburn, May 1843.

Morris, R. J. "Samuel Smiles and the Genesis of Self-Help: The Retreat to a Petit Bourgeois Utopia." *Historical Journal* 24, no. 1 (March 1981): 89–109.

Morton, Timothy. *The Ecological Thought.* Cambridge, MA: Harvard University Press, 2010.

Moses, A. Dirk. *Genocide and Settler Society: Frontier Violence and Stolen Indigenous Children in Australian History.* New York: Berghahn Books, 2004.

Moynahan, Julian. "The Hero's Guilt: The Case of *Great Expectations.*" *Essays in Criticism* 10 (1960): 60–79.

"My Brilliant Career." *Saturday Review of Politics, Literature, Science and Art* 92, no. 2395 (September 21, 1901): 373.

"New Colony of South Australia." *Morning Chronicle* 2,0231 (July 1, 1834).

Ngai, Sianne. *Our Aesthetic Categories: Zany, Cute, Interesting.* Cambridge, MA: Harvard University Press, 2015.

Nichols, Ashton. *Beyond Romantic Ecocriticism: Toward Urbanatural Roosting.* Basingstoke: Palgrave Macmillan, 2011.

"Obituary." *Academy* 807 (October 22, 1887): 269–70.

Oliphant, Margaret. "Mrs. Craik." *Macmillan's Magazine* 57, no. 338 (December 1887): 81–85.

Orwell, George. "Charles Dickens." *George Orwell: An Age like This 1920–1940 Vol. 1.* In *The Collected Essays, Journalism & Letters,* edited by Sonia Orwell and Ian Angus, 1–75. Boston: David R. Godine, 2000.

*Oxford English Dictionary Online.* Oxford University Press, 2020. www.oed.com.

Parker, David. "Thackeray's *Barry Lyndon.*" *ARIEL: A Review of International English Literature* 6, no. 4 (1975): 68–80.

Parker, Langston. "On the Effects of Certain Mental and Bodily States upon the Imagination." *Analyst: A Quarterly Journal of Science, Literature, Natural History, and the Fine Arts* 5 (June 1836): 53–73.

Pascoe, Bruce. *Dark Emu: Aboriginal Australia and the Birth of Agriculture*. Melbourne: Scribe, 2018.

Patel, Leigh. *Decolonizing Educational Research: From Ownership to Answerability*. New York: Routledge, 2016.

Paton, Walter B. "Work and Workers: VIII. Emigration." *Time* 19, no. 44 (August 1888): 129–42.

Pearce, Trevor. "From 'Circumstances' to 'Environment': Herbert Spencer and the Origins of the Idea of Organism-Environment Interaction." *Studies in History and Philosophy of Biological and Biomedical Sciences* 41 (2010): 241–52.

Perkin, Harold. *The Origins of Modern English Society*. 2nd ed. New York: Routledge, 2002.

Petersen, Anne Helen. *Can't Even: How Millennials Became the Burnout Generation*. Boston: Houghton Mifflin Harcourt, 2020.

Peterson, Linda H. *Becoming a Woman of Letters: Myths of Authorship and Facts of the Victorian Market*. Princeton, NJ: Princeton University Press, 2009.

———. "From French Revolution to English Reform: Hannah More, Harriet Martineau, and the 'Little Book.'" *Nineteenth-Century Literature* 60, no. 4 (2006): 409–50.

Pettigrove, Glen. "Ambitions." *Ethical Theory and Moral Practice* 10, no. 1 (February 2007): 53–68.

Pierce, Jennifer L. *Gender Trials: Emotional Lives in Contemporary Law Firms*. Berkeley: University of California, 1995.

Plotz, John. *The Crowd: British Literature and Public Politics*. Berkeley: University of California Press, 2000.

Polhemus, Robert M. *The Changing World of Anthony Trollope*. Berkeley: University of California Press, 1968.

———. *Comic Faith: The Great Tradition from Austen to Joyce*. Chicago: University of Chicago Press, 1980.

Poovey, Mary. *Genres of the Credit Economy*. Chicago: University of Chicago Press, 2008.

———. *Uneven Developments: The Ideological Work of Gender in Mid-Victorian England*. Chicago: University of Chicago Press, 1988.

Puckett, Kent. *Bad Form: Social Mistakes and the Nineteenth-Century Novel*. New York: Oxford University Press, 2008.

"The Pursuit of Knowledge under Difficulties." *New-Yorker* 8, no. 25 (March 7, 1840): 397.

Quayson, Ato. *Aesthetic Nervousness: Disability and the Crisis of Representation*. New York: Columbia University Press, 2007.

Radcliffe, David Hill. *Lady Morgan's Memoirs: Autobiography, Diaries and Correspondence*. Rev 2nd ed. Edited by Geraldine Endsor Jewsbury and William Hepworth Dixon. 2 vols. London: Wm. H. Allen, 1863; Blacksburg: Virginia Tech Center for Applied Technologies in the Humanities, 2010. http://lordbyron.org.

Rader, Ralph Wilson. "Thackeray's Injustice to Fielding." *Journal of English and Germanic Philology* 56 (1957): 203–12.

Richards, Ngaire (primary author). *Goulburn Mulwaree LGA Aboriginal Heritage Study*. Consultancy report to Goulburn Mulwaree Council. Sydney: Australian Museum Business Services, 2011.

Richardson, Rebecca. "Becky Sharp, Gender, and Likability: Adapting Thackeray's *Vanity Fair* after 2016 and #MeToo." *Nineteenth-Century Gender Studies* 16, no. 2 (Summer 2020). www.ncgsjournal.com/issue162/richardson.html.

———. "Bradley Headstone's Bad Example of Self-Help: Dickens and the Problem with Ambition." *Dickens Studies Annual: Essays on Victorian Fiction* 44 (2013): 267–88.

———. "Imagining Environmental and Economic Systems in Harriet Martineau's *Illustrations of Political Economy*." *Nineteenth-Century Prose* 47, no. 2 (Fall 2020): 62–88.

Rickey, Carrie. "*My Brilliant Career*: Unapologetic Women." The Criterion Collection (May 2, 2019). www.criterion.com/current/posts/6328-my-brilliant-career-unapologetic -women.

Rigby, Kate. *Dancing with Disaster: Environmental Histories, Narratives, and Ethics for Perilous Times*. Charlottesville: University of Virginia Press, 2015.

Ritchie, Anne. Introduction to *The Biographical Edition of the Works of William Makepeace Thackeray*. Vol. 4, *The Memoirs of Barry Lyndon, Esq., The Fitz-Boodle Papers, Men's Wives, Etc.*, xiii–xxxvi. London: Smith, Elder, 1898.

Robbins, Bruce. *Upward Mobility and the Common Good: Toward a Literary History of the Welfare State*. Princeton, NJ: Princeton University Press, 2007.

Robinson, William. *Self-Education; or, The Value of Mental Culture, with the Practicability of Its Attainment under Disadvantages*. 2nd ed. London: Hamilton, 1845.

Roderick, Colin. *Miles Franklin: Her Brilliant Career*. Sydney: Landsdowne, 2000.

Roe, Jill. *Her Brilliant Career: The Life of Stella Miles Franklin*. Cambridge, MA: Belknap Press of Harvard University Press, 2009.

———. "*My Brilliant Career* and 1890s Goulburn." *Australian Literary Studies* 20, no. 4 (October 2002): 359–69.

Rogers, Katharine M. "The Pressure of Convention on Thackeray's Women." *Modern Language Review* 67, no. 2 (April 1972): 257–63.

Rogers, Todd, and Moore, Don A. "The Motivating Power of Under-confidence: 'The Race Is Close but We're Losing.'" Harvard Kennedy School Faculty Research Working Paper Series (October 2014).

Rogers, Winslow. "Thackeray and Fielding's Amelia." *Criticism: A Quarterly for Literature and the Arts* 19 (1977): 141–57.

Rose, Jonathan. *The Intellectual Life of the British Working Classes*. New Haven, CT: Yale University Press, 2001.

Ross, Marlon B. "The Race of/in Romanticism: Notes toward a Critical Race Theory." In *Race, Romanticism, and the Atlantic*, edited by Paul Youngquist, 25–58. Burlington: Ashgate, 2013.

Royal Society of Literature. *Literature in Britain Today*, March 2017. https://rsliterature.org/wp -content/uploads/2017/02/RSL-Literature-in-Britain-Today_01.03.17.pdf.

Rubinstein, W. D. *Men of Property: The Very Wealthy in Britain since the Industrial Revolution*. New Brunswick, NJ: Rutgers University Press, 1981.

Ruskin, John. *The Stones of Venice*. New York: Da Capo Press, 2003.

Russell, Emily. *Reading Embodied Citizenship: Disability, Narrative, and the Body Politic*. New Brunswick, NJ: Rutgers University Press, 2011.

Ruth, Jennifer. *Novel Professions: Interested Disinterest and the Making of the Professional in the Victorian Novel*. Columbus: Ohio State University Press, 2006.

Sadleir, Michael. *Trollope: A Commentary*. London: Oxford University Press, 1961.

Samalin, Zachary. "Exploitation." In *From Political Economy to Economics through Nineteenth-Century Literature: Reclaiming the Social*, edited by Elaine Hadley, Audrey Jaffe, and Sarah Winter, 59–84. London: Palgrave Macmillan, 2019.

Sandberg, Sheryl. *Lean In: Women, Work, and the Will to Lead*. New York: Knopf, 2013.

Scates, Bruce. "*My Brilliant Career* and Radicalism." *Australian Literary Studies* 20, no. 4 (2002): 370–78.

Schalk, Sami. "Reevaluating the Supercrip." *Journal of Literary & Cultural Disability Studies* 10, no. 1 (2016): 71–86.

Schoeck, Helmut. *Envy: A Theory of Social Behaviour*. Indianapolis, IN: Liberty Press, 1987.

Schreiner, Olive. *The Story of an African Farm*. Oxford: Oxford University Press, 1992.

Schwerin, Friederike von. *High Shakespeare, Reception and Translation: Germany and Japan*. New York: Continuum Press, 2004.

Scott, Catherine. "Time Out of Joint: The Narcotic Effect of Prolepsis in Christopher Reeve's *Still Me*." *Biography: An Interdisciplinary Quarterly* 29, no. 2 (Spring 2006): 307–28.

"Self-Help." *Fraser's Magazine for Town and Country* 61, no. 366 (June 1860): 778–86.

"Self Help." *Tait's Edinburgh Magazine* (October 1860): 552–55.

"Self-Help, with Illustrations—Character and Conduct." *New Quarterly Review* 8, no. 32 (1859): 430.

Shaffi, Sarah. "Publishing Seeks to Address Industry's Lack of Diversity." *Bookseller*, November 4, 2016. www.thebookseller.com/news/publishing-seeks-address-industry-s-lack-diversity-426031.

Shanahan, Daniel. *Toward a Genealogy of Individualism*. Amherst: University of Massachusetts Press, 1992.

Shaylor, Joseph. Introduction to *John Halifax, Gentleman*, vii–xi. London: J. M. Dent & Sons, 1925. First issue of this edition published in 1906.

Shillingsburg, Peter L. "The 'Trade' of Literature." In *Vanity Fair*, 739–44. New York: Norton, 1994.

Showalter, Elaine. "Dinah Mulock Craik and the Tactics of Sentiment: A Case Study in Victorian Female Authorship." *Feminist Studies* 2, nos. 2/3 (1975): 5–23.

Shuman, Cathy. *Pedagogical Economies: The Examination and the Victorian Literary Man*. Stanford, CA: Stanford University Press, 2000.

Simon, Gary. "'Show Me the Money!' A Pecuniary Investigation of William Makepeace Thackeray's Early Victorian Journalism." *Victorian Periodicals Review* 45, no. 1 (2012): 64–96.

Sinnema, Peter W. Introduction to *Self-Help*, edited by Sinnema, vii–xxviii. Oxford: Oxford University Press, 2002.

Skilton, David. Introduction to Trollope, *An Autobiography*, edited by Skilton, vii–xx. London: Penguin, 1996.

Smiles, Samuel. *The Autobiography of Samuel Smiles*. Edited by Thomas Mackay. London: John Murray, 1905.

———. *Character*. London: John Murray, 1871.

———. *The Life of George Stephenson, Railway Engineer*. London: John Murray, 1857.

———. *Self-Help: With Illustrations of Character, Conduct, and Perseverance*. Oxford: Oxford University Press, 2002.

———. *Thrift*. London: John Murray, 1875.

Smith, Adam. *An Inquiry into the Nature and Causes of the Wealth of Nations*. London: T. Nelson and Sons, 1852.

Smith, Michelle J. "The 'Australian Girl' and the Domestic Ideal in Colonial Women's Fiction." In *Domestic Fiction in Colonial Australia and New Zealand*, edited by Tamara S. Wagner, 75–89. London: Pickering and Chatto, 2014.

———. *Empire in British Girls' Literature and Culture: Imperial Girls, 1880–1915*. New York: Palgrave Macmillan, 2011.

Smith, Rachel Greenwald. *Affect and American Literature in the Age of Neoliberalism*. Cambridge: Cambridge University Press, 2015.

So, Richard Jean, and Gus Wezerek. "Why Is Publishing So White?" *New York Times* (December 11, 2020).

Sparks, Tabitha. "Dinah Mulock Craik's *Olive*: Deformity, Gender, and Female Destiny." *Women's Writing* 20, no. 3 (June 2013): 358–69.

"The Spirit of Smiles." *Saturday Review of Politics, Literature, Science and Art* 100, no. 2609 (October 28, 1905): 551–52.

Spitzka, Edward Charles. *Insanity: Its Classification, Diagnosis, and Treatment.* New York: Bermingham, 1883.

Steinlight, Emily. *Populating the Novel: Literary Form and the Politics of Surplus Life.* Ithaca, NY: Cornell University Press, 2018.

Stephens, A. G. "A Bookful of Sunlight." *Bulletin* 22, no. 1128 (September 28, 1901): inside front cover.

Stevenson, Lionel. "*Vanity Fair* and Lady Morgan." *PMLA* 48, no. 2 (June 1933): 547–51.

Stewart, J. I. M. Introduction to *The History of Pendennis*, 7–22. London: Penguin Books, 1986.

Stoddard Holmes, Martha. *Fictions of Affliction: Physical Disability in Victorian Culture.* Ann Arbor: University of Michigan Press, 2004.

Stout, Daniel. *Corporate Romanticism: Liberalism, Justice, and the Novel.* New York: Fordham University Press, 2017.

"Success." *Saturday Review of Politics, Literature, Science and Art* 8, no. 215 (December 10, 1859): 700–701.

*Success in Life: A Book for Young Men.* London: T. Nelson and Sons, 1851.

Sundell, M. G. Introduction to *Twentieth Century Interpretations of Vanity Fair*, edited by Sundell, 1–12. Edgewood Cliffs: Prentice-Hall, 1969.

Super, R. H. "Truth and Fiction in Trollope's *Autobiography.*" *Nineteenth-Century Literature* 48, no. 1 (June 1993): 74–88.

Thackeray, William Makepeace. "A Brother of the Press on the History of a Literary Man, Laman Blanchard, and the Chances of the Literary Profession." *Fraser's Magazine* 33, no. 195 (March 1846): 332–42.

———. *A Collection of Letters of Thackeray, 1847–1855.* New York: Charles Scribner's Sons, 1888.

———. *The History of Pendennis.* New York: Penguin, 1972.

———. *The Luck of Barry Lyndon: A Romance of the Last Century.* Edited by Edgar F. Harden. Ann Arbor: University of Michigan Press, 1999.

———. *The Letters and Private Papers of William Makepeace Thackeray*, Vol. 1, *1817–1840.* Edited by Gordon N. Ray. London: Oxford University Press, 1945.

———. "May Gambols; or, Titmarsh in the Picture Galleries." *Fraser's Magazine* 29, no. 174 (June 1844): 700–716.

———. *The Newcomes.* New York: Penguin, 1996.

———. "On Men and Pictures: À Propos of a Walk in the Louvre." *Fraser's Magazine* 24, no. 139 (July 1841): 98–111.

———. *The Paris Sketch Book.* Vol. 16 of *The Works of William Makepeace Thackeray.* London: Smith, Edler, 1901.

———. "A Pictorial Rhapsody: Concluded." *Fraser's* 22, no. 127 (July 1840): 112–26.

———. "Small-Beer Chronicle." *Roundabout Papers. Cornhill Magazine* 4, July–December 1861, July 1861, 122–28. London: Smith, Elder, 1861.

———. *The Snobs of England* and *Punch's Prize Novelists.* Edited by Edgar F. Harden (general editor) and Peter L. Shillingsburg. Ann Arbor: University of Michigan Press, 2005.

———. *Vanity Fair.* New York: Norton, 1994.

Thompson, E. P. *The Making of the English Working Class.* New York: Pantheon Books, 1963.

Thompson, Noel W. *The People's Science: The Popular Political Economy of Exploitation and Crisis 1816–34.* Cambridge: Cambridge University Press, 2002.

Tiedens, Larissa Z., and Melissa J. Williams. "The Subtle Suspension of Backlash: A Meta-analysis of Penalties for Women's Implicit and Explicit Dominance Behavior." *Psychological Bulletin* 142, no. 2 (2016): 165–97.

Tillotson, Geoffrey. *Thackeray the Novelist.* Cambridge: Cambridge University Press, 1954.

Tobias, C. F. "Ella's Englishman." *Cape Illustrated Magazine* 2, no. 1 (September 1, 1891): 1–4.

Tracy, Robert. "Stranger Than Truth: Fictional Autobiography and Autobiographical Fiction." *Dickens Studies Annual* 15 (1986): 275–91.

Travers, Timothy. "Samuel Smiles and the Origins of 'Self-Help': Reform and the New Enlightenment." *Albion: A Quarterly Journal Concerned with British Studies* 9, no. 2 (Summer 1977): 161–87.

———. *Samuel Smiles and the Victorian Work Ethic*. New York: Garland, 1987.

Trendafilov, Vladimir. "The Origins of Self-Help: Samuel Smiles and the Formative Influences on an Ex-Seminal Work." *Victorian* 3, no. 1 (2015): 1–16.

Trilling, Lionel. "Little Dorrit." *Kenyon Review* 15, no. 4 (Autumn 1953): 577–90.

Trollope, Anthony. *An Autobiography*. New York: Penguin, 1993.

———. "The Civil Service." *Dublin University Magazine* 46, no. 274 (October 1855): 409–26.

———. "The Civil Service." *Fortnightly Review* 2 (October 15, 1865): 613–26.

———. "The Civil Service as a Profession." *Cornhill Magazine* 3, no. 14 (February 1861): 214–28.

———. *Thackeray*. London: MacMillan, 1925.

———. *The Three Clerks*. New York: Oxford University Press, 1989.

Tuck, Eve, and K. Wayne Yang. "Decolonization Is Not a Metaphor." *Decolonization: Indigeneity, Education & Society* 1, no. 1 (2012): 1–40.

Tyrrell, Alexander. "Class Consciousness in Early Victorian Britain: Samuel Smiles, Leeds Politics, and the Self-Help Creed." *Journal of British Studies* 9, no. 2 (May 1970): 102–25.

———. "Samuel Smiles and the Woman Question in Early Victorian Britain." *Journal of British Studies* 39, no. 2 (2000): 185–216.

Vandello, Joseph A., Nadav P. Goldschmied, and David A. R. Richards. "The Appeal of the Underdog." *Personality and Social Psychology Bulletin* 33, no. 12 (December 1, 2007): 1603–16.

Van Zuylen, Marina. *Monomania: The Flight from Everyday Life in Literature and Art*. Ithaca, NY: Cornell University Press, 2005.

Walker Gore, Clare. *Plotting Disability in the Nineteenth-Century Novel*. Edinburgh: Edinburgh University Press, 2020.

Walker, Melissa. "On the Move: Biography, Self-Help, and Feminism in the *Women's Union Journal*." *Victorian Periodicals Review* 50, no. 3 (Fall 2017): 585–618.

———. "Self-Made Maids: British Emigration to the Pacific Rim and Self-Help Narratives." *Victorian Literature and Culture* 43, no. 2 (2015): 281–304.

———. "Samuel Smiles and the Woman Question in Early Victorian Britain." *Journal of British Studies* 39, no. 2 (April 2000): 185–216.

Watt, Ian. *Myths of Modern Individualism: Faust, Don Quixote, Don Juan, Robinson Crusoe*. Cambridge: Cambridge University Press, 1996.

———. *The Rise of the Novel: Studies in Defoe, Richardson and Fielding*. Berkeley: University of California Press, 1971.

Webby, Elizabeth. "Reading *My Brilliant Career*." *Australian Literary Studies* 20, no. 4 (2002): 350–58.

Welsh, Alexander. *The City of Dickens*. Oxford: Clarendon Press, 1971.

———. *Dickens Redressed: The Art of "Bleak House" and "Hard Times."* New Haven, CT: Yale University Press, 2000.

———. *From Copyright to Copperfield: The Identity of Dickens*. Cambridge, MA: Harvard University Press, 1987.

Wilson, Angus. "The Heroes and Heroines of Dickens." In *Bloom's Modern Critical Views: Charles Dickens*, edited by Harold Bloom, 83–90. New York: Chelsea, 2006.

Wolfe, Patrick. *Settler Colonialism*. London: Continuum, 1999.

Woloch, Alex. *The One vs. the Many: Minor Characters and the Space of the Protagonist in the Novel*. Princeton, NJ: Princeton University Press, 2003.

Wright, Daniel. *Bad Logic: Reasoning about Desire in the Victorian Novel.* Baltimore: Johns Hopkins University Press, 2018.

Wright, Erika. *Reading for Health: Medical Narratives and the Nineteenth-Century Novel.* Athens: Ohio University Press, 2016.

Wyllie, Irvin G. *The Self-Made Man in America: The Myth of Rags to Riches.* New York: The Free Press, 1966.

Zeldin, Theodore. *A History of French Passions 1848–1945.* Vol. 2, *Intellect, Taste, and Anxiety.* Oxford: Clarendon Press, 1993.